Put Your Bodies Upon the Wheels

PUT YOUR BODIES UPON THE WHEELS

Student Revolt in the 1960s

Kenneth J. Heineman

The American Ways Series

IVAN R. DEE   *Chicago*

PUT YOUR BODIES UPON THE WHEELS. Copyright © 2001 by
Kenneth J. Heineman. All rights reserved, including the right to
reproduce this book or portions thereof in any form. For information,
address: Ivan R. Dee, Publisher, 1332 North Halsted Street, Chicago
60622. Manufactured in the United States of America and printed on
acid-free paper.

Library of Congress Cataloging-in-Publication Data:
Put your bodies upon the wheels : student revolt in the 1960s /
Kenneth J. Heineman.
        p.   cm. — (The American ways series)
    Includes bibliographical references and index.
    ISBN 1-56663-351-6 (cloth : alk. paper) — ISBN 1-56663-352-4
(paper : alk. paper)
    1. Student movements—United States—History—20th century.
2. College students—United States—Political activity—History—
20th century.   I. Title: Student revolt in the 1960s.   II. Heineman,
Kenneth J., 1962–   III. Series.

LA229 .P88 2001
378.1'981'0973—dc21   00-049371

For
Theresa Ann
and our daughters,
Natalie MacKenzie
and
Grace Ann

"There is a time when the operation of the machine becomes so odious, makes you so sick at heart, that you can't take part; and you've got to put your bodies upon the gears and upon the wheels, upon the levers, upon all the apparatus and you've got to make it stop. And you've got to indicate to the people who run it, to the people who own it, that unless you're free, the machine will be prevented from working at all."

—MARIO SAVIO
The Free Speech Movement,
Berkeley, 1964

Contents

Preface

IN THIS OVERVIEW of radical student protest and social unrest in the 1960s, I draw upon a great many monographs as well as my own research. Narrative and analytical chapters explore specific events, historical trends, and the social roots of campus protest in America. This book is *not* a celebration of the 1960s New Left and violent confrontation written by a participant turned scholar. Nor is it an attack on every social reform movement that arose in the sixties. I have tried to be evenhanded but clear-eyed.

I express my great appreciation to Tom Reeves, Greg Schneider, and Mitch Hall for reading this book in manuscript and helping me correct flaws in analysis, composition, and fact. I also must thank Mitch's student Carrie Hoefferle for giving me the opportunity to read a draft of her ambitious dissertation on the American and British student movements of the 1960s. Her work provided me with several campus anecdotes which I incorporated in this book.

I am especially grateful to John Braeman and Ivan Dee for the opportunity to contribute to Ivan R. Dee's American Ways Series. I must acknowledge as well the students in my course on "The U.S. and the 1960s" at the Lancaster Campus of Ohio University. Their questions proved enormously helpful in my writing. (As one of my first-generation-in-college students said after viewing a PBS documentary on the confrontation at the 1968 Democratic convention in Chicago, "How could those students think they wouldn't get their asses kicked for calling the cops names and throwing rocks at them?") Finally, I thank Niko Pfund for giving me permission to use—and revise—

some portions of my previous work published by New York
University Press.

K. H.

Lancaster, Ohio
January 2001

Put Your Bodies Upon the Wheels

1

Campus Wars and Culture Wars

STUDENT PROTEST in the 1960s, which began as a rejection of parental authority and the Vietnam War, rapidly evolved into a social movement. The Students for a Democratic Society (SDS), the chief organization of the campus-based New Left, gained strength as Democratic politicians lost control of the war in Vietnam and the unrest in America's inner cities. SDS, which began the 1960s with just a few members, ended the decade 100,000 strong. By then it had committed itself to violent confrontation with university and government officials.

More than three hundred of the nation's two thousand campuses experienced sit-ins, building takeovers, riots, and strikes in the sixties. In a period of a year and a half—between January 1969 and April 1970—young radicals bombed five thousand police stations, corporate offices, military facilities, and campus buildings set aside for the Reserve Officers' Training Corps (ROTC). Twenty-six thousand students—of a campus population of ten million—were arrested and thousands injured or expelled while engaged in protest activities. (Fifty-seven thousand youths, many of whom lacked the financial means to attend college and secure draft deferments [II-S], died in Vietnam.) Against a backdrop of student protest, the campus drug culture blossomed. The proportion of college students who had smoked marijuana jumped from 4 percent in the early 1960s to 60 percent by 1972.

At the same time many American cities became combat zones. Violent crime, which was largely concentrated in America's poorest urban precincts, in the sixties rose 126 percent. In 1968, 125 cities experienced riots that left 225 dead and caused $112 billion in property damage. While politicians such as Alabama governor George Wallace blamed social unrest on "lawless" blacks and students, leftist intellectuals justified rioting as revolutionary acts against "white racism." Sadly for the Democratic party—which since the era of Franklin Roosevelt had dominated national politics—divisions over Vietnam, sexual liberation, recreational drug use, and urban crime spelled its decline. As social conflict grew, Southern whites, union members, and Northern Catholics parted ways with their former black, Jewish, and professorial allies.

Although these developments are ample reasons for the importance of the 1960s, another force is at work to ensure that the era does not fade into the mists of time. Manufacturers of America's popular culture have found that the events of the 1960s offer compelling plots around which to construct films and television shows. For example, in *Wild in the Streets* (1968), a young rock-and-roll star becomes President of the United States when the voting age is lowered to fourteen. He immediately establishes a dictatorship of "love," sending citizens over the age of thirty to concentration camps where they are fed LSD. A decade later *Animal House* (1978) created "Faber College," a fictional 1960s-era campus. At Faber, students smoke dope, sleep around, fail their classes, and gleefully destroy property.

In contrast to *Animal House, Forrest Gump* (1994) depicts the 1960s as an era of class and cultural polarization. While young working-class men like the title character fight in the Vietnam War, college students take drugs, denounce the military, and embrace the Black Panthers. In one of the most vivid scenes of this film, Gump punches out the abusive, weasel-like president of the Berkeley SDS during the 1967 march on the Pentagon. Perhaps unknown to the scriptwriters, the president of the

Berkeley SDS in 1967, Michael Lerner, had become, by the date of the film's release, an adviser to First Lady Hillary Rodham Clinton.

If films on the 1960s span the ideological spectrum, network television series and specials more consistently support Baby Boomer activists. (An unprecedented U.S. population boom occurred in the fifteen years following the end of World War II. The millions of American children born in those years soon became known as Baby Boomers.) In 1998 the NBC series "Law and Order" aired a fictional, retrospective account of the 1968 SDS takeover of Columbia University. Police investigators, working on the case of a militant who had been murdered in 1968, discover that the radical had been an undercover New York police officer. Then the investigators, and a district attorney who had himself been an anti-war demonstrator, learn that nearly all of the most outspoken radicals at "Kensington College" were police spies sent to provoke violence and discredit the SDS. While such agent provocateurs did exist in real life, "Law and Order" suggested that the violence of the New Left was nothing more than the work of a manipulative Establishment.

Despite television series and films, most Americans' memories of the 1960s are evoked by rock songs. Jefferson Airplane's lively 1967 song "Somebody to Love" has endured as an anthem of countercultural liberation. Whenever Hollywood scriptwriters want to conjure among viewers images of free love and psychedelics—without having to create fully realized characters—they turn to singer Grace Slick.

Equally evocative, the Rolling Stones' 1968 hit "Streetfighting Man" celebrated "violent revolution" against cops and "compromised solutions." After the Stones released "Streetfighting Man," no campus riot was complete without this tune being blasted over the stereo speakers. Finally there was Crosby, Stills, Nash, and Young's 1970 dirge "Ohio," commemorating the slaying of four students at Kent State University by the Ohio National Guard. To this day, as soon as a disc jockey plays "Ohio" in a student bar, conversation turns to the song's origins in the Kent State tragedy.

Looking past popular culture to the historical record, we can say that "The 1960s" began as myth and reality in Greensboro, North Carolina, in 1960, when a handful of black college students challenged local segregation ordinances. These religious pacifists asked to be served a cup of coffee at a Woolworth five-and-ten lunch counter. When they were refused service, they inspired thousands of other Southern black students to imitate their example. Soon black youths established a new civil rights organization to promote racial equality in Dixie—the Student Nonviolent Coordinating Committee (SNCC, often pronounced as Snick).

At the same time young white radicals at the University of Michigan were founding the Students for a Democratic Society. SDSers condemned Washington's anti-Communist foreign policy and the "racism" of the Democratic and Republican parties. Often forgotten is that even as students were building a New Left, conservative white youths were laying the basis for a New Right, founding the anti-Communist, free-market-oriented Young Americans for Freedom (YAF).

The student-led phase of the civil rights movement peaked in 1964 during the Mississippi Freedom Summer campaign. As white and black students battled Southern racists, they also began to fall out among themselves. Returning to their campuses in the fall of 1964, young activists at Berkeley initiated their own freedom struggle against college administrators. The Berkeley Free Speech Movement (FSM) inaugurated a spiral of conflict that transformed many tranquil college campuses into battlefields over university regulations and a widening war in Indochina.

America's initial military involvement in Indochina dated from World War II. Determined to defeat Imperial Japan, the Roosevelt administration had sent weapons and military advisers to Ho Chi Minh and his Vietnamese Communist guerrillas. After World War II, when France insisted on reclaiming its Indochina empire and ousting Ho Chi Minh as the leader of Vietnam, the United States stood on the sidelines. President Harry Truman did not consider Ho Chi Minh to be a threat to American security interests in Asia. But Truman did not wish to alienate a needed European ally by trying to awaken France from its colonial dreams. After the Korean War began in 1950, and the United States found itself fighting hundreds of thousands of Chinese soldiers, Truman decided that France's Indochina war was part of a broader struggle against Communist expansion.

Although Washington ultimately underwrote 80 percent of France's doomed military effort in Vietnam, neither Truman nor President Dwight Eisenhower were eager to commit American combat troops to Indochina. The Korean War had turned into a wrenching stalemate. Eisenhower, though desirous of checking the Soviet-backed Vietnamese Communists, had no intention of getting involved in another Asian land war. Instead he supported the creation of an independent South Vietnamese government. He hoped that American financial and technical assistance to Saigon would buy President Ngo Dinh Diem the time he needed to consolidate his power and stabilize the economy. But South Vietnamese insurgents, with the backing of North Vietnam, China, and the Soviet Union, launched a wave of political assassinations and terrorism at the end of the 1950s that rocked Diem's government. Diem responded ineptly to Communist terrorism, alienating peasants and Buddhist monks.

Most South Vietnamese tried to take a neutral stance, wanting nothing to do with the urban, Roman Catholic Diem or Ho Chi Minh. They knew that Ho Chi Minh had imprisoned or exterminated thousands of capitalist "class enemies" in 1954 upon taking power in Hanoi. Unfortunately for Diem, Communist terrorism escalated, and the thousands of American military advisers that President John F. Kennedy sent to assist Saigon were more than matched by the troops that infiltrated South Vietnam from the North.

When Lee Harvey Oswald assassinated Kennedy in November 1963, newly installed President Lyndon Johnson found the military situation in South Vietnam rapidly deteriorating. South Vietnamese military officers, with the tacit support of U.S. leaders, had killed Diem earlier in November 1963. The generals and their American patrons erroneously thought they were better equipped to impose order. Johnson ran for election in 1964 publicly proclaiming his unwillingness to send American combat troops to South Vietnam. Privately he was biding his time until the conclusion of his campaign against Republican challenger Barry Goldwater, whom he depicted as a wild-eyed, bomb-throwing extremist.

To the Democratic heirs of former First Lady Eleanor Roosevelt and two-time presidential candidate Adlai Stevenson, Johnson insisted that he, unlike Goldwater, was a responsible anti-Communist who would deploy force only as a last resort and then only in careful measure. The Stevenson–Eleanor Roosevelt Democrats believed that accommodation with China and the Soviet Union was possible. Such Democrats, most of whom came from suburban, white-collar Protestant and secular Jewish backgrounds, were also suspicious of politicians who wore their anti-communism on their sleeves.

The revolt of the white-collar Democrats began in February 1965 when President Johnson bombed military targets in North Vietnam. Hanoi responded by deploying more Communist troops to South Vietnam. Johnson's decision to introduce American combat troops into South Vietnam in March 1965 prompted thousands of college faculty and middle-class suburban students to hold teach-ins on the war. These special sessions served largely as forums for condemning U.S. military action against the North Vietnamese army and its southern guerrilla wing, the National Liberation Front (or Viet Cong). SDS president Carl Oglesby proclaimed that corporate-serving Democrats were behind the escalation of the Vietnam conflict.

It quickly became evident that winning the Vietnam War

would not be easy. The first major clash between American and North Vietnamese army regulars took place in 1965 in the Ia Drang Valley. U.S. troops, despite being outnumbered seven to one, managed to kill three thousand Communist soldiers. Two hundred forty Americans died. The Hanoi regime realized that its army would have to pursue hit-and-run attacks, blend into the local population, and retreat to Cambodian and Laotian sanctuaries which the United States could not assault. Such a strategy, Hanoi anticipated, would lead Washington to bomb South Vietnam indiscriminately and, as a consequence, turn the South Vietnamese people against the United States and its Saigon ally. Hanoi's strategy made for a protracted war that frustrated the American electorate.

While the Vietnam War grew bloodier, campus protest against the draft, university research for the military, and related matters mounted. At the same time Northern black activists—who were not as religious or as committed to nonviolence as their Southern brethren—expelled whites from SNCC. Black militants established organizations such as the Black Panthers in the San Francisco Bay Area. By 1967, confrontations escalated on the nation's college campuses and in the cities of the North. White and black radicals advocated "picking up the gun" to destroy "American imperialism."

1968, one of the most traumatic years in recent American history, began with the North Vietnamese army and the Viet Cong launching the Tet offensive. Despite the loss of several thousand American and South Vietnamese soldiers, the Communist forces were decimated. The U.S. army and air force eliminated the Viet Cong as a military threat to Saigon. Yet President Johnson and the elite media misread the results of the Tet offensive, regarding it as a devastating American defeat. (The Johnson administration had not believed the Communists were capable of launching such a massive attack. Many journalists felt they had been lied to, and Johnson himself felt deflated.) Weary of anti-war protest and unwilling to invade North Vietnam lest China intervene, Johnson announced that he would open peace negotiations with Hanoi—and that he would not seek reelection.

With the assassination of civil rights leader Martin Luther King, Jr., in the spring of 1968, a new wave of rioting struck America's urban black neighborhoods. No sooner had the riots subsided when SDSers at Columbia University seized control of their campus in an effort to spark a student revolt across America. As the national SDS argued in 1968, "The whole education system now—from grade schools on up—is used to tie the allegiance of youth to the capitalist system by building up an ideological army for the ruling class." Higher education, far from being an Ivory Tower, was, according to SDS, a citadel of U.S. imperialism that had to be liberated or destroyed.

In August 1968, ten thousand demonstrators gathered in Chicago to disrupt the Democratic National Convention. The violence that occurred in the streets of Chicago, much of it intentionally provoked by partisans of the New Left, shattered the Democratic electoral coalition and led to the party's capture by anti-war activists. Such Democrats rejected America's anti-Communist foreign policy and embraced abortion, racial hiring quotas, and gay rights, among other causes.

In 1969 campus protest in support of black power, and against defense contracting by the universities, accelerated. Where just one-quarter of the nation's campuses could claim a leftist student organization in 1965, four years later 46 percent had one. Bombings, building seizures, and assaults against faculty and students who did not embrace SDS and the Black Panthers became the norm at Berkeley, Cornell, and Kent State. One faction of SDS split off and dedicated itself to armed revolution. Meanwhile, "do-your-own-thing" libertarians in the Young Americans for Freedom—who accounted for a third of the organization's membership—divided the conservative student movement. Boomer libertarians protested the draft and believed that government should not regulate the marketplace or the bedroom.

The wave of violence that hit hundreds of campuses in 1969 continued unabated into the early months of 1970. In April 1970, President Nixon announced that U.S. forces had invaded Cambodia. The Cambodian incursion sparked rioting at several campuses and led to the Ohio National Guard occupation of Kent State. After the Ohio Guard killed four Kent State students on May 4, 1970, America witnessed the greatest student strike in its history. Four million youths protested the slayings and the invasion of Cambodia.

Thinking that their campus had cooled down with the end of the spring quarter, University of Wisconsin administrators were not prepared when a bomb with the equivalent destructive power of 3,400 sticks of dynamite exploded outside the Army Mathematics Research Center. (Twenty-eight full-time mathematicians at the center helped develop infrared detection devices which the army deployed in Vietnam to root out Communist troops.) The blast killed Robert Fassnacht, a doctoral physics student, blinded a night watchman, and damaged 28 campus buildings. Paradoxically, "Army Math" emerged unscathed.

Campus unrest must be understood in the context of several important post–World War II developments that transformed American higher education. Foremost among the changes America experienced during the 1960s were the coming of age of the Boomers and the rapid growth of universities. Between 1960 and 1972, 45 million youths—many of them the offspring of the Great Depression–World War II generation—turned 18. College enrollment swelled as the American economy continued its post–World War II expansion. In 1960, 3 million youths attended college. By 1970, 10 million young men and women were enrolled in an institution of higher education. In just 31 years, from 1939 to 1970, the proportion of American youths between 18 and 21 years of age in college rose from 15 percent to 50 percent.

Before World War II, not one American university enrolled

more than fifteen thousand students. In 1970 America claimed
fifty colleges with at least fifteen thousand students. Eight universities enrolled more than thirty thousand, including Ohio
State and Wisconsin (at Madison). The University of Minnesota
was not atypical in having two thousand students enrolled in a
single introductory psychology course. Not wishing to burden
research-oriented faculty with undergraduates, colleges relied
on poorly compensated, sometimes incompetent graduate students to teach the larger classes. At Berkeley graduate students
taught two-thirds of all introductory courses.

An implicit bargain kept graduate programs well stocked
with willing workers. (Berkeley's history department alone enrolled four hundred graduate students.) Most male graduate
students accepted short-term exploitation by their universities
in exchange for draft deferments—at least until deferments for
attending graduate school ended in the summer of 1967. (Deferments remained for the rapidly growing number of male
graduate students who announced their intention to attend divinity school.) Doctoral students received advanced degrees
that were subsidized at the public schools by taxpayers, while
those attending private colleges lived off the tuition income
generated by well-off undergraduates. Once they had obtained
their doctorates, freshly minted professors could expect to walk
into tenure-track jobs. All they had to do was finish graduate
school before the market for Ph.D.s became saturated.

The rapid expansion of the student body in the 1960s created
the social base for campus activism. At Berkeley, which stood in
the vanguard of campus activism, just 3,000 of the university's
27,000 students in 1964 and 1965—11 percent—took part in
protests over free speech and the Vietnam War. More Berkeley
students participated in fraternity and sorority events than in
protest activities. The problem for university administrators
and law enforcement agencies, however, was that a minority
movement with only 3,000 members was still large enough to
disrupt a campus, paralyze administrators, and divide a faculty.

Nationally just six million Americans—barely 5 percent of the population—participated in any form of moderate or radical anti-war and civil rights protest. In a democratic society, however, one in which most elected officials are reluctant to deploy force against its citizens, a minority intent upon disruption can immobilize a government and polarize a people.

Students in the 1960s, who had gone away to college in an effort to escape parental authority, found that schools routinely practiced *in loco parentis* (in place of the parents). In other words, the universities functioned as surrogate parents, demanding that their "children" not drink beer until they were of legal age (twenty-one), consume narcotics, or copulate in the dormitories or in off-campus apartments. As events transpired, the university regulation of student sex became nearly impossible once pharmaceutical companies introduced the birth-control pill in 1960 and local clinics provided penicillin for the syphilis-infected. Sex without the consequences of unwanted pregnancy and incurable social disease proved extremely alluring for many members of the 1960s generation. Most Boomer students, in contrast to their parents, had never known deprivation, regarded a university education as a birthright, romanticized the social pathologies of the black underclass, and largely lacked a sense of limits.

In addition to fighting an uphill battle against sexual liberation and a drug-laced counterculture, college administrators sought to regulate campus politics. Fearful of state legislatures still dominated by conservative rural interests—and that supplied needed funding for additional classrooms and dormitories—public universities from Berkeley to Ohio State banned radical speakers. A few universities also denied tenure to leftist professors.

But those were the exception rather than the rule. In earlier decades, in the 1940s and 1950s, no more than 300 faculty, out of nearly 200,000, had been denied tenure on political grounds. Such professors were usually booted off campus for turning

their classrooms into political rallies and for refusing to cooperate with legislative and law enforcement agencies investigating
Communist infiltration of higher education and the federal
government. Typically, elite research-oriented universities such
as Wisconsin and Harvard shielded their faculty radicals from
outside censure—as long as professors did not flaunt their
Marxism off campus. The sheltered radical professors and
graduate students of the 1950s became the core of the 1960s
campus-based New Left.

Radical students complained that the liberal arts courses
taught by the World War II generation of faculty made society
too complex to understand. Confrontation cleared the mind.
Liberation came with struggle. To many SDSers, Karl Marx
provided the answers. As Michigan SDSer Robert Meeropol recalled, he had become "enchanted by the beauty of Marx's for-
mulations" and began "to realize that his [Marx's] vocabulary
was not used to obfuscate but rather to crystallize meaning."
(Meeropol's parents, Julius and Ethel Rosenberg, had been executed in the 1950s as Soviet espionage agents.) SDS leader Carl
Oglesby added a caveat: students had to do more than read
Marx; they needed to get out of the classroom and into the
streets, because "the policeman's riot club functions like a magic
wand under whose hard caress the banal soul grows vivid and
the nameless recover their authenticity—a bestower, this wand
of the lost charisma of the modern self—I bleed, therefore I
am."

The students who followed Oglesby saw America as a profoundly racist and imperialist nation. The New Left vanguard,
as well as its foot soldiers, viewed the Vietnam War as a criminal act of genocide, not as a mistaken policy of well-intentioned
anti-Communist Democrats. Indeed, SDS ridiculed moderate
peace groups such as the Committee for a Sane Nuclear Policy
(SANE). SDSers also berated Minnesota senator Eugene
McCarthy and other Democratic party reformers. New Leftists
saw no difference between cold war Democrats who clung to

the banner of Franklin Roosevelt and anti–New Deal Republicans. Vice President Hubert Humphrey and California governor Ronald Reagan merely represented two sides of the same imperialist, racist coin.

Lyndon Johnson was unable to persuade many middle-class youths—even those who did not join SDS—that a Communist victory in Vietnam would pose a security risk to the United States. Millions of Americans did not believe that the fall of Vietnam might result in a "domino effect," plunging Laos, Cambodia, and other Southeast Asian countries one by one into the Soviet Empire. They were also not persuaded by the "Munich Analogy." According to Johnson, the failure of the democracies to stop Hitler in 1938 in Czechoslovakia had led to World War II. It followed that compromise and negotiation with Ho Chi Minh would be like dealing with Hitler; they only invited further aggression. America had to fight in Vietnam today to avoid World War III tomorrow.

The difficulties with this line of reasoning were aggravated when Johnson tried to explain to the American people that the Vietnam War was not really about Vietnam—it was about Communist China and the Soviet Union. After World War II, America had committed itself to containing the Soviet Union and Communist China. The chief problem with containment, however, was that since the Communist superpowers also had atomic weapons, America could not take them on directly. Consequently the United States found itself fighting Soviet proxies in Korea (1950–1953) and Indochina (1965–1973). Nixon's decision in the early 1970s to normalize relations with China and negotiate arms control with the Soviet Union effectively ended America's policy of containment and *officially* made Vietnam irrelevant. (In the 1980s President Ronald Reagan renewed America's *Soviet* containment policy.)

One of the most fateful of Johnson's Vietnam-related decisions was to continue draft deferments to college students and to exempt nearly all National Guard and military reserve units from combat. Only in 1968 did Johnson reluctantly send fifteen thousand reservists and Guardsmen to Vietnam. (*Seven hundred thousand* Guardsmen and reservists had fought in the Korean War.) Johnson's initiative unleashed a firestorm of criticism, since the deployment of Guardsmen and reservists in their twenties and thirties disrupted families and inconvenienced employers. Wilting, Johnson reversed policy and once again exempted National Guard and military reserve units from combat duty.

In order to promote his domestic legislative agenda—the War on Poverty—Johnson did not want Congress and the public to believe that America had become involved in a shooting match with Asian Communists. If Johnson admitted that the nation was on a war footing, Congress would expect him to defeat Ho Chi Minh first, then resume the War on Poverty. Unwilling to shelve his domestic programs, Johnson upset the American economy as well as the Selective Service program. Refusing to raise taxes, which would have been a clear signal that the nation was at war, Johnson pursued a policy of deficit spending. Given that it cost the United States $400,000 to kill just *one* Viet Cong or North Vietnamese army soldier, the Vietnam War became a financial quagmire.

Johnson's draft policy in effect targeted eighteen-year-old working-class males who lacked the finances to attend college or the political connections to get a berth in a National Guard unit. Selective Service identified males in their mid-twenties as undesirable draftees. By that age men were more likely to resent being ordered around and, in any event, had established themselves in a community that would notice their absence. With six months of basic training followed by a one-year tour in Vietnam, people were likely to ask the newly discharged nineteen-year-old combat veteran what his plans were after he graduated from high school. (The average age of an American soldier in Vietnam was nineteen, compared with twenty-six in World War II. Although younger soldiers were easier to command, the Pentagon failed to consider that older and more emotionally mature veterans would find it easier to readjust to civilian life.)

Given the generous provision of student deferments, it was not surprising that 60 percent of draft-age men avoided military service. Just 17 percent of all university students in the 1960s came from working- and lower-middle-class backgrounds, making the college deferment a largely middle- and upper-middle-class entitlement. Consequently 80 percent of the young Americans sent to Vietnam came from the working class. Just one student each from Harvard, Princeton, and Yale died in combat. Where America's elite had trooped off to fight in 1942, their children avoided the Vietnam War. Many of the children of the elite, including the son of Johnson's defense secretary, Robert S. McNamara, identified with the New Left.

In response to criticism that they were taking advantage of their privileged backgrounds and shirking their patriotic duty, the sons of the middle class had an excellent rejoinder: If Johnson thought the Vietnam War was all that important, why did he continue to provide student draft deferments and exempt Guard and military reserve units from service in Indochina? The answer was that Johnson allowed domestic political considerations to hinder America's ability to fight the Vietnam War. He gave Americans the impression that Vietnam was not important enough to risk sacrificing anyone other than working-class, black, or Hispanic youths.

Robert Timberg, a Vietnam veteran who later became a reporter for the *Washington Post*, offered a telling commentary on the class and ideological divisions that tore apart his generation. In a discussion of James Webb, who served as Ronald Reagan's secretary of the navy, Timberg related this story. When Webb was attending Georgetown Law School after returning from Vietnam, an anti-war faculty member used Webb's name in an essay question. The law professor posed a fictional situation in which Webb was smuggling jade home from Vietnam inside the bodies of two dead comrades. While the leftist academic would never ridicule blacks, he felt that Vietnam veterans—baby killers all—were fair game. Timberg concluded that:

> The generational schism broadened with the blossoming of the antiwar movement and the counterculture that accompanied it. Ultimately, those who opposed the war prevailed, but along the way they made a strategic error. They did not attempt to make common cause with their peers in uniform. Instead, they portrayed the men fighting the war with contempt, spitting on them, calling them fascists and baby killers, as if by a simple act of labeling they could transform them into beings different from and less worthy than themselves, with less reason to live.

As Webb learned when he enrolled at Georgetown, the Vietnam War had radicalized many students and faculty—even at a Jesuit institution that in the 1950s had been famous for its cold war ardor. (Both Nixon and Joseph McCarthy had sought political advice from anti-Communist faculty at Georgetown.) Thousands of students, professors, and recent college graduates rejected the policy of Communist containment. Campus constituencies were frustrated with an unending war and repulsed by the mounting American and Vietnamese death toll. Campus peace activists, or "doves," and hard-core leftists came to see the universities as complicit in the promotion of America's "immoral war" in Vietnam. ROTC programs and, more particularly, defense contracts awarded to university faculty became targets of campus protest.

Campus-based military research deeply involved higher education in the formulation and execution of American foreign policy. During World War II, Berkeley, the University of Chicago, and Columbia worked to defeat Germany and Japan. Scientists developed new weapons, including the atomic bomb. Harvard scientists created napalm, a jellied gasoline substance that U.S. aircraft used in 1945 to firebomb Tokyo. After the war, with tensions with the Soviet Union and China mounting, scores of universities enlisted in the crusade to contain communism. By 1968 universities were spending $3 billion annually for research and development. Seventy percent of these funds came from the federal government, of which half originated in defense-related agencies. In 1969 the Pentagon underwrote 80 percent of the budget of the Massachusetts Institute for Technology (MIT).

MIT was far from the only university to feed at the cold war defense trough. Shortly after World War II, Penn State's Ordnance Research Laboratory (ORL) became one of five university-based naval weapons testing facilities. The ORL developed the nuclear-tipped Polaris missile and a variety of torpedo prototypes. In 1949 Penn State and the navy built the world's largest water tunnel to test the noise level of submarine and torpedo propellers. Between 1945 and 1965 the navy awarded Penn State $62 million in grants and underwrote 76 percent of the engineering college's budget.

Unlike the submarine and missile research at Penn State, Michigan State faculty worked on projects directly related to the anti-Communist struggle in Vietnam. From 1955 to 1962 the Michigan State Vietnam Project represented what was then the largest federally directed technical assistance program in American history. Michigan State economists and political scientists created the South Vietnamese governmental structure while the School of Police Administration established Saigon's security forces and equipped them with five hundred 60mm mortars, among other crowd-control devices. The Michigan State Vietnam Project also served as cover for Central Intelligence Agency operations in Indochina, with several dozen CIA agents obtaining faculty rank at the university.

In all, one thousand Michigan State personnel traveled to South Vietnam, and the university received $25 million from the U.S. Foreign Operations Administration (later renamed the Agency for International Development). By 1962 Michigan State had become one of the largest university players in third world technical assistance programs, accounting for 10 percent of the total number of American faculty serving overseas. Michigan State improved security forces in such anti-Communist states as Colombia, South Korea, and Taiwan. Before becoming president of South Vietnam in the 1950s, Ngo Dinh Diem had been a graduate student at Michigan State.

To the faculty critics of American foreign policy, undertakings like the Michigan State Vietnam Project soiled higher education. (As the 1960s wore on, disaffected faculty were joined by larger numbers of white-collar professionals in publishing, the media, and the entertainment industry.) To the dismay of anti-Communist university administrators, the ranks of the faculty left grew—a consequence of the demand for additional faculty to teach the burgeoning student population. In 1948 there had been 196,000 college professors; by 1970, 500,000 had taken their place. For every faculty member who retired in 1966, five young, often radicalized, professors replaced them.

A number of junior faculty—most of them concentrated in liberal arts and social science departments—did not share the anti-Communist beliefs of their older colleagues. Too young to remember much of the Great Depression, the Stalin-Hitler pact, and World War II, they seemed to lack a sense of history—not to mention gratitude to the university for hiring them in the first place. Some of the newer faculty were children of 1930s-era Communist party activists. While student opinion generally divided over Vietnam, and barely a quarter participated in demonstrations on a regular basis, 70 percent of faculty embraced the anti-war movement. Faculty supported the New Left more vigorously than students themselves. Such professors provided the base for what anti-war activists called the "constituency of conscience." Not so kind critics called anti-war faculty the "constituency of chaos."

Not surprisingly, a period as disruptive as the 1960s has spawned continuing controversy and conflicting interpretations. One school of thought has championed the notion of

"The Good 1960s." Historian Paul Buhle, a former Wisconsin SDSer, has contended that the "hysterical" critics of the New Left are nothing more than stooges of the radical right. According to Buhle, conservatives have grown more vocal in their treatment of the 1960s because the "Reagan Revolution" failed to change the leftist culture of the universities. Hence the right has "thirsted for the revenge that eluded them." Writing in 1990, Buhle defended his former comrades who bombed the Army Mathematics Research Center at Wisconsin. Although one young scientist died, leaving behind a wife and three children, that fatality, Buhle pointed out, was "less than that in any one village in any one day of fighting in Vietnam."

Sociologist Sheldon Wolin, who had been a faculty champion of the Berkeley Free Speech Movement, concurred with Buhle. As Wolin asserted in 1997, vengeful conservatives have fixated on the few excesses of the 1960s because they know they can mobilize a coalition of racist reactionaries against black rights and in favor of an imperialist foreign policy.

In her 1991 book *The Vietnam Wars*, historian Marilyn Young, a student activist at Michigan in the 1960s, called U.S. military intervention in Indochina the "American invasion of South Vietnam." Young, a participant in the 1965 Michigan teach-in on Indochina, argued that the Vietnam War advanced a capitalist foreign policy. The United States, she claimed, imposed its will on other nations through violence. Fortunately for the world's exploited peoples, Young's generation rebelled against American racism, sexism, and imperialism. Their rebellion, Young boasted, contributed to Hanoi's victory in 1975.

Terry Anderson, a Boomer historian like Young and Buhle, praises the revolutionary spirit of the 1960s. In his 1995 book *The Movement and the Sixties*, Anderson compared the Boomers to their less admirable elders who had came of age in the 1950s. In his discussion of the so-called Silent Generation, which opposed the campus and culture wars of the 1960s, Anderson wrote:

Perhaps their label—the Silent Generation—was unfair, for they did talk, but they sounded just like their parents, so void of thought that they should have held their breath. Appropriately, a decade or so later when the nation was inflamed with protest and when the Silent Generation was relaxing into middle age, many of them earned a new label—the Silent Majority.

Continuing his survey of recent generations, Anderson argued that World War II veterans had built a stifling, repressive social order that deserved overturning. "Coming of age in the Great Depression, the older generation saved for the future, worked for the family, and followed the roles and the rules. The counterculture challenged that, encouraged experimentation, and provoked millions to consider, or reconsider, their lives." Anderson admitted that the counterculture had its problems, but ultimately he defended the liberated Boomers. They could not, Anderson insisted, be blamed for failing to transcend the values of their corrupt parents and a sick society.

Morris Dickstein, a professor of English and celebrant of the 1960s counterculture, seconded Anderson's view. In 1997 Dickstein noted that the students of the 1960s and their intellectual mentors had successfully fostered "a cultural division that fractured the artificial, often repressive consensus of the postwar years" on matters like America's anti-Communist foreign policy, recreational drug usage, and sexual preference.

Significant voices outside academia have also endorsed the New Left interpretation of the 1960s. In 1994 the *New York Times* praised the youth of the 1960s and touted the anti-war movement as an "exercise in mass sanity." Reacting to Republican House Speaker Newt Gingrich's bitter characterization of President Bill Clinton as a child of the 1960s counterculture, the *Times* underlined its contempt for moral traditionalists by titling its editorial rebuttal "In Praise of the Counterculture." (Arthur Ochs Sulzberger, Jr., who succeeded his father as publisher of the *New York Times* in the early 1990s, had been a 1960s-era activist and countercultural enthusiast.)

The *Christian Science Monitor,* reviewing Terry Anderson's book, argued that he had written a "valuable counterpart to the reductionist and revisionist views now prevalent." Echoing Buhle and Wolin, the *Monitor* dismissed critiques of leftist campus violence in the 1960s as provoked by the conservative partisans of war, racism, and sexual repression.

Journalist and historian David Caute, in his 1988 book *The Year of the Barricades,* described the Vietnam War as "worse than a blunder, it was a crime"—a "murderous exercise"—committed by cold war Democrats. Caute then praised SDS: "The innovative ideas of the New Left—frequently, though not invariably, expressed with clarity and sophistication—constitute a treasury whose present dilapidation impoverishes us." (In 1965 Caute had organized a Vietnam teach-in at Oxford University which, critics complained, he stacked with anti-American speakers.)

1960s activists, like their media, political, and academic supporters, have remained vocal. Abbie Hoffman, a leader of the Yippies, an anarchist group that mixed LSD, group sex, and radical protest, observed in 1989 that "We were young, we were reckless, arrogant, silly, headstrong—and we were right. I regret nothing!" (Hoffman committed suicide shortly after making this statement.)

In 1988 Carl Oglesby claimed that the assassinations of Martin Luther King, Jr., and Robert Kennedy had pushed the New Left to violence and revolution. As Oglesby insisted, "reform had been made to seem like a dead-end street. How many times do you climb that tree just to have it chopped down beneath you?" Berkeley sociologist and onetime SDS president Todd Gitlin picked up Oglesby's theme, arguing in the 1980s that the deaths of Robert Kennedy and King meant that "a promise of redemption not only passed out of American politics, it passed out of ourselves." Former 1960s radicals Peter Collier and David Horowitz charged that Gitlin and Oglesby were revising the history of the New Left with little regard to the facts: in the 1960s SDSers denounced anti-war liberals such as Robert Kennedy and sided with the Black Panthers against the moderate civil rights leader whom they called "Martin Luther Queen."

Although the "Good 1960s" school represents a dominant view in the worlds of publishing and higher education, a "Bad 1960s" school has mounted a vigorous counteroffensive. Russell Baker, a syndicated newspaper columnist, World War II veteran, and critic of contemporary conservatism, wrote in 1998 what may be seen as a rebuttal to Dickstein and Anderson. Taking aim at *Pleasantville*, a film that mocked the sterile, drab, "black and white 1950s," Baker argued that the Boomers resented their elders because:

> Their parents lived in a heroic age, prevailing against poverty and tyranny [during the depression and World War II], leaving their children doomed to know only unheroic peace and prosperity.
>
> Born too late to get in on the big show, and being only human, the children might naturally resent their parents' triumph and take vengeance by belittling what the old folks made of their moment of glory. Which, of course, was the 1950s.

Historian Stephen Ambrose in 1997 provided his own take on the campus radicalism of the 1960s. The New Left, Ambrose charged,

> took its opportunity to print a license to riot, to scandalize, to do drugs and group sex, to talk and dress dirty, to call for revolution and burn flags, to condemn parents and indeed anyone over 30 years of age, in an excess of free will and childish misjudgment seldom matched and never exceeded.

(Ambrose, who came of age in the 1950s, had been a long-haired, left-of-center historian at Kansas State. He reassessed his politics in the 1970s when it became clear that a Communist-dominated Indochina was not the socialist paradise the New Left had envisioned.)

In 1988 sociologist Edward Shils argued that the New Left

had taken "over most of the heritage of Stalinist totalitarianism." Shils saw the 1960s activists as "antinomians" who had liberated themselves from social obligation. They were accountable to no higher law. Ultimately Shils regarded 1960s radicals and their liberal apologists as anti-American; they were "unable to see where liberalism ends and treason and subversion begin."

Peter Collier, who had been active in SNCC and the Berkeley Free Speech Movement, said of his former comrades, "Their god could never fail because they were atheists to begin with. They never really believed *in* anything: they were *against* patriotic commitment; they hated the *idea* of America."

In the early 1960s Collier and his friend David Horowitz had seen SDS as an "opportunity to be leftists in a new way: not as servile agents of a foreign power [like the 1930s-era Communist party] but as the shapers of an indigenous radicalism." Later Collier and Horowitz decided they had been wrong. Collier saw a "chic hatred of America" and a rationalization for violence. "Vietnam made us special," Collier contended. "It justified every excess, every violent thought and deed."

As Horowitz concluded, "The more I thought about the posturing of the left, the more I saw that its genius lay not in reforms but in framing indictments. Resentment and retribution were the radical passions." Horowitz was no minor, easily dismissed, New Left figure. He had edited *Ramparts* which, with a circulation of 100,000 in the 1960s, was the largest radical magazine published in the United States. Three of his books, *The Free World Colossus* (1965), *Containment and Revolution* (1967), and *Empire and Revolution* (1969) were oft-cited condemnations of America's cold war foreign policy. Horowitz's subsequent "apostasy," as he wryly called it, made him a particular target of abuse in the media and academia.

Years before Collier and Horowitz went public with their "second thoughts" about the 1960s, historian William O'Neill had bemoaned "the dreary propaganda about youth's insurgent idealism." (For that matter, O'Neill had nothing kind to say about the counterculture and posturing rock-and-roll stars. "The difference between a rock king and a robber baron," O'Neill claimed, "was about six inches of hair.") In the early 1970s O'Neill observed that leftist faculty and intellectuals had created "the conventional eulogy of the young as the best-educated, most altruistic generation in history." O'Neill charged that the New Left produced "moral arrogance," not idealism. Intellectuals who promoted SDS and the Panthers, O'Neill wrote, were part of the "national pathology" that afflicted America in the 1960s. Memorably, O'Neill described the 1968 Columbia SDS uprising as "a mixture of living theater, cowboys and Indians, the Russian Revolution, and nursery school. Afterward, everyone got a good spanking for being naughty."

Tied closely to the debate between the partisans of the "Good 1960s" and the "Bad 1960s" is the question of what role campus activists played in ending the Vietnam War and "redeeming" the Democratic party. Former South Dakota senator and 1972 Democratic presidential candidate George McGovern, for instance, has argued that the peace movement ended the Vietnam War. Indeed, McGovern, ironically mirroring the complaints of anti-Communist conservatives, has observed that the Vietnam War was lost on the streets of America, as students rumbled with police, and not on the battlefields of Indochina.

Historian Jeffrey Herf, who had belonged to the Wisconsin SDS in the 1960s, eventually concluded that the New Left's disruption of American society forced Nixon to make a bad peace with the Vietnamese Communists. Worse, the anti-war movement encouraged Hanoi to pretend to negotiate a settlement while continuing to kill South Vietnamese and American soldiers.

Unlike Herf and McGovern, who believed that campus protest had, at least indirectly, ended the war in Vietnam, other commentators took a different tack. Andrew Greeley, a sociologist, as well as a Catholic priest, argued in the early 1970s that the New Left, with its radicalism, anti-Americanism, and upper-class elitism and hostility to white workers, delayed the public rejection of the Vietnam conflict. SDS extremism encouraged ordinary citizens to rally around Lyndon Johnson, thereby prolonging the war.

Political scientist Guenter Lewy concluded in his 1990 book *The Cause That Failed* that the public rejection of the Vietnam War had little to do with campus protest. Rather, people grew weary of a war that went on for too long with too many American deaths and no victory in sight. Campus unrest, Lewy felt, was not a significant factor in ending the Indochinese conflict.

Although most Americans, including Boomers, did not accept the New Left view of Washington's foreign policy, Lewy overstated his case. A number of writers have tried to distinguish among the positive and negative influences of campus protest on presidential politics and the conduct of the Vietnam War. Historians Charles DeBenedetti and Charles Chatfield, in their 1990 book *An American Ordeal,* went to great lengths to dissociate the peace movement from what they saw as the irresponsible radical campus fringe. There was, the authors insisted, a socially responsible, implicitly good peace movement in the late 1950s. But after the military escalation of the Vietnam War in 1965, media attention shifted from respectable, moderate organizations, such as SANE, to the militant SDS. Once SDS imploded in 1969, DeBenedetti and Chatfield argued, the more mature, nonviolent activists regained their momentum and, working within electoral channels, captured control of the Democratic party.

If the responsible anti-war movement should not be conflated with other crusades of the 1960s, we are still confronted with the fact that the general public made (and makes) few distinctions in the anti-war movement between moderates and radicals, peace partisans and gay liberation advocates. As the combative pundit Patrick Buchanan observed in the 1996 Republican presidential primaries, it is no more fair to criticize him for the beliefs of some of his more extremist followers than it was for Southerners in 1859 to view all anti-slavery people as being no different from John Brown. It may not be fair, but politics is frequently unfair—the perception of reality, not necessarily reality itself, can shape belief.

On the other hand, the negative public perception of the 1960s anti-war movement was not entirely unjustified. As Lewy argued, the peace movement's principle of inclusion attracted the violence-prone and the lawless. Moderate activists were powerless to correct this situation. SDS pursued a political strategy intended to create as much social disruption as possible. The New Left, Lewy believed, alienated the great majority of Americans and brought about the elections of Richard Nixon and Ronald Reagan.

Historian Leo Ribuffo observed in 1994 that the 1960s was a polarized era, not a radical one. When we move beyond the radicalized, affluent confines of Ann Arbor, Berkeley, and Cambridge, a portrait of America emerges that is quite different from the one painted by veterans of the student movement. For every radical student who admired North Vietnam's Ho Chi Minh, many more conservative youths became politically active as a result of Arizona senator Barry Goldwater's 1964 presidential campaign. Goldwater may have lost the election to Johnson, but the young conservatives he inspired became the architects of Ronald Reagan's triumph in the 1980 presidential election.

We should also remember that in 1968 the hawkish populist George Wallace scored best among voters under the age of thirty, while a 1970 Gallup public opinion poll showed that 73 percent of people between twenty and twenty-nine years of age opposed student anti-war strikes. It is also some cause for amusement that Generation X member and former Christian Coalition director Ralph Reed credited the campus anti-war movement for inspiring his own conservative activism. Reed earned a Ph.D. in history from Emory University, where he read the works of Tom Hayden and other stalwarts of the New Left.

In trying to sum up "the 1960's Experience," Ribuffo asked

an excellent question: "Might the [Vietnam] war have ended sooner if the debate between the hawks and doves had not been embedded in cultural conflicts that were largely irrelevant to foreign policy?" But can historians separate class and cultural conflicts from foreign policy issues? Foreign policy is a reflection, if not an extension, of domestic conflicts and accommodations. A foreign policy in the 1960s that exacerbated class and cultural divisions by sending one group to fight and exempting another from combat altogether led to grief. This may well be the only lesson of the 1960s that everyone who writes about its campus and culture wars can endorse.

2

Civil Rights and Wrongs

AT THE DAWNING of the twentieth century, Southern "reformers" had removed nearly all blacks and one-third of poor whites from the voter rolls. They hoped to eliminate the issues of race and poverty from future elections. Through the imposition of poll taxes and literacy tests, voter turnout in the South plunged—from 58 percent in 1892 to 28 percent by 1904. In Louisiana, for instance, 130,000 blacks had participated in the 1896 elections. By 1906, just 1,342 blacks voted.

As impoverished Southern blacks and whites lost their voting rights, lynching and segregation became commonplace. From the 1870s to the 1950s, Southerners lynched 3,400 blacks and 1,300 whites. Meanwhile the U.S. Supreme Court, in *Plessy v. Ferguson* (1896), sanctioned "separate but equal" racial segregation. Soon separate public accommodations, toilets, and drinking fountains blanketed the South. Most public schools had been segregated since the 1870s. Black teachers received half the salary of whites—who did not fare all that well either, given Southern indifference to public education. Mississippi did not establish a public school system until 1919, more than 70 years after New England.

By the 1930s President Franklin Roosevelt had identified the South as "America's number one economic problem." Economic statistics, as well as the social trends that Roosevelt did not mention, told a woeful tale. More than eight million white and black tenant farmers and sharecroppers lived barely at a level of subsistence. One-quarter of Southern textile workers were under the age of sixteen. They were four times more likely to be illiterate than Southern children who did not work in mills. Two million Southerners had hookworm, and the South had the highest illegitimacy and syphilis infection rates in the United States. Six Dixie states led the nation in black-on-black homicide.

In 1935 a few Northern politicians, responding to the demands of their black constituents, attempted to make lynching a federal crime. Southern Democrats shot down the proposal—a not unexpected development, since of the fourteen standing committees in the Senate that originated legislation, Southerners chaired ten. Roosevelt confided to the leaders of the National Association for the Advancement of Colored People (NAACP) that he was powerless to deal with the South. "The southerners by reason of the seniority rule in Congress are chairmen or occupy strategic places on most of the Senate and House committees," the president moaned. "If I come out for [an] anti-lynching bill now they will block every bill I ask Congress to pass and to keep America from collapsing. I just can't take that risk."

Other New Deal liberals, especially those who did not have to campaign in the South, were less circumspect than Roosevelt. Harvard Law School professor Felix Frankfurter called the South "the greatest immoral factor in American politics, and to the extent that northerners help to perpetuate it they are accomplices in all the evils that flow from it." (When Roosevelt later appointed Frankfurter to the U.S. Supreme Court, he handed down judicial rulings against segregation and voter disfranchisement.) The left-leaning *Nation* magazine went further than Frankfurter, arguing that the South was "so sick from its old infections of prejudice and poverty that it is a menace to the nation."

The advent of World War II forced Roosevelt to support limited civil rights initiatives. In 1941 union leader A. Philip

Randolph had threatened to lead a protest march on Washington that would undermine America's claim to being the defender of global freedom. Bypassing Congress, Roosevelt signed an executive order prohibiting discrimination on federally funded defense projects. He also established the Fair Employment Practices Committee (FEPC), though the agency had no direct enforcement power. Southerners were outraged. As Senator Theodore Bilbo of Mississippi said of the FEPC: "If you go through the government departments there are so many niggers it's like a black cloud all around you. . . . The niggers and the Jews of New York are working hand in hand on this damnable, Communist, poisonous piece of legislation."

A year after Roosevelt's death, Southerners denied funding to the FEPC, in effect abolishing the agency. Eager to shore up his support among the tens of thousands of new black voters who had moved north during the war in search of good-paying factory jobs, President Harry Truman proposed outlawing lynching. At the 1948 National Democratic Convention, Minneapolis mayor Hubert Humphrey led the fight for a civil rights plank in the party platform. Addressing himself to seething Southerners, Humphrey said, "To those who say that this civil rights program is an infringement on states' rights, I say this, that the time has arrived in America for the Democratic Party to get out of the shadows of states' rights and walk forthrightly into the bright sunshine of human rights."

Birmingham, Alabama, police commissioner "Bull" Connor and half the Alabama delegation stalked out of the convention, along with all the Mississippi delegates. Alabama election officials subsequently removed Truman from the presidential ballot. South Carolina governor Strom Thurmond also walked out of the convention and headed up the States' Rights party to challenge Truman. "There's not enough troops in the army to force the southern people to break down segregation and admit the Negro race into our theaters, into our swimming pools, into homes, and into our churches," Thurmond fumed. Although most of the South held firm for the victorious Truman, the 1948 election served warning that civil rights might tear apart the Democratic party.

Southern politicians calmed down after Truman's reelection—at least until 1954 when the U.S. Supreme Court, in *Brown v. Board of Education of Topeka,* overturned the separate-but-equal doctrine. President Dwight Eisenhower condemned the federal judiciary for—in his opinion—trying to dictate morals. If people in their heart of hearts, Eisenhower insisted, believed in segregation, the federal government could not and should not impose its own morality on unwilling individuals. Before the announcement of the *Brown* decision, Eisenhower had taken Chief Justice Earl Warren aside at a dinner party and said of the Southern segregationists, "These are not bad people. All they are concerned about is to see that their sweet little girls are not required to sit in school alongside some big overgrown Negroes." Despite his qualms, however, Eisenhower felt duty bound to enforce *Brown.*

A little more than a year after *Brown,* Martin Luther King, Jr., a twenty-six-year-old Baptist minister, took over leadership of a boycott of city buses in Montgomery, Alabama. Even though three-quarters of Montgomery's bus passengers were black, they had to give up their seats and move to the back if a white wanted their seat. If there was no seating available in the rear, blacks had to stand. In opposing this policy, King insisted that blacks follow the path of nonviolence and work for the Christian redemption of their oppressors. As the founder of the Southern Christian Leadership Conference (SCLC) later explained to friend and foe alike,

> Nonviolence offers a method by which [people] can fight evil with which they cannot live. It offers a unique weapon which, without firing a single bullet, disarms the adversary. It exposes his moral defenses, weakens his morale and at the same time works on his conscience.

Sadly for King, some white Southerners had untroubled consciences. These bitter-end racists felt threatened by the

Montgomery bus boycott and the *Brown* decision. By 1956 a reinvigorated Ku Klux Klan had enrolled 200,000 Southerners. In Congress, 101 Dixie politicians signed the "Southern Manifesto," vowing "massive resistance" against racial integration. Just three Southern congressmen refused to sign: Tennessee senators Albert Gore, Sr., and Estes Kefauver, and Senate Majority Leader Lyndon Johnson of Texas.

The advocates of massive resistance made a stand in Little Rock, Arkansas. Governor Orval Faubus, running for reelection in 1957, egged on a mob of several thousand who had gathered at Central High School to prevent nine black children from enrolling. The Arkansas National Guard abetted the segregationists, preventing the Little Rock school board from complying with *Brown*. Faced with an overt challenge to the authority of the United States government, Eisenhower sent the 101st Airborne Division to Little Rock. Illinois senator Paul Douglas (who had been a University of Chicago professor) spoke for many Northern liberals when he said to a national television audience that he "would be very happy" if Southern whites "should leave the Democratic Party" for "their spiritual home of the Republican Party."

In February 1960 four freshman at the North Carolina Agricultural & Technical College ushered in a new era of black student activism. With great dignity the quartet politely requested service at a Woolworth store lunch counter in Greensboro. When refused, they went outside and recited the Lord's Prayer. Their challenge to racism sparked similar protests in fifteen Southern cities by fifty thousand black and white students. Three thousand six hundred were arrested. Two months after the Greensboro incident, a new interracial youth organization came into existence: the Student Nonviolent Coordinating Committee (SNCC). SNCC's founders made it clear that they were Christian pacifists, not violent Marxist revolutionaries:

> Nonviolence as it grows from Judaic-Christian tradition seeks a social order of justice permeated by love. . . . By ap-

pealing to conscience and standing on the moral nature of human existence, nonviolence nurtures the atmosphere in which reconciliation and justice become actual possibilities.

Although SNCC members felt an initial surge of exhilaration in 1960 and 1961—having successfully integrated businesses in 200 cities—the events of 1962 proved disheartening. At the University of Mississippi a riot erupted when James Meredith sought to become the first black to attend Ole Miss. Mississippi governor Ross Barnett and retired Major General Edwin Walker incited a crowd of thousands. Fearful that Meredith would be killed, President John F. Kennedy and U.S. Attorney General Robert Kennedy dispatched federal marshals to the campus. Under strict orders not to shoot white rioters who screamed, "You nigger-lovers go to hell!" and "You goddamn Communists!", the marshals were hit with bats, bricks, and bullets. Of the 166 marshals injured in the riot, 28 had been shot. Two civilians—who got in the way of the rioters' guns—died. Unwilling to look at the Ole Miss incident with any measure of objectivity, North Carolina senator Sam Ervin blamed blacks for provoking the rioting.

Before the Ole Miss incident, SNCC and the Southern Christian Leadership Conference had forged an alliance to challenge discrimination in Albany, Georgia. Albany police chief Laurie Pritchett, not wanting to provoke a bloody confrontation that would bring sympathetic Northern media coverage and radicalize more Southern blacks, draped himself in the banner of Christian nonviolence. Pritchett joined SNCC and SCLC demonstrators in prayer and then gently hauled one thousand of them to county jails. Frustrated, SNCC militants—largely the Northern blacks and whites who had descended upon Albany—denounced their leaders.

Bayard Rustin, head of the pacifist Congress of Racial Equality (CORE), urged King to seek a more politically advantageous locale. After all, Rustin argued, "protest becomes an effective tactic to the degree that it elicits brutality and oppression from the power structure." Rustin told King to go to Birmingham, Alabama. Bull Connor's vicious police officers would certainly capture the attention of the national media and, perhaps, bring the SNCC radicals back into the fold.

From the late 1950s to 1963, when King arrived in Birmingham, the city had experienced eighteen racially motivated bombings. Most of Birmingham's black clergy refused to join SCLC, SNCC, or CORE. They considered King to be an outsider and preferred to maintain a boycott of white businesses that was succeeding in driving a wedge between the worried economic elite and Police Commissioner Connor. Unable to gain the cooperation of the community's adult black population, King and his Birmingham ally, the Rev. Fred Shuttlesworth, encouraged children to face down police dogs, fire hoses, and clubs. Connor's men battered and then arrested one thousand black youths. The youngest black protester jailed was six years old. After white extremists bombed King's hotel room, black juveniles rioted. Reporters focused on Connor's brutality, thereby building congressional support for civil rights legislation.

Growing weary of civil rights marches, SNCC opted in 1964 to push for voter registration in Mississippi. On the face of it, much work was to be done there. Although 45 percent of the state's population was black, just 5 percent could vote. Civil rights workers, however, could have selected a more hospitable state. Mississippi elected the most racist politicians in the South. While the forces of economic change and growth were leading greater numbers of businessmen in cities such as Atlanta and Birmingham to reconsider segregation and disfranchisement, Mississippi remained a backwater. By 1964 it was becoming an *atypical* Southern state. But that fact in itself was a primary motivation for Northern white radicals to go to Mississippi. White leftists had already decided that the South (and America at large) was hopelessly racist. They were not about to have their preconceptions challenged by going elsewhere.

Nine hundred white students from such elite campuses as

Berkeley, Harvard, Swarthmore, and Yale descended upon America's poorest state. Over half the white volunteers during the so-called Mississippi Freedom Summer were Jews; the majority had parents affiliated with the Communist party and other Marxist organizations. Bankrolled by their parents, the white volunteers stood out against the impoverished Mississippi backdrop. The men tended to wear their hair long, both males and females smoked marijuana, and the women engaged in sexual intercourse with black men. Some of SNCC's black men demanded that the white female volunteers have sex with them to prove they were not racist. Black "sisters," however, were berated if they expressed interest in a white college student.

SNCC's white radicals identified with the Southern (and Northern) black underclass which they regarded as the most liberated from middle-class norms. As British journalist Godfrey Hodgson, a sympathizer of the New Left, noted, white student activists wanted to associate "with those who lived outside the code of respectability." The Mississippi Freedom Summer volunteers, Hodgson wrote, rejected the "future-oriented system of Puritan values" and embraced the underclass penchant for sexual promiscuity and narcotics. (Years later, historian Terry Anderson asserted that "sexual rules and double standards were not as strict in the black community, which appealed to hippies" and the young leftists who stormed the South in 1964. Tellingly, Anderson confused the values of the underclass with the majority of Southern blacks who regularly attended church, did not sleep around, and never smoked dope.)

Many white Mississippi Freedom Summer volunteers spent evenings "having sex in a field in the countryside" and hanging out in "Blind Pigs" dancing, drinking, and getting stoned till dawn. For some, the threat of violent retribution from Southern whites created "an erotic feeling." Confrontation was the ultimate aphrodisiac. As one giddy male volunteer noted, his sojourn in the South represented his "first time of real sexual experimentation. During my time in Mississippi, I slept with more different [white] women than I had up to that point." In short order, the Northern white volunteers embraced the liberated lifestyle of the black underclass. Hoping to become "authentically black," the white civil rights activists purchased bib overall "uniforms" and adopted the obscenity-filled language of their role models.

Mississippi whites—and most black adults—were not amused by the behavior of the Northern radicals. Mississippi senator James Eastland had already charged that SNCC and CORE were "carrying on the fight for a Soviet America." Less refined than Senator Eastland, Lieutenant Governor Paul Johnson joked that the initials NAACP stood for "Niggers, Alligators, Apes, Coons, and Possums."

Local law enforcement officers, working closely with the reactionary White Citizens Councils and the Ku Klux Klan, murdered six civil rights workers and burned thirty-five black churches that summer. In an incident that led to the intervention of the Federal Bureau of Investigation (FBI), police officers and town officials in Philadelphia, Mississippi, killed civil rights workers James Chaney, Andrew Goodman, and Michael Schwerner. Afterward they buried the young men in an earthen dam. One of the Klansmen complained on the night of the slayings that his friends got to kill the two Jews, leaving him with just "a nigger." FBI Director J. Edgar Hoover, no friend of the civil rights movement, concluded that Mississippi was ruled by lawless white trash.

Mississippi Freedom Summer did more than antagonize whites and create "Movement Martyrs"; it resulted in the eventual self-destruction of SNCC. Black women resented the cosmopolitan white women who had sex with "their men," going as far as to claim that "the Jews" were spreading social diseases across Mississippi. Soon anti-Semitic doggerel began appearing in SNCC offices:

> The Jews have stolen our bread
> Their filthy women tricked our men into bed
> So I won't rest until the Jews are dead.

SNCC's religiously motivated members were appalled by the sight of white women and black men parading hand in hand and groping each other in Southern streets. SNCC's militant faction, led by Stokely Carmichael, a native of Trinidad and a recent graduate of Howard University in Washington, D.C., also frowned on interracial sex. Carmichael, however, had no more use for religious pacifists such as SNCC leader John Lewis. Where Lewis believed that the civil rights struggle would redeem black and white alike in Christian brotherhood, Carmichael identified with such revolutionary Marxists as Che Guevara, Ho Chi Minh, and Frantz Fanon—the black Caribbean writer who in the 1950s had argued that "violence [against whites] is a cleansing force. It frees the native from his inferiority complex" and "restores self-respect."

Carmichael detested the profound religiosity of SNCC's Southern contingent and had no real commitment to registering blacks to vote. As far as Carmichael was concerned, "the only good the vote could do was to wreck the Democratic Party and spring off a revolution in America." For Carmichael and his followers who organized the Mississippi Freedom Democratic party in the summer of 1964, Northern cold war Democrats were just as racist as Southern whites. Northern white Democrats "raped" Vietnamese Communists while Southern white Democrats oppressed blacks. As Carmichael and SNCC were to argue, "We believe the United States government has been deceptive in claims of concern for the freedom of the Vietnamese people. . . . The United States government has never guaranteed the freedom of oppressed citizens and is not yet truly determined to end the rule of terror and oppression within its own borders."

Mississippi Freedom Summer underscored SNCC's declining religiosity and growing identification with sexual liberation and revolutionary communism. Although young black extremists would not admit it, their actions in 1964 helped discredit the cause of civil rights in the South among whites who might otherwise have supported King—or at least would have remained neutral. Public opinion polls conducted *before* the summer of 1964 showed that 95 percent of Southern whites thought blacks should have the right to vote. A slim majority of white Southerners even stated that they did not mind sharing a bus seat with a black.

After Mississippi Freedom Summer, Southern white acceptance of civil rights ebbed, giving King little choice but to take the road to Selma, Alabama. In 1965, as King prepared for Selma, he noted that "Bull Connor gave us the civil rights bill [of 1964] and [Dallas County Sheriff] Jim Clark is going to give us the voting rights bill." King's forecast proved accurate. While network television cameras recorded the scene, several hundred blacks and whites set out on a march from Selma to the state capitol in Montgomery. Sheriff Clark and his deputies savagely clubbed the marchers when they reached Selma's Edmund Pettus Bridge.

Exulting in his victory, Clark informed the media that one should not "hit a nigger with your first because his head is too hard." Clubs were better. King had the "sound bite" he needed. With six million Southern blacks having moved to Northern cities since 1942, the national Democratic party could no longer ignore civil rights. Black Democratic voters in Illinois, Michigan, and Ohio had been key to expelling the GOP from the White House in 1960. Clark's brutality ensured the passage of the 1965 Voting Rights Act.

In the 1950s and early 1960s religious organizations had been central to the civil rights struggle. The predominantly white (and Protestant) National Council of Churches, for instance, spent $400,000 lobbying Congress to pass the Civil Rights Act of 1964. Meanwhile the U.S. Catholic Conference of Bishops supported the 1964 bill so intensely that Republican senator Karl Mundt of South Dakota felt compelled to vote for it. Privately Mundt told friends, "I hope that satisfies those two goddamned bishops that called me last night."

In Dixie the black church loomed large in the civil rights struggle. It was no accident that in 1957 King had called his organization the Southern *Christian* Leadership Conference. By 1964, however, secularized Northerners were swamping the civil rights movement. Less than a third of the white and black activists who joined SNCC and CORE claimed that religion had any role to play in social reform. As belief in Christian non-violence waned, revolutionary Marxism and nihilism filled the void.

It was impossible to ignore the rising spirit of nihilism and militancy that swept up tens of thousands of young blacks in the early 1960s. That spirit was most visible in the Los Angeles neighborhood of Watts. In 1965, after Los Angeles police officers arrested a drunken black motorist, a rumor spread in the ghetto that the "pigs" had killed him. The rioting that erupted left 34 dead, 900 injured, and 977 buildings damaged or destroyed. It took 15,000 California National Guardsmen to stop the rioting and arrest 4,300 of the worst offenders. The Watts riot, or "rebellion," as leftists called it, caused $40 million in property damage. Nearly all the businesses destroyed belonged to middle-class blacks, who quickly decided to move to the safer suburbs. In the future, Watts would do without grocery stores and other vital services.

Despite the decimation of Watts, half of Los Angeles' black population informed pollsters that the riot had a positive effect on their community. The rioters, many blacks believed, had chastised the white power structure. They were mistaken. One year after the Watts riot, former Hollywood actor Ronald Reagan rode a wave of public revulsion against urban (and campus) rioting to the governor's mansion in Sacramento. An ardent supporter of President Roosevelt in the 1930s, Reagan had become a Republican by the 1960s after his clashes with Communists in the Screen Actors Guild in the 1940s and his dismay with the growth of the federal bureaucracy in the 1950s.

The black militants who came to the fore in the 1960s were often inspired by the Nation of Islam. Established a generation earlier, this religious sect of Black Muslims began the 1960s with thirty thousand members. They believed that whites were literally devils and, following the lead of Muslim convert Malcolm X, derided King as a "twentieth-century Uncle Tom." According to Malcolm, Southern Klansmen and the cold war Democrats who supported racial equality belonged to the same species. "The job of the civil rights leader is to make the Negro forget that the wolf [southern Klansmen] and fox [northern Democrats] belong to the [same] family," Malcolm said. "Both are canines; and no matter which one of them the Negro places his trust in, he never ends up in the White House but always in the doghouse."

Malcolm X, who became a secular saint of the New Left, worked hard to promote separatism and anti-Semitism among poor urban blacks. He frequently called Jews parasites, slum lords, and leaders of the pre–Civil War slave trade. (In reality, Arab *Muslims* had been instrumental in promoting the African slave trade.) Malcolm also dismissed the Nazi Holocaust, arguing that the Jews had it coming.

So deeply did Malcolm believe in racial separatism and anti-Semitism that in 1961 he had forged an alliance with the Ku Klux Klan. Malcolm knew that the white supremacists and the Nation of Islam shared the same goal of segregating the races and curbing what black nationalists called "Kosher Power." Apologists rationalized that Malcolm later recanted some of his racist positions; but a shadow racism remained a strong undercurrent among black activists. (An internal power struggle within the Nation of Islam led in 1965 to Malcolm X's assassination.)

Many SNCC partisans enthusiastically followed in Malcolm's footsteps. As one SNCC activist said in homage to the members of the black underclass who, like Malcolm X, had spent time in prison, "We crap on the clean, antiseptic, acceptable, decent middle-class 'image.'" Having turned SNCC chief John Lewis out of office in 1966, Stokely Carmichael expelled whites. A 1966 SNCC position paper justified Carmichael's course of action, contending that "All white people are racists." Still smarting from the Mississippi Freedom Summer fiasco,

Carmichael's supporters called whites a "contaminating" influence.

The SNCC hard-liners went on to list other reasons why white leftists could no longer be permitted to associate with the civil rights movement:

> The inability of whites to relate to the cultural aspects of Black society; attitudes that whites, consciously or unconsciously, bring to Black communities about themselves (western superiority) and about Black people (paternalism); inability to shatter white-sponsored community myths of Black inferiority and self-negation; inability to combat the views of the Black community that white organizers, being "white," control Black organizers as puppets . . . the unwillingness of whites to deal with the roots of racism which lie within the white community; whites though individually "liberal" are symbols of oppression to the Black community—due to the collective power that whites have over Black lives.

Julius Lester, a graduate of Fisk and a veteran of Mississippi Freedom Summer, privately expressed his dismay with the black separatists and Carmichael. He wondered how it was that even though Southern blacks like himself grew up with segregation, the Northern blacks who followed Carmichael were angrier. "Why," Lester asked, "do they hate white people and we don't?" Lester also disapproved of Carmichael's enormous drug consumption and violent rhetoric, which inspired young blacks to riot wherever the SNCC leader spoke. "I sit here with the Mick Jagger of revolution," Lester privately fretted, "and think about all the people who believe in him, and I am frightened." (Carmichael's ego, Lester observed, was no little matter either. The walls of Carmichael's Atlanta office were plastered with photographs of himself.)

Other black activists sought to emulate the examples of Carmichael and Malcolm X. As early as 1964, extremists in the New Orleans chapter of the Congress of Racial Equality had threatened to riot unless white politicians immediately met their demands. In Atlanta, CORE demonstrators, not content with a prayerful sit-in, urinated on the floor of a restaurant that had refused them service. By 1966 Floyd McKissick, the newly installed head of CORE, dismissed nonviolence as "a dying philosophy."

CORE, like SNCC and the Nation of Islam, fantasized about carving out an independent black nation from several Southern states. (The notion that blacks were a subjugated internal colony that deserved independence or "self-determination" was first advanced in the 1920s by the Soviet Union and the American Communist party. Malcolm X and Carmichael simply put a radical *white* idea in black power garb.) Whites who refused to leave the South would be expelled or killed. Sometimes black separatists called their nation the "Republic of Gamal"—Georgia, Alabama, Mississippi, Arkansas, and Louisiana. Why the growing number of middle-class blacks in the North would willingly relocate to an area that in the 1960s claimed America's worst schools and housing stock was never adequately explained. Implicitly, McKissick and Carmichael had no intention of allowing blacks any choice in where they lived.

Roy Wilkins, executive secretary of the NAACP, scorned the black separatists. The cry for black power that Carmichael's supporters raised in 1966, Wilkins said, represented "the father of hate and the mother of violence." Martin Luther King also chided the black separatists in 1966, insisting that "This is no time for romantic illusion and empty philosophical debates about freedom. What is needed is a strategy for change, a tactical program that will bring the Negro into the mainstream of American life as quickly as possible."

Outside the South, in the federally subsidized North Oakland Poverty Center, a new revolutionary organization came into existence in 1966: the Black Panthers. San Francisco Bay Area leftists fell in love with the gun-toting, black beret–wearing Panthers. They were, in the words of the white New

Left, "authentic" and "heavy." Panther leader Eldridge Cleaver, who had spent time in prison for drug dealing, titillated white radicals by arguing that the rape of white women by black men represented "an insurrectionary act" against racism. (The Bay-area-based *Ramparts* magazine served as the unofficial press of the Black Panthers and published a series of essays by Cleaver. In 1968 these essays became the basis for Cleaver's best-selling book, *Soul on Ice.*) Part intellectual and, in fellow Panther Huey Newton's words, part "brother off the block," Cleaver pistol-whipped dissenters in the Panther party and questioned Martin Luther King's sexual orientation, calling him "Martin Luther Queen."

As a child growing up in Oakland, Panther co-founder Bobby Seale mugged white children at knifepoint. He later rationalized that his criminal activities were the only way he could strike a blow against racism. Newton, Seale's comrade in arms, beat Panther women and ingested massive quantities of narcotics. (Two decades later a rival crack dealer in Oakland killed Newton.) Discovering a loophole in the California penal code that allowed residents to carry weapons in the open, Newton and Seale brandished their guns around Oakland and San Francisco policemen. The Panthers said they were "patrolling the pigs." Newton liked to tell followers, "Every time you go to execute a white racist Gestapo cop, you are defending yourself." Not surprisingly, police officers and Panthers had frequent run-ins. After one such standoff, James Forman, the former executive director of SNCC, warned that for every Panther killed in a shoot-out with "the pigs," five hundred cops would die.

Seale and Newton identified black ministers as "Uncle Toms" who had helped maintain slavery before the Civil War and now continued to keep blacks under their thumbs. They demanded reparations for the "50 million" Africans supposedly killed by whites and characterized black Americans as "a colonized people in every sense of the term." Seale argued that "while the aggression of the racist American government escalates in Vietnam, the police agencies of America escalate the re-

pression of black people throughout the ghetto." Although
Seale and Newton wished to "liberate" inner-city blacks from a
white army of occupation, they no doubt had other reasons for
wanting the police removed. Nearly all the Panthers were ha-
bitual criminals. Their two thousand well-armed members included killers, drug dealers, rapists, and extortionists.

Initially Seale and Newton raised money by selling copies of
the *Thoughts of Chairman Mao* on the Berkeley campus. Soon,
however, wealthy white leftists such as symphony conductor
Leonard Bernstein and Democratic party leaders who hoped to
buy them off showered the Panthers with contributions and
grants. With great fanfare the Panthers established a free
breakfast program for black children in Oakland as leftists and
white liberals cheered. This Panther endeavor, however, served
as a front for drug dealing and the extortion of Bay Area merchants. The Panthers also took the opportunity to indoctrinate
black children. Before breakfast, the Panthers led the children
in chanting, "I want a pork chop. Off the pig!"

Like other black revolutionaries, the Panthers were virulent
anti-Semites. This was peculiar to say the least, given the central role that Jews had played in the twentieth-century civil
rights movement. The Anti-Defamation League, the American
Jewish Committee, and the American Jewish Congress lobbied
Congress for civil rights legislation in the early 1960s. Earlier,
Jews and blacks had worked together to end racial and religious discrimination in housing, employment, and university
admissions. Moreover, Jews felt they had the same enemy: conservative Southern Democrats. Jewish reformers wanted to
drive racist Southerners out of the Democratic party.

Far from appreciating Jewish support, however, the young
militants in SNCC, the Panthers, CORE, and the Nation of
Islam resented Jews. In part they felt that blacks were being
used to open doors for Jews who had also felt the sting of discrimination. Addressing their appeals to the urban underclass,
black revolutionaries sought to discredit their middle-class inte-

grationist rivals by deploying anti-Semitic canards. This made civil rights leaders such as King feel extremely vulnerable, since their organizations depended on Jewish contributors and lawyers who provided free legal assistance. Although unwilling to sever his ties to the Jewish community, King found himself making questionable, unrealistic concessions to the black left. After the Watts riot, when larger numbers of white Northerners were failing to make distinctions between working-class and underclass blacks, King insisted that President Johnson spend an additional $12 billion on welfare.

Conservative Republicans, who had opposed the 1964 Civil Rights Act and the 1965 Voting Rights Act, could not believe their luck. Black radicals, with King following reluctantly in their wake, were setting the stage for the end of the Democratic electoral majority as working-class whites in the North and the South grew restless with Johnson's War on Poverty and urban rioting. Although Senator Barry Goldwater, who had voted against the 1964 Civil Rights Act, was no racist, some self-described conservatives would not and did not hesitate to appeal to the prejudices of Southern and Northern whites.

Unlike the affluent white radicals who came South for short visits in the 1960s and then returned to their sheltered campuses, Lyndon Johnson had grown up in an environment of violence and poverty. In 1921 his father, Texas state representative Sam Johnson, had championed a resolution denouncing the Ku Klux Klan. One evening a Klansman called Sam Johnson with a death threat. Visibly angry, Sam Johnson shouted into the receiver, "Now listen here, you Kukluxklansonofabitch, if you and your goddamned gang think you're man enough to shoot me, you come on ahead. My brothers and I will be waiting for you out on the front porch. Just come on ahead, you yellow bastards." The Klan decided to leave Sam Johnson alone.

Seven years later Lyndon Johnson was working as a teacher in a Hispanic school district. He never forgot his experience:

My students were poor and they often came to class without breakfast, hungry. They knew even in their youth the pain of prejudice. They never seemed to know why people disliked them. But they knew it was so, because I saw it in their eyes. I often walked home late in the afternoon, after classes were finished, wishing there was more that I could do. But all I knew was to teach the little that I knew, hoping it might help them against the hardships that lay ahead. Somehow you never forget what poverty and hatred can do when you see its scars on the hopeful face of a young child.

In 1935 Johnson became the Texas director of the National Youth Administration, a New Deal agency that provided financial assistance to youths so they could remain in college or high school. Quietly defying local practice, Johnson hired Hispanic and black youths. Two years later Johnson entered the U.S. House of Representatives, determined to bring federal work relief and farm reclamation projects to his impoverished neighbors.

Although many Texans admired Johnson, others did not. As the Democratic vice presidential candidate in 1960, Johnson and his wife Lady Bird met with a rough reception in Dallas. A mob of unruly right-wingers, led by Texas congressman Bruce Alger, rushed Lyndon Johnson, screaming, "He sold out to Yankee Socialists!" They spat on the Johnsons, ripped Lady Bird's gloves off her hands, and beat them with picket signs. The New Right had given notice that its partisans could be just as obnoxious and intolerant as the New Left.

When Kennedy's assassination elevated Johnson to the presidency in 1963, the Texan embraced a legislative program of social reform that would, he hoped, surpass that of his idol, Franklin Roosevelt. In the span of one Congress alone (1965–1966), Johnson presented 200 bills. His liberal Democratic majority passed 181, giving Johnson the best legislative success rate for a president since the 1930s.

The White House, Johnson believed, could promote racial

justice and wage a victorious War on Poverty. So far as the civil rights agenda stood, Johnson's expectations were met. The 1964 Civil Rights Act forthrightly attacked segregation. Title VII of the act, for instance, created the Equal Employment Opportunity Commission (EEOC) to end discrimination in hiring. (Although Senator Hubert Humphrey insisted that companies would not have to adopt hiring quotas to prove that they were not discriminating, quotas, or as Johnson called it, "affirmative action," eventually became the norm.)

With the passage of the 1965 Voting Rights Act, four million blacks immediately registered to vote in eleven Southern states. Once Southern blacks became part of the political process, they tossed the Bull Connors and Jim Clarks out of office. In 1966 Virginia senator A. Willis Robertson, who had urged massive resistance against racial integration, lost his seat. Robertson's son, Pat, a Pentecostal minister and founder of the Christian Broadcasting Network (CBN), declined to campaign for his father. Pat Robertson—a member of the "Silent Generation"—proclaimed his belief in racial equality:

> I was much more open toward assimilation to the blacks in society than were the Old-Guard southerners. I was uncomfortable with the massive resistance that went on, the unwillingness to allow black people into school, and segregation in general, which put one class of people down. They had a feeling of white superiority. That was their culture and it was a blind spot, although those people were mostly Christians who just couldn't accommodate the emerging status of blacks.

If Johnson's civil rights crusade appeared successful, his War on Poverty was another matter. Although the president argued that he was carrying on the tradition of the New Deal, in reality the War on Poverty represented a dramatic political departure. To begin with, the global depression of the 1930s had given Franklin Roosevelt the pretext for erecting a limited social welfare state. In the 1960s there was no comparable economic crisis.

Quite the contrary, the economy was booming. Second, there was no great cry in the 1960s for the federal promotion of social welfare. Instead of millions of unemployed people demanding relief from Congress, there was a small anti-poverty movement whose origins could be found in the nation's universities. Third, while New Dealers expected work in exchange for federal checks—with Roosevelt disdaining outright cash relief as a spiritually debilitating narcotic—the architects of Johnson's Great Society had a different view. There would be no "racist" distinction between the "deserving" and "undeserving" poor.

As part of the War on Poverty, overall federal spending on inner cities increased 198 percent. Federal appropriations for various anti-poverty measures expanded 400 percent. The case-load for Aid to Families with Dependent Children (a New Deal program originally created through the Social Security Act of 1935 to benefit widows with children) rose 125 percent. In New York City the number of welfare recipients went from 84,700 in 1965 to 175,400 in 1968. By 1970 more than a million New Yorkers received welfare even though the economy was robust. Welfare activist Beulah Sanders told New York law-makers, "I do not believe that we should be forced to work. . . . The welfare recipients are tired. They are tired of people dictating to them, telling them how they must live."

Believing that the federal government could create attractive jobs for inner-city youths, the White House Office of Economic Opportunity (OEO) established the Community Action Program. In Chicago, Johnson's Community Action Program awarded grants to "authentic" black community leaders, in most cases bypassing the clergy. In part, government reformers and their academic advisers chose this course of action because the black church had not established itself as firmly in Northern soil as in the South. (The federal government's decision to avoid involving Northern black ministers in anti-poverty initiatives made the clergy appear even more irrelevant to impressionable youths.) Secular liberals also wished to maintain the separation of church and state while radicals disdained most black ministers. One Brooklyn minister conceded that the church was a "training ground for equipping folks with the middle-class values of upward mobility." Few black clergy called for the overthrow of capitalism.

Federal anti-poverty officials believed that the black recipients of Community Action grants would establish businesses catering to the underclass population. Unfortunately, among the new minority business organizations created in Chicago were the Vice Lords and the El Rukns—street gangs. Chicago Democrats, white *and black*, were not amused that Washington bureaucrats were using their taxes to subsidize drug dealing, extortion, murder, and prostitution. Great Society liberals denied the problems and accused critics of racism.

In Harlem a group with grants from the OEO formed a black organization called the "Five Percenters." They believed that 85 percent of American blacks were mindless cattle. The other 10 percent were "Uncle Toms." Thus the Five Percenters were the only real blacks in America. Wasting little time, the Five Percenters put four thousand black teenagers on their payroll. Five hundred well-paid administrators supervised the youths. Among the projects undertaken by the Five Percenters was the Black Arts Repertory Theater School, which produced plays attacking Jews, middle-class blacks, and black clergy. One of its playwrights, LeRoi Jones, defended his art, asserting that "there are a lot of people in black nations all over the world who want to kill white people." Jones, who took the Black Muslim name Amiri Baraka and went on to become a professor at Rutgers University, also composed a provocative poem: "I got something for you . . . I got the extermination blues, Jew boy."

Undaunted, the OEO forged ahead, creating the Job Corps program. It proved to be a disaster. In Oregon and Kalamazoo, Michigan, young white and black trainees rioted. Edison, New Jersey, Job Corps trainees were arrested for dealing narcotics. A St. Petersburg, Florida, Job Corps training facility designed to teach young women to learn typing and nursing skills became instead a center for prostitution. (The St. Petersburg project hired 122 administrators to serve 237 Job Corps students.) In Indiana, authorities arrested several Job Corpsmen for raping a fellow male trainee. Job Corps recruits in San Antonio, Texas, shot two air force enlisted men during a holdup. At Kentucky's Camp Breckinridge, which was managed by Southern Illinois University, Job Corpsmen extorted money from other trainees for "life insurance." During a riot at Camp Breckinridge, half the trainees fled as the other half assaulted members of the local fire department that tried to put out the fires. Overall, barely a fifth of the welfare recipients who enrolled in any kind of federal or state job-training program finished their training.

One U.S. senator noted that it cost $8,000 a year to feed, clothe, house, and train a single Job Corps volunteer ($32,000 in 2000 dollars). It would be cheaper, the senator said, to send the trainee to Harvard for a year. OEO director Sargent Shriver—a Kennedy family member by marriage—retorted that the actual cost would cover only two-thirds of the expenses necessary to pay for a year at Harvard. Other congressional critics wondered why the Job Corps trainees, many of whom had criminal records and, consequently were exempt from military service, could avoid Vietnam and get a government check. Meanwhile law-abiding, working-class white and black youths were being drafted to fight in Vietnam instead of being enrolled in the Job Corps program. As Republican representative Paul Fino of New York put it in 1966, "Why should juvenile virtue be rewarded with military service in the Vietnamese nightmare while a record of delinquency exempts punks from the army and puts them in line for Job Corps codlings?"

Congressman Fino did not appreciate what Stokely Carmichael and other militants had realized at the inception of the War on Poverty. Every time a riot broke out in America's cities, Johnson created another anti-poverty program that inevitably fell under the militants' control. San Francisco radicals found that actual rioting was not even necessary. Mere threats proved effective. Whenever San Francisco mayor John Shelley talked about reducing funds to various community groups, militants put on a menacing show and the cuts were rescinded. This marked the beginning of a process which author Tom Wolfe called "Mau-Mauing the Flakcatchers." (The term "Mau-Mauing" came from the example of black revolutionaries in Kenya—Mau-Maus, who in the 1950s and 1960s had used terrorism to drive out European settlers.) San Francisco's black radicals boasted that their tactics paid off, "You made the white man quake. You brought *fear* into his face."

Big-city Democratic mayors were livid, blaming Great Society liberals and leftist firebrands for rewarding "criminals." As the violent crime rate rose 126 percent in the 1960s, disaffection swelled among Northern Democrats. A few of them, notably Daniel Patrick Moynihan of the U.S. Labor Department, pointed to a black illegitimacy rate of 25 percent in 1965 and noted that nearly all children growing up in fatherless households lived in poverty. Criticized for "stigmatizing" illegitimate black children and "blaming the victims" of racism, Moynihan retreated while the OEO created more anti-poverty programs and wrote more checks. Within a few years the number of single black teenage mothers grew 800 percent and the proportion of black children who did not have fathers increased from one-quarter to one-third.

Those most affected by the mounting street crime of the 1960s and accelerating dissolution of poor families were blacks and urban Roman Catholics, or "white ethnics." The affluent suburbs where Great Society reformers and leftist academics lived remained safe havens. Not surprisingly, resentment against such "liberal hypocrisy" swelled. Chief Justice Earl Warren and Senator George McGovern of South Dakota, both of whom were ardent advocates of integration, sent their children to private schools or to mostly white suburban schools.

Similarly, federal Judge Frank Johnson in Alabama, an enemy of Governor George Wallace and proponent of racial integration, founded a private academy for his own son. Governor Wallace's children went to integrated public schools; Judge Johnson's son attended school with wealthy Episcopalians and

Unitarians. (In the mid-1960s Frank Johnson's son obtained a college student deferment and joined SDS. With so many Southerners perishing in Vietnam, the judge had few friends outside his *segregated* country club.) George Wallace tartly said of the Great Society liberals in Washington, "They're building a new bridge over the Potomac for all of the white liberals fleeing to Virginia."

As "white backlash" mounted and leftists hailed the riotous underclass, Lyndon Johnson's and Martin Luther King's dream of racial peace and social reform died. Tragically, with each passing year most blacks found themselves feeling locked out of a Republican party that played to white working-class fears and trapped in a Democratic party that increasingly embraced menacing urban militants and self-righteous campus leftists. In the "politics of authenticity" that Great Society reformers, campus activists, and black power advocates practiced, there was no room for anyone, regardless of race, who thought that Martin Luther King and John Lewis had anything worthwhile to offer minorities.

Surveying the political wasteland created in the wake of the insurgent 1960s, historian Christopher Lasch wrote a damning epitaph for the Stokely Carmichaels of the decade and their white apologists:

> The rhetoric of black power corrupted the white left and the black left alike, substituting a politics of the media for the civil rights struggles earlier waged in deadly earnest in the South. As the black power rhetoricians co-opted the civil rights movement, they also captivated white liberals who sought to appease the guilt associated with "white skin privilege" by adopting the gestures and language of black militancy. Both whites and blacks embraced radical style in place of radical substance.

3

Who Protested?

BEFORE the military escalation of the Vietnam War in 1965, several activist student organizations had appeared on select college campuses. Undergraduates and faculty at Lake Forest College, a suburban Chicago school, in 1960 established the Student Peace Union. The Union took a "Third Camp" position, meaning that its members regarded the United States and the Soviet Union as equally at fault for perpetuating the nuclear arms race. By 1963 the group had grown from 100 members to 3,500. As a result of establishing affiliates at Harvard and the University of Chicago—where small Marxist sects flourished—the Student Peace Union became decidedly anti-anti-Communist. It berated "capitalist imperialism" while expressing little criticism of the Soviet Union. Shortly before President Kennedy's assassination, Student Peace Union leader Gail Paradise claimed that cold war Democrats were the chief threat to world peace.

The Harvard affiliate of the Student Peace Union, Tocsin, similarly regarded cold war Democrats with contempt. (Tocsin was not an acronym.) Tocsin's leader, Todd Gitlin, a native of New York City, had protested Kennedy's efforts in 1962 to force the Soviet Union to withdraw its nuclear missiles from Cuba. Gitlin, who would shortly merge Tocsin with the Students for a Democratic Society, had little use for anti-Communist Democrats. On the other hand, most Harvard students had little use for Tocsin. Gitlin cheerfully acknowledged that Tocsin was a "little [Jewish] enclave" away from Harvard's white Anglo-Saxon Protestants (WASPs). (In fact, the over-whelming majority of Jewish students, like their WASP coun-terparts, had no use for Tocsin either.)

In addition to the Student Peace Union, two other radical campus-based groups had emerged by 1962: the Youth Against War and Fascism (YAWF) and the Progressive Labor party (PL). Created by exiles from the Trotskyite Socialist Workers party in Buffalo, YAWF's members were largely the children of depression-era Marxists. Although its numbers were small, YAWF played a significant role in campus anti-war activism at the Buffalo campus of the State University of New York. YAWF also proved to be a national trendsetter: its members were the first "anti-imperialists" to carry Viet Cong flags at peace demonstrations.

The Progressive Labor party came into existence when the American Communist party split between followers of the So-viet Union and of China. Initially PL founders Milt Rosen, Mort Sheer, Fred Jerome, and Bill Epton tried to incite racial unrest in Harlem. As Epton argued, "We're going to have to kill a lot of cops, a lot of these judges, and we'll have to go against their army." Having failed to organize the black under-class, Progressive Labor activists turned their attention to white workers. By 1966, having recruited little more than fourteen hundred members, the PL leadership opted to "bore within" the much larger SDS.

SDS had been founded in 1960, the offspring of the Socialist party's League for Industrial Democracy. Within a year, the Ann Arbor–based group had a thousand members and chap-ters at some of America's most elite institutions of higher edu-cation, including Oberlin College and Swarthmore. In 1962 SDS held a national convention at Port Huron, Michigan. Fifty-nine delegates attended, of which forty-three belonged to SDS and the remainder represented the Student Nonviolent Coordinating Committee and various groups associated with the Communist party. Tom Hayden, a University of Michigan student, wrote the SDS manifesto, the so-called Port Huron Statement.

In drafting the statement, Hayden drew upon two sources of inspiration. While visiting Berkeley in 1959 he had become enchanted with an activist campus organization called SLATE. An affiliate of the Student Peace Union, SLATE, which had been established by anti–cold war Democrats and Marxists in 1957, sought to gain control of student government and abolish the ROTC training for male undergraduates that was mandatory at land-grant institutions. (In 1963 the Department of Defense and the land-grant colleges set aside the compulsory ROTC requirement.) Hayden's second source of inspiration was Columbia sociologist C. Wright Mills, a vocal critic of America's anti-Communist foreign policy and an ardent defender of Cuban dictator Fidel Castro.

By the time Hayden had completed his college education and written the Port Huron Statement, he had shunted aside the values of his own anti-Communist Catholicism. Berkeley activist David Horowitz, who knew Hayden well in the 1960s, believed that Hayden's "radicalism seems to have sprung full-blown from what [socialist intellectual] Irving Howe once described as an 'obscure personal rage.' The son of an alcoholic father with whom he was not on speaking terms, Tom was indeed an angry man who seemed in perpetual search of enemies."

In the Port Huron Statement, Hayden argued that the United States hindered the cause of nuclear disarmament because of its unreasonable hostility to the Soviet Union and China. Anti-Communist politicians like the Kennedys, Hayden believed, were more dangerous to American youth than all the Joseph Stalins and Mao Tse-tungs in the world put together. As Hayden contended in the Port Huron Statement, "McCarthyism and other forms of exaggerated and conservative anti-Communism seriously weaken democratic movements and spawn movements contrary to the interests of basic freedoms and peace." Hayden became president of SDS after the Port Huron convention, serving until 1963 when Todd Gitlin took over.

Both Gitlin and Hayden have argued that the SDS of the early 1960s simply wanted the university and American society at large to live up to their democratic promise. Far from being a subversive, militant organization, the pre–Vietnam War SDS, Hayden and Gitlin insist, was idealistic, nonviolent, and committed to "participatory democracy." Critics then and now, however, have countered that SDS did not degenerate into a self-indulgent, anti-American organization intolerant of dissenting views—it was that way from the start. Al Haber, the first SDS president, was the son of a University of Michigan professor who had belonged to the League for Industrial Democracy. In 1961 Haber called conservative student members of the Young Americans for Freedom "racist, militaristic, imperialist butchers." A year later Roger Leed, a champion of SDS, referred to YAF activists as "hollow men" who were "virtually maniacal" and "irrational."

From the beginning, SDSers tolerated no one who disagreed with them. The SDS slogan "Let the People Decide," ex-leftists Peter Collier and David Horowitz have argued, actually meant that SDSers would do the deciding since they represented the authentic people. Horowitz recounted, "Participatory democracy was really a code of what our parents' generation would have called 'soviet democracy.'" As Horowitz concluded, "From its beginnings, the New Left was not an innocent experiment in American utopianism but a self-conscious effort to rescue the Communist project from its Soviet fate." The founders of SDS, Horowitz argued two decades after the Port Huron convention, wanted to create a Soviet America without the ossified bureaucracy that characterized post–World War II Russia.

Al Haber and the SDS founders, dismayed by the role that union leaders Philip Murray and Walter Reuther had played in purging organized labor of Communists after World War II, felt justified in arguing that the working class was hopeless. "If any really radical liberal force is going to develop in America," Haber insisted, "it is going to come from the colleges and the young." In 1964 Haber and his wife Barbara urged SDSers not to vote for Lyndon Johnson since the president was a tool of the racist right. By 1965 Haber was denouncing America's anti-Communist foreign policy because it served to "justify political imperialism abroad" and thwarted the "expression of radical vision and dialogue at home."

In 1968 a University of Maine student, Stephen King, discovered for himself how intolerant young leftists were of anyone who challenged their worldview. Although King disliked the Vietnam War and had imbibed psychedelic drugs, the future novelist recoiled from the paranoid, lockstep mentality of SDS and the Black Panther party:

> I went to a big assembly where three Panthers from Boston were talking about the war and racism and poverty and discrimination and how all these things tied together. They were talking about some kind of capitalist conspiracy that sounded more paranoid the more they went on. So finally I stood up in the question-and-answer period and said, "Look. Are you really trying to say that Rockefeller, Dupont, and all these people have got some great underground cavern where they go to plan Vietnam and discrimination and all this other stuff?"—and this huge wave of BOOOOOS came from the audience! I immediately sat down. It was embarrassing! And this Panther said [softly, smugly], "You got a surprise, didn't you, man?"

Stephen King would have found that matters differed little at the University of Wisconsin. James Rowen of the Wisconsin SDS was much like the University of Maine radicals in his hostile attitude toward anyone who questioned the New Left vision. The son of a *Washington Post* columnist, Rowen had married the daughter of Senator George McGovern of South Dakota. When he took his place among the Wisconsin SDS "heavies," he participated in some of the university's most violent confrontations with campus and city police. As an editor of the campus newspaper, the *Daily Cardinal,* Rowen berated students who opposed violent protest. Such students, Rowen claimed, were "politically chickenshit." Rowen also hurled another insult at the proponents of nonviolence: they were "liberals."

On the face of it, Carl Oglesby appeared to have little in common with Rowen and Haber. Oglesby, the national SDS president from 1965 to 1966, was a rare radical who came from a blue-collar background. The son of a South Carolina sharecropper who had relocated to Akron, Ohio, to work in a rubber factory, Oglesby felt he had grown up in America's cultural equivalent of the third world. His education at Kent State in the 1950s, financed by a debate scholarship, led him to connect the economic exploitation of poor Americans to that of third-world citizens. Oglesby's background also made him sympathetic to the Marxist revolutionaries who sought to free themselves from American economic domination. While many blue-collar youths who went to college in the 1950s and 1960s tended to become more conservative, Oglesby had moved in the opposite direction. He concluded that American and global politics could be summed up as a struggle between capitalists and the poor.

When Oglesby assumed leadership of SDS he was nearly thirty years old. He had fathered three children, had bought a house in Ann Arbor, and worked as a technical writer for the Bendix Aerospace Systems Division. His initial attraction to SDS had little to do with politics. Oglesby later recounted that the Michigan SDS "had the best parties, the prettiest girls. It was the sexiest show in town." Becoming ever more immersed in the 1960s counterculture of easy sex and abundant drugs, Oglesby eventually parted company with his wife and children.

A desire to "do my own thing," coupled with a hostility toward white workers, Southerners, authority figures, and a government that waged war on Marxist guerrillas in Southeast Asia, formed the basis of New Left ideology. Cold war Democrats, the politicians who stood at the "vital center" of American society, represented the true adversaries of progressive reform. Some SDSers ultimately became revolutionaries, robbing banks, bombing military bases, and rumbling with white policemen—the occupation army of America's ghetto colonies.

Other New Leftists sought control of the Democratic party, intending to drive out its "racist" urban machine bosses and anti-Communist labor leaders. Still more dreamed of making "the long march through the professions," moving into positions of cultural power in the universities, the media, and Hollywood. Radicals also entered the legal profession in order to shape the federal judiciary. Just as they nationalized the civil rights conflict, challenging repressive local ordinances in the federal courts, radicals planned other legal crusades. In their minds, Northern communities that prohibited abortion and gay sex were little different from the Southern states that enforced segregation.

In part, the student left's antagonism toward white workers derived from the overwhelming support that the American Federation of Labor–Congress of Industrial Organizations' (AFL-CIO) leadership threw behind America's cold war foreign policy. In 1967, 1,368 labor union representatives had urged Lyndon Johnson to escalate the Vietnam War, compared to 276 who wanted an immediate withdrawal from Indochina. Vividly, one AFL-CIO vice president in 1970 rendered his judgment of leftist students:

> They burn books, loot stores, tear apart institutions of learning; they physically assault educators, public officials and others who disagree—all in the name of destroying the establishment and gaining "freedom." . . . Most of them never did a day's work, let alone know a day's suffering, and are still amply cared for by their parents.

If middle-class student activists had examined rank-and-file sentiment, they would have learned that, according to a University of Michigan study, working-class whites were no more pro-war than college-educated professionals. Why Boomer activists failed to see this may have had much to do with their own class blinders. Dan Lichty of the Princeton SDS sadly noted at the end of the 1960s that his fellow Ivy League radicals were indifferent to, when not outright contemptuous of, working-class whites:

> Princeton is just that kind of place. It's all shade trees and lawns and rich people's kids. They don't think about workers here. The students all know they've got it made. A friend of mine was talking like a revolutionary for a few months and now he says he's going to be a corporate lawyer.

Most students on the left majored in liberal arts and the social sciences. At Michigan State, for instance, 76 percent of anti-war students generally and 84 percent of New Left partisans were liberal arts and social science majors. The story was the same at Penn State, Kent State, and the elite universities. Of the 733 student supporters of the Berkeley Free Speech Movement arrested in a December 1964 building sit-in, none majored in business. Most pursued just three fields of study: English, history, and philosophy.

(It is ironic that Michigan State president John Hannah, a stout anti-Communist, had gone out of his way to enhance the university's liberal arts and social science departments. Envious of the University of Michigan, Hannah wanted Michigan State to acquire greater academic prestige—not knowing that in the process he was enlarging the pool of potential student activists. In 1960, 20 percent of Michigan State students were liberal arts and social science majors. By 1970, as twelve thousand Michigan State undergraduates went on strike following the Kent State slayings, 54 percent of students were liberal arts and social science majors. Berkeley underwent a similar shift in academic emphasis as anti-Communist business and engineering majors were steadily overwhelmed by the more left-leaning students of history and literature.)

Student anti-war activists often had urban and "out-of-state" backgrounds. Fifty-two percent of Michigan State SDSers were not natives of the state, and 53 percent came from far more cosmopolitan and metropolitan areas than East Lansing. Although fewer Penn State SDSers (21 percent) were from out of state compared to their peers at Michigan State, nearly two-thirds of the "Happy Valley's" radicals hailed from a metropolitan area—chiefly Philadelphia and its affluent suburbs. At Kent State, 41 percent of SDSers were not natives of Ohio, and more than half claimed metropolitan origins. Twenty-one percent of Kent State SDSers were products of Cleveland and its middle-class suburbs. At the University of Wisconsin, SDS would not have existed without cadres from New York City and the upscale community of Scarsdale. Conversely, at Wisconsin—as well as at Kent State—the students who felt repelled by the anti-war movement tended to be homegrown, small-town natives.

Looking at the ethnic and religious backgrounds of campus activists, one sees few Roman Catholics. Those Catholics in the ranks of the student anti-war movement and the New Left had Irish, not Eastern European, antecedents. The reasons for this are not difficult to fathom. Well into the 1960s, the Soviet occupation of Eastern Europe remained a sore spot among Americans of Eastern European ancestry. On top of that, youths with Eastern European Catholic backgrounds frequently did not go to college—they went to Vietnam.

In contrast, Irish-Americans could—more readily, though not always—distance themselves from the plight of their Eastern European co-religionists. Moreover, among American Catholics, the Irish claimed the largest middle class. It followed that most of the Catholic students who received college deferments from the Vietnam draft were Irish. And ever larger numbers of Irish attended secular schools with professors who were less inclined to embrace the anti-Communist cause than was the case at Catholic colleges.

Catholic students did not need to go to secular universities, however, to be exposed to anti–cold war faculty. For instance, by the end of the 1960s faculty and administrators at the Catholic universities of Georgetown and Notre Dame were turning against America's cold war foreign policy. Their desire to be competitive with the Ivy League led Notre Dame and Georgetown to distance themselves from traditional Catholic anti-communism and social conservatism. Few parents seemingly objected to the growing anti-war culture at America's prominent Catholic colleges. One in every four Notre Dame students, for instance, reported that their parents urged them to avoid the draft by any means.

The vast majority of anti-war student activists came from Jewish and WASP families. Although Jews represented 3 percent of the U.S. population and accounted for 10 percent of the total number of college students in 1970, 23 percent of youths from Jewish families identified with the New Left. In contrast, just 4 percent of Protestant students and 2 percent of Catholic students embraced the New Left. At the elite institutions of higher education, Jews dominated the New Left. Sixty-three percent of the student radicals at the University of Chicago came from Jewish backgrounds. In Ann Arbor, 90 percent of the student left came from Jewish backgrounds, though few were religiously observant.

Even at less academically competitive schools where there were fewer Jews, their influence in the New Left remained great. Forty-two percent of Penn State's SDS chapter was Jewish, though Jews accounted for just 10 percent of the student body. Nationally, 60 percent of SDSers were Jewish. (It should not be forgotten, however, that the majority of Jewish students did *not* join SDS. As was true with the 1930s-era Old Left, though Jewish students dominated the New Left, most Jewish Boomers were not radicals.)

SDS founder Bob Ross had the impression that there were hardly any non-Jews in the Wisconsin and Minnesota SDS chapters. Ross was not mistaken. Wisconsin SDSer Paul Buhle fondly recalled that "Radical Madison was a goyishe city with a

Jewish heart of passionate intellectual-political commitment."
As fellow Wisconsin SDSer Paul Breines observed, "The real
yeast in the whole scene had been the New York Jewish students in Madison." Breines also praised the "rootless cosmopoli-
tanism" of the Wisconsin New Left. It was precisely this lack of
attachment to place, and disregard for local moral and patriotic
values, that deepened class and cultural divisions between
"town and gown" in the 1960s.

Many Jewish students, regardless of their degree of assimila-
tion, had absorbed from their Eastern European backgrounds a
propensity toward social activism. Uprooted in the late nine-
teenth and early twentieth centuries, Jewish immigrants confronted a culturally ambiguous environment in America.
Unlike other ethnic groups (including German Jews) that,
upon gaining higher socioeconomic status, became conservative, Eastern European Jews did not tend to forsake their con-
cept of what constituted a better society. In the 1930s, at a time
when Jews were leaving the sweatshops behind to go to college,
half the membership of the Communist party had Jewish backgrounds. By 1946 one-third of America's Jews—as opposed to
13 percent of non-Jews—felt some sympathy for the Soviet
Union. Hitler, after all, was a right-winger, and the Red Army
had liberated Auschwitz.

Possibly some Jews clung to leftist causes because of their
persistent cultural anxiety. Their social mobility had arrived
after World War II and was achieved largely in the independent
professions of law, medicine, and teaching. Pursuing a career in
the corporations was out of the question since Protestant businessmen barred their doors to Jews and Catholics.

Some conservative Jewish scholars, however, have not put
such a sympathetic spin on post–World War II Jewish social activism. Stanley Rothman and S. Robert Lichter, for instance,
have argued that "the aim of the Jewish radical is to estrange
the Christian from society, as he feels estranged from it." To
them, Jewish student radicals represented "the advance guard

of the liberal-cosmopolitan sensibility" that penetrated the heartland by the end of the 1960s from both the West and East coasts.

Rothman and Lichter concluded that many Jewish SDSers had parents who in the 1950s had abandoned Orthodoxy for Reform Judaism. Reform Jews became so assimilated and secularized that they developed an even deeper attachment to the "god" of left-liberal politics. Without elaborate rituals and self-sacrificing obedience to God, there was nothing to do in temple—or in church—but talk about secular politics. Jewish Boomer activists, Rothman and Lichter believed, merely evolved one step further than their parents—becoming alienated agnostics, atheists, or born-again Buddhists.

In any event, religious faith and SDS politics did not tend to mix well. Describing his thoughts at his first anti-war demonstration, one SDSer best summed up the New Left attitude toward religion: "I felt the way I did when I gave up religion. I felt I had kicked something. I was free." Another Boomer leftist, Osha Neumann, whose father had been a Columbia University professor, took his hatred of organized religion to its logical conclusion. (Neumann belonged to a militant New York–based group called "The Motherfuckers." The organization took its name from a poem—"Up Against the Wall, Motherfucker"—written by black militant LeRoi Jones.) In 1966 Neumann and his friends disrupted a Mass at St. Patrick's Cathedral. They were protesting Francis Cardinal Spellman's support for the Vietnam War. After a confrontation with parishioners and police officers, Neumann wrote down his feelings about Catholics:

> I imagine Cardinal Spellman stripped naked in front of his congregation, beaten, defiled, shit upon, forced to kneel down in a circle of raw bleeding ass holes of the sodomized choir boys and be fahrted upon, forced to eat the flesh of burnt children, forced to shiver in icy puke for all eternity.
>
> His congregation will observe this spectacle while submitting themselves to a number of tortures. Their clothes will be

taken away from them and they will be made to beat each
other with whips. Their children will be brought to them
and before their eyes married to dope-addicted Negro
prostitutes. The marriages will be consummated in the
aisles.

Two extreme varieties of Jewish student activists stood out in
the 1960s: those who regarded their religious heritage as a political road map to the future, and those who rejected Judaism as
counterrevolutionary. The majority took the second position
and were more likely to believe that Judaism was an imperialistic faith, as evidenced by Israel's "subjugation" of the Palestini-
ans. Typical was Columbia SDSer Steven Cohen. The son of a
Baltimore businessman, Cohen had spent his teen years at a socialist summer camp playing games that pitted workers against
capitalists instead of cowboys against Indians. Accompanying
his father around Baltimore, Cohen observed, "After a while I
began looking around and seeing that the ghetto merchants and
landlords were all Jewish and were exploiting blacks like mad.
And all those self-righteous Jewish liberals openly spout the
most incredible racism. That finally clinched it for me." Abandoning his Jewish faith, Cohen identified himself as an "inter-
nationalist" dedicated to supporting the Arab liberation
movement. Cohen became such a committed foe of Israel that
at one Columbia debate in the 1960s he accused the Zionists of
cutting a deal with Nazi Germany. According to Cohen, Germany had allowed six thousand Jews to go to Palestine in exchange for Zionist assistance in exterminating the other six
million Jews.

In contrast to Cohen, Penn State activist Leverett Millen believed that rooted religious conviction represented the means by
which to achieve moral salvation. Millen, who was one of the
few Orthodox Jews in the national SDS, sought to mobilize
Penn State's Jewish student population. In 1966 he founded the
Hillel Liberation Front (HLF) and praised biblical and more
contemporary prophets:

... The HLF does not intend to be representative of the Jewish students at Hillel. Like the prophet Jeremiah, we say, "I am in derision daily; everyone mocketh me daily." For the prophets who spoke the words: "seek justice, undo oppression; defend the fatherless, plead for the widow," were, unfortunately, not representative of the Jewish people of their time. And the few Germans like the sainted [Dietrich] Bonhoeffer, who spoke out against the horrors of Auschwitz were, unfortunately, not representative of the German people. In our unrepresentativeness, then, we claim good company.

... Many of the more "representative" students have suggested to us that taking part in the street protests and denouncing the atrocities inflicted by Americans on innocent Vietnamese is not good public relations, and that as Jews we cannot become involved in this matter. We say to these more "representative" students that you have an intimate moral kinship with the millions in Nazi Germany whose only moral guide was, "Don't get involved!"

Given their ideological lineage, Boomer radicals whose parents had been leftists during the Great Depression became known as "red diaper babies." As early as the 1950s, Madison, Wisconsin, was a virtual nursery for red diaper babies. With perhaps one exception, the Wisconsin students who belonged to the campus "Joe Must Go" chapter—dedicated to ousting Republican senator Joseph McCarthy from office—were New Yorkers, and often the children of Communist party stalwarts. They deliberately concealed their political affiliations and residential origins from the local media to avoid being tagged as "outside agitators." Many of the radical graduate students who took part in the "Joe Must Go" movement at Wisconsin became activist professors in the 1960s.

The red diaper babies—who accounted for at least a third of SDS's membership in the 1960s—liked to believe that the New Left represented an ideological departure from the Communist party of their parents. In reality, the New Left and the Old Left were more alike than different. At best, one distinction between Old Left and New Left may be made. The depression-era Communist party had regarded the working class as the agency of radical change. SDSers turned their backs on white workers, contending that intellectuals, blacks, and third-world Marxists represented the revolutionary vanguard. Even that distinction, however, should not be so sharply drawn. By the 1940s, when the CIO expelled Communists from leadership roles, Old Leftists had grown disenchanted with the conservative, largely Catholic, working class.

Both Old and New Left partisans called the United States an imperialist, repressive nation. Conversely they idealized foreign revolutionaries—whether Joseph Stalin in the 1930s or Ho Chi Minh in the 1960s. Red diaper babies, like their parents, also reached out to America's "internal black colony." Finally, it should not be forgotten that the Old and New Left recruited their members from the same pool—college students. Although the Communist party of the 1930s imagined itself to be an organization of workers, its appeal was greatest at Berkeley, Chicago, the City College of New York, Columbia, Harvard, and Swarthmore. Even the Communists who became CIO organizers tended to be college graduates.

The influence of red diaper babies in the New Left should not be underestimated. Ronald Radosh, a graduate history student at the University of Iowa who became a leading critic of America's cold war foreign policy, had spent his childhood at a private New York academy for "little reds." His classmates included Kathy Boudin and Michael and Robert Meeropol. Kathy Boudin, whose father was a radical lawyer and had been a major Communist party figure, helped found the terrorist SDS–Weather Underground. Michael and Robert Meeropol, whose father was a Soviet spy convicted of conveying atomic bomb secrets to Moscow, were vocal members of the Michigan and Wisconsin SDS chapters.

Three of the founders of SDS, Richard Flacks and Bob Ross of the University of Michigan, and Steve Max of New York

City, were red diaper babies. Max's father had edited the Communist party's newspaper, the *Daily Worker.* Ross grew up in
such a radical, politically insulated environment that only upon
marriage did he discover "Jewish families without socialists or
Communists in them. I thought it came with the territory."

Frank Emspak, leader of the National Coordinating
Committee to End the War in Vietnam, which organized
Washington-bound protest rallies, had been a leftist graduate
history student at Wisconsin and head of the Communist
party's DuBois Clubs. His father, Julius Emspak, was one of the
Communist labor leaders expelled from the CIO after World
War II. (Frank Emspak later wrote an academic monograph
claiming that the CIO lost any claim to being an agency for social justice when Catholic labor leaders such as Philip Murray
expelled the Communists.) Another graduate of the Wisconsin
New Left, Gene Dennis, was the son of the general secretary of
the American Communist party. The senior Dennis had also
been an agent of the Communist International (Comintern),
performing errands for the Soviet Union in the Philippines,
South Africa, and China.

Robert Starobin, a Berkeley Free Speech Movement veteran
and history professor, had much in common with Gene Dennis.
Starobin's father, Joseph, had been a major figure in the American Community party. In 1954 the elder Starobin had published
Eyewitness to Indochina, a book that celebrated the revolutionary freedom struggles of the Soviet Union, China, and Vietnam
from the Western "feudal and colonial order." Joseph Starobin,
anticipating an analysis of U.S. cold war foreign policy that
would become popular in the historical profession in the 1960s,
argued that America had provoked North Korea to invade
South Korea in 1950. Joseph and Robert Starobin, and their
counterparts at the Marxist journal *Monthly Review,* spent the
1950s and 1960s praising North Vietnam as a socialist paradise
and describing Ho Chi Minh as a gentle, warmhearted leader.
The United States, in contrast, was an imperialist enemy of democracy.

On the West Coast, two red diaper babies made history in the 1960s. Folk singer "Country Joe" McDonald, a fixture at Berkeley's coffeehouses, wrote the 1965 anti-war anthem, "I Feel Like I'm Fixin' to Die Rag." (Four years later McDonald achieved national notoriety when he led an audience of 250,000 at Woodstock in chanting the word, "Fuck.") In "I Feel Like I'm Fixin' to Die Rag," McDonald, sounding much like his Communist parents, argued that American youths were dying in Vietnam in order to advance the fortunes of corporate imperialism. Concurring with Mao that revolutionaries had to move among the unsuspecting populace like fish in a sea, McDonald called his group "Country Joe and the Fish."

(Contrary to Country Joe McDonald, American corporations were not the driving force behind Washington's anti-Communist foreign policy. American capitalists, as Lenin had predicted, were willing to sell the Communists the rope they needed to hang businessmen. In 1965, for instance, the Firestone Tire and Rubber Company announced plans to build a synthetic tire plant in Romania. Firestone's Romanian-fabricated tires would have likely ended up on North Vietnamese army trucks. Only a national protest by the Young Americans for Freedom and congressional conservatives forced Firestone to cancel its plans.)

While Country Joe McDonald gained national renown, Paul Richards achieved great notoriety in the Bay Area. In 1961 Richards and his parents received invitations from the Soviet Women's Committee to make a Communist propaganda film called "Women in Russia." Given his family background, it was not surprising that Richards vehemently protested compulsory ROTC when he enrolled at Berkeley. To the annoyance of his classmates, Richards would shout obscenities at the officers who ordered him to wear his uniform. In 1964 Richards helped lead the 1964 Berkeley Free Speech Movement and presided over the local chapter of the Communist party's DuBois Clubs. (At Berkeley the campus SDS chapter and the DuBois Clubs were virtually one and the same.)

Beyond red diaper babies and Jews, the 1960s antiwar movement and the New Left recruited tens of thousands of hitherto apolitical WASPs. While Jewish activists often had parents who supported their children's activism, this was more rare for middle-class Protestant SDSers who, Texas activist Jeff Shero noted, had to break with their past:

> ... If you were a New York student [in other words, Jewish] and became a member of SDS, it was essentially joining a political organization, which was a common experience. In Texas to join SDS meant breaking with your family, it meant being cut off—it was like in early Rome joining a Christian sect—and the break was so much more total, getting involved with something like SDS you had to be much more highly committed, and you were in a sense freed, 'cause you'd get written off. If you were from Texas, in SDS, you were a bad motherfucker, you couldn't go home for Christmas. Your mother didn't say, "Oh, isn't that nice, you're involved. We supported the republicans in the Spanish Civil War, and now you're in SDS and I'm glad to see you're socially concerned." In most of those places it meant, *"You Goddamn Communist."*

What is especially intriguing from a psychological standpoint is the number of radicalized young WASPs who were the alienated children of the men who led America into Vietnam. Craig McNamara, the son of Secretary of Defense Robert McNamara, threw himself into anti-war organizing at Stanford University. Beyond displaying the Viet Cong flag in his room, Craig McNamara joined fifteen thousand Bay Area students in trashing businesses and breaking windows—believing this would end the Vietnam War. He admitted that he felt nothing but "rage, pure rage" toward his father. Craig's sister, Kathy McNamara, also became a student anti-war activist and befriended Sam Brown, the leader of the October 1969 Vietnam Moratorium which sponsored anti-war lectures and pickets across the country. Paradoxically, while Robert McNamara issued ever larger draft calls, his son and other upper-middle-class Stanford males clung tightly to their student deferments.

Senior Pentagon official Paul Nitze had three children taking part in the militant 1967 "Confront the Warmakers" rally in Washington. One of them was affiliated with the Columbia SDS chapter. Secretary of Army Stanley Resor had two sons who were anti-war organizers, while Under Secretary of the Army Ted Beal had a daughter in the anti-war movement. Attorney General Nicholas Katzenbach's son joined Craig McNamara in the ranks of the Stanford anti-war movement. National Security Adviser McGeorge Bundy also had an anti-war activist son. (Although his father was not associated with the Johnson administration, Rennie Davis, a founder of the Michigan SDS, is worth mentioning. Davis's father had, in the Truman administration, been an architect of West Germany's rehabilitation as an ally against Soviet communism. The senior Davis was a rare Jew among the WASPs who created America's cold war foreign policy.)

One of President Johnson's staunchest supporters in Congress, Senator Albert Gore, Sr., of Tennessee, ended up, like the McNamaras and the Bundys, in a generational shouting match over Vietnam. Albert Gore, Jr., a Harvard student, informed his father that he opposed the war because:

We do have an inveterate antipathy for Communism—or paranoia as I like to put it. My own belief is that this form of psychological ailment—in this case a national madness—leads the victim to actually create the thing which is feared the most. It strikes me that this is precisely what the U.S. has been doing. Creating—if not creating, energetically supporting—fascist, totalitarian regimes in the name of fighting—totalitarians. Greece, South Vietnam, a good deal of Latin America. For me, the best example is the U.S. Army.

(When Senator Gore faced a tough reelection in 1970, his son volunteered to serve in Vietnam. The younger Gore donned a uniform, sat on a horse, and filmed a campaign commercial before shipping out. He became an army photographer and was able to avoid combat. Interestingly, in 1988, while challenging Massachusetts governor Michael Dukakis for the Democratic presidential nomination, Albert Gore, Jr., accused Dukakis of being anti-military as well as insufficiently anti-Communist.)

Given that 95 percent of the youths who joined the anti-war movement and identified with SDS came from Democratic and Old Left households, it might not be surprising to see generational divisions within the Johnson White House. To find such cleavages within the administration of Richard Nixon *is* noteworthy. Nixon Defense Secretary Melvin Laird's son participated in anti-war protests at the Eau Claire campus of the University of Wisconsin. Susan Haldeman, the daughter of White House Chief of Staff—and future Watergate defendant—H. R. Haldeman, demonstrated against the war at Stanford. At the same time Deputy Attorney General Richard Kleindienst and Secretary of the Interior Walter Hickel watched their children march against the Vietnam War.

Ideological and generational divisions over America's cold war foreign policy were also fought out by WASPs within the ranks of the Peace Corps. The Kennedy appointees who led the Peace Corps in the 1960s cultivated the image of rugged volunteers who journeyed into the "Heart of Darkness" to construct hydroelectric dams. In reality, far from dwelling in thatched huts, most of the seventy thousand Peace Corps volunteers had comfortable situations and worked as English, drama, and math teachers. In Ghana, for example, 90 percent of the volunteers had servants. Many others lived in African and Asian neighborhoods that reminded them of Scarsdale. The upper-middle-class, Ivy League–educated Peace Corps volunteers largely lived and worked with their social counterparts overseas.

The World War II generation of Washington bureaucrats

who ran the Peace Corps complained that many of these young volunteers smoked dope, engaged in "macho" sexual conquests, and, on balance, were "neurotic, infantile whiners." The generational schism that ripped the foreign policy–making elite apart in America was replicated throughout the Peace Corps ranks. Given that joining the Peace Corps was one way for young males to avoid military service in Vietnam, it is not surprising that a number of volunteers viewed America's anti-Communist foreign policy with disdain. That disdain, after having been continuously exposed to the third-world Marxism of some members of the postcolonial elite, often grew into vigorous dissent.

A few former Peace Corps volunteers became moderate antiwar activists while others joined New Left organizations and denounced America as an imperialist power. Overall, 43 percent of the volunteers returned home critical of America's crusade against communism. (By the 1970s, hundreds of Peace Corps veterans had worked their way up through the ranks of the Agency for International Development and other federal programs related to the execution of American foreign policy in Africa, Asia, and Latin America.)

Beyond creating a generational and political schism within the elite, the Vietnam War and the rise of the New Left underscored another fact of life in the 1960s: class had its privileges. Fifty-five percent of the youths who joined SDS came from upper-middle-class households. The children of white-collar professionals were far more likely to identify themselves as radicals than was the case for working-class Boomers. Just 17 percent of SDSers could claim blue-collar origins. Of course, only 17 percent of *all* college students in the 1960s came from working and lower-middle-class backgrounds.

Working-class Boomers who attended college were often more career oriented than their elite counterparts and, in any event, did not have parents with sufficient financial and political clout to bail them out if they got into trouble. Significantly, if working-class college students did become radicalized in the

1960s, they tended to embrace the right. Thirty-nine percent of the members of the Young Americans for Freedom, the anti-Communist, free-market vanguard of the New Right, had working-class origins—more than twice the proportion for SDS.

One had only to look at the face of America and its army in Vietnam to see the class divisions that separated affluent Scarsdale from blue-collar Queens. While greater numbers of youths were attending college in the 1960s, few Americans (just 6 percent) had ever set foot on a university campus. Forty-three percent of Americans had no more than an eighth-grade education. Of the 29 million males who turned 18 between 1965 and 1972, just 2 million went to Vietnam. Eighty percent of the soldiers who fought in Vietnam came from blue-collar families. In 1965, one-quarter of the American soldiers in Vietnam were black. (Horrified at that statistic, by 1968 the Defense Department cut the proportion of blacks in combat units in half.) SDSers may have posted pictures of Stokely Carmichael on their dormitory room walls, but they still allowed working-class blacks to go to Vietnam in their place.

Although 450,000 middle- and upper-middle-class youths broke the nation's draft laws, just 3,250 received jail sentences. (Families who could afford to hire good lawyers tied the Justice Department into knots. It was easier to imprison poor people than well-off ones.) Among 1,203 (male) members of the Harvard class of 1968, only 26 went to Vietnam—none were killed. In contrast, 35 members of the Harvard class of 1941 had perished in World War II and hundreds of others had seen combat. As former *Newsweek* editor Robert Christopher observed (in 1989), "It was essentially the children of the disproportionately WASP middle class who ultimately destroyed public support for the Vietnam War by refusing to fight in it."

When the Johnson administration finally abolished graduate school deferments, Harvard's student newspaper, *The Crimson*, wailed that the government was guilty of "careless expediency" and of acting in an "unfair" manner. One Rhodes Scholar and future corporate lawyer justified his avoidance of military service, observing that "There are certain people who can do more good in a lifetime in politics or academics or medicine than by getting killed in a trench." At Berkeley, a Free Speech Movement veteran admitted that he never brought up the issue of class privilege and the draft. "I'm frankly appalled at the fear of alienating students," he said, "by raising the II-S [student deferment] issue." Of the members of the New England Resistance who called upon youths to abandon their college deferments and allow themselves to go on trial as draft resisters, 90 percent kept their own student deferments.

According to various surveys of campus opinion, three-quarters of male college students confessed that they were deliberately avoiding the draft. The inquisitive dean of one prestigious graduate business school discovered that 90 percent of his twelve hundred male candidates for admission were seeking to continue their evasion of the Vietnam War. When New York City's draft boards announced in 1968 that school-teachers would be exempt from the draft, twenty thousand youths beyond the number expected applied for positions. Meanwhile enrollment in New York's education colleges increased 800 percent.

Beyond going to college, there were other ways to avoid Vietnam. Joe Namath's draft board labeled him physically unfit for Vietnam but well enough to play professional football for the New York Jets. New York Knicks basketball star Bill Bradley arranged to be posted to a reserve unit. (The Pentagon found that 71 percent of reservists had joined up to avoid Vietnam. Nearly all reservists and National Guard members were college graduates.) Players for the Baltimore Colts and the Detroit Lions football teams received automatic draft exemptions or postings in the reserves while the Dallas Cowboys—along with the sons of such wealthy Texas politicians as Lloyd Bentsen and George Bush—went into the National Guard.

Actor George Hamilton received a hardship deferment: he was the sole provider for his mother, who lived with him in his

Hollywood mansion. Rock-and-roll stars flocked to Beckley, West Virginia. Selective Service allowed males to report to any draft board of their choosing, and Beckley's reputation for exempting males with long hair, beards, and evidence of drug consumption made the locale attractive to rockers. God-fearing mountaineers preferred to send the military nice blue-collar boys with crew cuts. If all else failed, there was always the ploy adopted by a member of the Michigan State SDS. During his physical examination, the doctor noticed an object protruding from the SDSer's anus. Bewildered, the doctor sought an explanation. The SDSer replied, "Oh, that's my pet rat." He was not drafted.

Although millions of youths escaped Vietnam, draft boards could be vindictive. For instance, Selective Service informed rock-and-roll star Gary Lewis—the son of comedian Jerry Lewis—that if he performed at recruitment events he would not be sent to Vietnam. Not wishing to entice youths into a war he would be exempt from fighting in, Gary Lewis told the army no. As punishment, the younger Lewis was sent to Vietnam. By the time he returned at the end of 1967, the sweet melodies of "Gary Lewis and the Playboys" had given way to acid rock. Lewis's career was finished.

While Boomer radicals avoided military service and captured national media attention, the emergence of a conservative student movement went largely unnoticed. Like SDS, the Young Americans for Freedom, established in 1960 with the help of *National Review* editor William F. Buckley, Jr., despised cold war Democrats. YAF activists objected to federal intervention in the South and what they regarded as the destruction of states' rights. Student conservatives, however, were not necessarily the racists their critics accused them of being. They believed that if Southern blacks wanted equal rights, they should move to the North and leave Mississippi to wallow in its racism and economic backwardness.

At least half of YAF's sixty thousand members were "cradle conservatives" from Republican, anti-union backgrounds. Others tended to be anti-Communist, socially conservative Irish and German Catholics who were repulsed by campus and urban rioting. Their parents, though they had remained nominal Democrats in the 1950s, enthusiastically championed Republican Senator Joseph McCarthy, a fellow anti-Communist Catholic.

Catholic conservatives were more likely to attend a community college or less prestigious state university than their libertarian colleagues and SDS counterparts. Such student conservatives, like Penn State YAF leader Carl Thormeyer and Daniel Manion—whose father was a onetime dean of the Notre Dame Law School—were also more likely to go to Vietnam after graduation. Student conservatives often found themselves alienated by their anti-war professors. YAF founder and social conservative Scott Stanley recalled:

> Our ideas were [the] subject of ridicule and attack and viciousness on the college campus. Everyone hears endlessly about the McCarthy era, but there's no talk about the terrible harassment that went on against college students and professors who were anti-Communists and anti-collectivists. . . . We felt ourselves persecuted for our ideas.

The partisans of YAF were an uneasy mixture of middle-class, secularized libertarians and lower-middle-class Catholic social conservatives. YAF counted homosexuals among its leaders and patrons. Many Boomer conservatives also championed the cause of cultural liberation. At Berkeley, for instance, YAF members participated in the 1965 *Filthy* Speech Movement. As early as 1960, libertarians had objected to including any references to God in YAF's founding document the "Sharon [Connecticut] Statement."

A few observers on the right noticed that thousands of the young conservatives were no less hedonistic than their counterparts in the New Left. The *National Review,* reflecting the angst of its conservative Catholic editors, warned that the libertarians were headed down the road to anarchy. Scrapping a federal bureaucracy that interfered with the conduct of business was one thing, but the wholesale repudiation of all moral authority was another matter. Libertarian-anarchists wanted to legalize marijuana, dismantle the "Warfare-Welfare State," and abolish the draft—or what they called the "Selective Slavery System." (Only the poor would be compelled by the free market to enlist.) *National Review* columnist Frank Meyer groused that

> The libertine impulse that masquerades as libertarianism . . . disregards all moral responsibility, ranges itself against the minimum needs of social order, and raises the freedom of the individual person (regarded as the unbridled expression of every desire, intellectual or emotional) to the status of an absolute end.

Penn State's libertarian-anarchists joined SDS in anti-war protests and helped create an "underground railroad" to Canada for draft evaders. At Berkeley, the campus YAF chapter organized demonstrations against the draft and campaigned for the legalization of narcotics. Two former California state chairs of YAF were, as Berkeley libertarian Sharon Presley said, "known to be druggies." In 1966 Presley and the two California YAF "druggies" were expelled from the organization.

Even though the libertarian right and the New Left stood at opposite ends of the political spectrum, they had much in common. Both wanted control over the federal government to further their own agenda. Libertarian extremists and leftists smoked pot, avoided the Vietnam War through college student deferments, and, after graduation, entered the ranks of the upper middle class. Such Boomer activists were fated to be the shock troops of a cultural and political revolution that undermined the cold war Democratic party and polarized the nation.

4

Other Dissenters—and Their Critics

BY THE TIME the 1950s gave way to the 1960s, many American intellectuals had turned their backs on the white working class and the cold war Democratic party. In 1948 Columbia sociologist C. Wright Mills had published *The New Men of Power*. It was clear that, with the onset of the cold war, Mills was put off by anti-Communist labor leaders. Eight years later, with the publication of *The Power Elite,* Mills warned that American democracy had been subverted by the "warlords" of the military establishment and Wall Street. (Mills failed to note that the "warlords" could not prevent President Eisenhower from slashing their budgets and that Wall Street had no qualms about doing business with the Communists.) By 1960, in his essay "Letter to the New Left," the Ivy League professor argued that young radicals should forget the racist, reactionary white workers who had been co-opted by capitalism. Students, and their intellectual mentors in the university and the world of letters, Mills believed, were destined to be the vanguard of revolutionary change in America.

Herbert Marcuse, a radical philosophy professor at Brandeis University, agreed with Mills. Marcuse claimed that the American working class possessed a "false consciousness." Consequently, white workers were impossible to organize because they had been bought off by Wall Street. Since workers could not think for themselves, intellectuals had to lead the revolution. Despite his hostility to American capitalism, Marcuse had no problem fitting in at Brandeis. The elite university was quite liberated even in the relatively tame 1950s. Abbie Hoffman—who had attended Brandeis in the 1950s—fondly recalled that his professors used the word "fuck" in the classroom.

To Marcuse, American democracy was Nazi totalitarianism in disguise. By promoting free speech and intellectual diversity, liberals were practicing what Marcuse called "repressive tolerance." Constitutional guarantees of free speech, and the promotion of scholarship characterized by complex, objective analysis, Marcuse asserted, sapped the revolutionary spirit, co-opted students, and muddied the left's clarity of vision. As Marcuse argued, Democrats were more despicable than Republicans since they hid their real agenda of repression under the cloak of tolerance. At least conservatives were open about their program of oppression, racism, and exploitation.

In order to promote authentic—meaning Marxist—free speech, Marcuse contended, all who opposed the left had to be silenced—or, at the very least, ignored. In 1962 Marcuse refused to debate a fellow Brandeis professor on the Cuban missile crisis. It was pointless, the philosopher said, to discuss issues with liberal "fascists" who supported President Kennedy. National SDS leaders eagerly read Marcuse, finding in his works the philosophical arguments that justified their efforts to scourge university administrators, students, faculty, and politicians who held ideologically incorrect views.

Having built an intellectual reputation with his 1962 book *One-Dimensional Man*, which melded Freudian psychoanalysis with Marx's musings on alienation in a capitalist society, Marcuse became an international icon of the New Left. He flew to Berlin in 1967 to support radical student demonstrations and hailed the German and American left as "the authentic voice of recovered Marxism." In his 1969 work, *An Essay on Liberation*, Marcuse spared no praise for the New Left and the counterculture. But he warned that unrestrained drug consumption might spawn an army of inchoate stoners incapable of carrying out revolutionary action.

While Marcuse and Mills dismissed white workers and castigated the ideological underpinnings of American civil society, New York writer Paul Goodman set his sights on moral traditionalists. In his best-selling 1960 book *Growing Up Absurd,* Goodman called on youths to revolt against the double standards and repressive sexual mores of cold war society. A popular speaker on college campuses in the 1960s as well as a source of inspiration for Tom Hayden and the founders of SDS, Goodman wished to liberate sexual conduct from all social and criminal sanctions. He particularly railed against the "social surveillance" of streetlights and the sterility of suburban life. In 1962 Goodman moaned that "without alleys and basements how will kids, who can't afford hotels, ever have sex?" (Goodman had a personal stake in changing the legal and social customs regarding sexual conduct. He enjoyed having sex with young boys.)

The cultural elite of the 1950s and 1960s concerned themselves with more than sexual liberation and exposing the fascist nature of democracy. They also rebelled against America's cold war foreign policy. In 1959 University of Wisconsin historian William Appleman Williams published the seminal New Left historical interpretation of American foreign policy, *The Tragedy of American Diplomacy.* Williams argued that American economic expansion and corporate imperialism precipitated the cold war and placed the Soviet Union in a defensive posture. In 1967, in *The Nation*, Williams elaborated on his thoughts and blamed the United States for provoking the cold war. Indeed, he argued, "the increasingly militarized holy war mounted by American leaders was grossly irrelevant to the situation and highly conducive to producing problems that were more dangerous than those the policy was supposed to resolve."

Williams's scholarship echoed the views of Franklin Roosevelt's onetime vice president, Henry Wallace. As Truman's secretary of commerce, Wallace had equated the Soviet military occupation of Eastern Europe with U.S. economic influence in Latin America. There was, Wallace thought, a moral-geopolitical equivalence between the two world powers. Moreover the Soviets, Wallace contended, feared "capitalist encirclement." Consequently American anti-Communists had placed Stalin in a purely defensive posture.

Williams influenced a generation of graduate history students and redirected nearly the entire field of diplomatic history to the New Left point of view. Boomer historians became anti-anti-Communists, convinced that U.S. actions had provoked the Soviet Union to take defensive measures—which the West then viewed as aggressive.

In 1959 Williams and his students established *Studies on the Left,* a journal which served as a forum for New Left scholarship. Typically, one of Williams's graduate students hailed him for analyzing historical documents by "reading in more than the document seemed to say." Traditional scholars made the same observation about Williams but did not mean it as a compliment. They believed that Williams took creative license in analyzing U.S. State Department materials, deconstructing meaning from the most banal of boilerplate missives. Diplomatic historian Robert James Maddox, for instance, minced no words in 1973 when he wrote, "Where Williams had the facts he used them, and where he could find none he claimed their very absence corroborated his interpretation." Maddox also noted that Williams often constructed "imaginary speeches and dialogues [of historical figures] by splicing together phrases uttered at different times and on diverse subjects."

Given the mind-set of Williams and his graduate students, it is not surprising that in a 1959 editorial, *Studies on the Left* dismissed the idea of "objectivity" in scholarship. Only "browbeaten" scholars embraced objectivity. Objective scholarship merely reinforced a status quo that was at heart imperialist and capitalist. Scholars, the Wisconsin historians contended, had a duty to promote radical social change in the classroom and in their publications.

A host of academics endorsed Williams, including University of Pennsylvania historian Gabriel Kolko. Kolko, whose father had been a radical CIO organizer in the 1930s and 1940s, blamed the United States for starting the cold war. He also dismissed the "myth" of Soviet repression and mass murder in Poland during World War II. In his 1968 book *The Politics of War*, and in other works, Kolko argued that Washington sought to promote global capitalist domination by waging war against independent nations. America was fundamentally a counterrevolutionary imperialist force in the world, and treated the Soviet Union and other nations as if they were colonial subjects. (In 1987 Kolko published what informally became known as Hanoi's history of the Indochina conflict, *Vietnam: Anatomy of a War*.)

Other New Left historians similarly believed that the United States had provoked the cold war and actively subverted democracy around the world. And they argued that President Truman had dropped atomic bombs on Hiroshima and Nagasaki in 1945 in order to keep Stalin from acquiring a zone of occupation in Japan. They did not believe that Truman, by hastening the end of the war with atomic bombs, had prevented an even greater loss of Asian and American lives which would have occurred if the United States had been forced to invade Japan. New Left academics ignored Japan's bloody resistance at Iwo Jima and Okinawa. (Most of the revisionists had never studied military history, and very few had any firsthand acquaintance with Kamikaze planes. Williams, at least, had been a World War II naval officer.) The Boomer leftists dismissed Japan's genocidal policies in China and Southeast Asia. In fact, they regarded Japan as the first cold war victim of American imperialism and racism. It followed, then, that North Vietnam represented the most recent target of American-sponsored genocide.

Yale historian Staughton Lynd, whose parents had been leftist sociologists in the 1930s and Wallace supporters in 1948, threw himself into the anti–Vietnam War movement. After he and Tom Hayden visited Hanoi in 1965, they published *The Other Side* (1966). Lynd and Hayden spared no praise for the North Vietnamese, pointing out (incorrectly) that even non-Communists had a political voice in their "rice-roots" democratic society. In 1967 Lynd wrote a scorching essay in *Studies on the Left*, in which he compared U.S. foreign policy to "rape" and called America "imperialist, ethnocentric," and racist.

Having been a member of two Communist-front organizations while a student at Harvard—the American Youth for Democracy and the John Reed Club—Lynd did not shy away from expressing his support for the Old Left. He urged 1930s-era Communists and 1960s New Leftists to unite because both had a "historic responsibility to keep American imperialism from destroying the unprecedented upsurge of revolution in the Third World." In spite of initial objections from SANE and other moderate peace organizations, he also wanted to invite Communists into the anti-war movement. (Sociologist Peter Berger, who was active in SANE, did not welcome the prospect of embracing anti-anti-Communist students either. "Observing the radicals in action," Berger said of the campus militants, "I was repeatedly reminded of the storm troopers that marched through my childhood in Europe.")

Before the escalation of the Vietnam War, Lynd and Howard Zinn, a leftist historian later employed by Boston University, sought to radicalize SNCC. In 1962 Lynd, Zinn, and a few SNCC activists had protested Kennedy's naval blockade of Cuba. (Howard Zinn's 1967 book *Vietnam: The Logic of Withdrawal*, depicted the United States as a racist bully who sought to stymie peaceful social change. Zinn hoped for a Communist victory in Indochina and concluded that the ideals of Ho Chi Minh and Mao were superior to the corrupt values of an imperialist America.)

In 1965 Lynd denounced Bayard Rustin of CORE for con-

tinuing to work with President Johnson on civil rights. By associating with a president who waged war in Vietnam, Lynd
fumed, Rustin had created a "coalition with the Marines." Yale
ultimately denied Lynd tenure. His defenders claimed that
Lynd had been persecuted because of his radical politics. Lynd's
detractors retorted that the leftist historian had been denied
tenure for the simple reason that he had given scant attention to
his scholarly and teaching obligations.

Lynd, Williams, and other revisionists received important
assistance from some members of the clergy. In January 1966
anti–cold war religious activists founded Clergy and Laymen
Concerned About Vietnam (CALCAV). By 1967 CALCAV
claimed seventy-eight chapters with twelve thousand members.
Three-quarters of CALCAV's board of directors came from the
Philadelphia–New York–Boston corridor. Its leaders, as well as
CALCAV's rank and file, were mainly Reform Jews, middle-
and upper-middle-class Presbyterians and Episcopalians, and a
handful of Catholics. Conversely, Pentecostals, fundamentalists, and more traditional Protestant clergy—chiefly Southern
Baptists and Missouri Synod Lutherans—tended to support
America's Vietnam War effort. A mid-1960s survey of funda-
mentalist clerics in California showed that they favored military escalation of the Vietnam War over withdrawal by a
margin of 76 percent to 3 percent.

CALCAV's leaders included Yale chaplain William Sloane
Coffin, Stanford professor Robert McAfee Brown, and Har-
vard Divinity School professor Harvey Cox. They warned that
Johnson's efforts to escalate the war would only damage Amer-
ica's relations with the Soviet Union and antagonize China.
Brown and Cox castigated the Saigon government and urged
Washington to open negotiations with the National Liberation
Front, which they saw as the authentic representative of the
South Vietnamese people. Both Brown and CALCAV board
member John C. Bennett, president of the Union Theological
Seminary in New York, observed that their allegiance to God,
and the shame they felt as a result of America's Indochina pol-

icy, prompted their dissent. In 1966 Bennett had said that "The escalation of the war in Vietnam makes it difficult to be an American." A year later Brown stated that "Our ultimate loyalty can never be to nation—it must be to God."

In early 1967 CALCAV gave official voice to the sentiments Brown and Bennett had expressed:

> Each day we find allegiance to our nation's policy more difficult to reconcile with allegiance to our God. . . . We add our voice to those who protest a war in which civilian casualties are greater than military; in which whole populations are deported against their will; in which the widespread use of napalm and other explosives is killing and maiming women, children, and the aged.

Despite their alienation from American society, CALCAV's directors made it clear that they rejected the incivility and violence that characterized SDS. The student left held no higher opinion of their religiously motivated counterparts in the anti-war movement. SDS leaders characterized such activists as "mindless, moralistic masochists." At Cornell University, SDS and anti-war Catholic students and clerics had promoted intense draft resistance. As the first Catholic chaplain ever appointed to Cornell, Daniel Berrigan, a CALCAV founder, could claim considerable credit for nurturing the campus religious left. But relations between the Marxists and the pacifists steadily deteriorated. By 1968 Cornell SDSers referred to the campus pacifists as "those damn Catholics." (Father Blaise Bopane, a Maryknoll priest, concurred with SDS. "Nonviolence is an imperialistic solution!" Father Bopane proclaimed at one academic anti-war conference. "Only guerrilla warfare will alleviate the misery of the masses in the underdeveloped countries.")

CALCAV's most notable recruit was Martin Luther King, Jr. When Lyndon Johnson escalated the Vietnam War in 1965, King urged the president to negotiate with the Viet Cong, halt the bombing of North Vietnam, and give diplomatic recognition to Communist China, which was supplying advisers and weapons to Hanoi. King insisted at the time that he did not believe the United States should unilaterally withdraw from South Vietnam. And the Baptist minister reassured his allies in the Johnson White House that he had no intention of turning from civil rights to foreign policy issues.

In February 1967 King, along with Senator George McGovern, attended an anti-war forum sponsored by *The Nation*. Concerned that the Vietnam conflict would siphon federal money from the War on Poverty, King decided that he had to devote more attention to the cold war. As King asserted, "The promises of the Great Society have been shot down on the battlefield of Vietnam." A few weeks later King became the cochairman of CALCAV. Among his aides he talked about the prospects of going to Hanoi to negotiate personally with Ho Chi Minh.

King's most famous anti-war speech took place in April 1967 from the pulpit of New York City's Riverside Church. There he recounted his conversations with ghetto youths about urban riots and the Vietnam War:

> As I walked among the desperate, rejected, and angry young men I have told them that Molotov cocktails and rifles would not solve their problems. . . . But they asked—and rightly so, what about Vietnam? . . . Their questions hit home, and I knew that I could never again raise my voice against the violence of the oppressed in the ghettos without having first spoken clearly to the greatest purveyor of violence in the world today—my own government.

The civil rights leader then called on young men to become conscientious objectors. To King, the Vietnam War was not an aberration or honest mistake. Taking a leaf from SDS leader Carl Oglesby, King insisted that there was something fundamentally sick about "the American spirit." But he backed away from a formal endorsement of the Viet Cong struggle. Instead he emphasized that the nation's soul could be redeemed if

America returned "to her true home of brotherhood and peaceful pursuits." Nearly three-quarters of the public disapproved of King's anti-war activism. Even among blacks, only a quarter thought the Nobel Peace Prize–winner was right to oppose the war. The *Chicago Tribune*, a bastion of conservative journalism, editorialized that King had taken "the Communist side in the war in Vietnam."

Other, less famous church figures joined King and CAL-CAV. Because the American Roman Catholic church was so well known for its staunch anti-communism, anti-war priests and laity were especially newsworthy and attracted media attention well beyond their small numbers. Monsignor Charles Owen Rice of Pittsburgh was notable for his opposition to the war, given his own past. Rice, who had lent important support to the steelworkers' union during the Great Depression and, as a founder of the Association of Catholic Trade Unionists, had fought Communist influence in the CIO in the 1940s, had since rethought his politics. By the 1960s he went as far as to join the children of his former Stalinist foes in protesting the Vietnam War. It did not help his local reputation that while working-class, largely Catholic Pittsburghers were fighting in South Vietnam, Radio Hanoi was quoting from Rice's anti-war magazine and newspaper articles. In a 1970 issue of the *Catholic World*, Rice argued that reformers should purge the church of its regressive majority:

> The rank and file are a problem, not only because they do not appreciate the outspoken and rebellious young, but because they tend to be racially bigoted and militaristic. One is tempted to say that we must push ahead regardless of cost, even if the cost should turn out to be a good proportion of the rank and file; after all, Catholicism has not been making much of an impression on them nor influencing their lives in the most important areas of conduct. However, one has to have compassion for all, even the bigoted ordinary Catholic with his narrow outlook. He himself is exploited and his family endangered from above and below; he needs under-

standing and help, although he cannot be allowed to run the show. We have to reassure these people, but never hide the truth or discard principles.

In 1965 Rice, writing in the diocesan newspaper, the *Pittsburgh Catholic*, contended that the United States was the aggressor in Vietnam. A number of radical graduate students at the University of Pittsburgh and Carnegie Mellon University helped Rice in building the city's anti-war movement. Rice attended the 1967 Spring Mobilization in New York City and the National Mobilization against the War in Washington. Dressed in priestly regalia at the national anti-war events, he gave respectability to the cause. At home, however, Rice was a prophet without honor. Most of his organizing took place at Pitt and Carnegie Mellon, not at Duquesne University, a Catholic institution operated by the Congregation of the Holy Spirit. When Rice ran as a peace candidate for the city council in 1971, he scored best in Pittsburgh's secular university and Jewish precincts. He trailed miserably in the city's Catholic and working-class neighborhoods.

Thomas Merton, a Trappist monk whose mystical writings became the rage on college campuses in the 1960s, viewed the Vietnam War as a continuation of America's history of genocide and racism. Similarly Father Philip Berrigan, a professor at a Josephite seminary in Newburgh, New York, and the brother of Daniel Berrigan, asserted that Western civilization was "the enemy of man." Another Catholic activist, James Douglass, a theology professor at Bellarmine College in Louisville, Kentucky (an independent Catholic educational institution), went further, comparing Ho Chi Minh to Jesus Christ and Lyndon Johnson to Satan:

> Depart from me, you cursed Americans, into the eternal fire for the devil and his angels; for I was a hungry North Vietnamese and you gave me no food, I was a thirsty Viet Cong and you gave me no drink, I was a napalmed child and you did not welcome me. . . . In fact, it is you who made me, the

Vietnamese Christ, hungry and thirsty, an outlaw hiding out
in my own forests, and it is you who maintain my suffering
by bombing my people and villages and razing my land.

Given the revulsion even religious activists felt for America's
Vietnam policy, it was not unexpected that the most radical
anti-anti-Communist intellectuals and their sympathizers readily rationalized violent student protest. Wisconsin historian
Harvey Goldberg, rhetorically a Marxist revolutionary who se-
cretly made millions on his Wall Street investments, insisted
that violence was the best path to world peace. Only the complete shredding of America's social fabric, Goldberg felt, could
bring about the end of the Vietnam War. Goldberg did not
hesitate to turn his history courses into revolutionary forums.
Students were required to read Frantz Fanon's *Wretched of
the Earth* while SDSers freely leafleted his large classes. Students frequently went directly to demonstrations after his lectures.

A self-conscious cosmopolitan, Goldberg boasted that
"Madison is where I work; Paris is where I live." His favored
students might receive an invitation to summer in Paris with
him. When President Johnson opened the Paris peace talks
with Hanoi in 1968, Goldberg and his students socialized with
Vietnamese Communist officials.

Maurice Zeitlin and Dwight Macdonald were among other
intellectual notables who justified student militancy. As a graduate sociology student at Berkeley in 1962, Zeitlin, whose parents were 1930s-era leftists, had participated in the first campus
demonstration against U.S. military assistance to South Vietnam. He had also supported Fidel Castro's dictatorship and in
1962 even journeyed to Cuba. There he interviewed the revolutionary Che Guevara for *Root and Branch*, a radical magazine
published in Berkeley and edited by David Horowitz. Once he
became a professor at the University of Wisconsin, Zeitlin defended SDS's confrontational tactics. According to Zeitlin, the
occupation of campus buildings by SDS was a more effective

political tactic than picketing. Building seizures and other forms of disruption, Zeitlin thought, raised the cost of the Vietnam War to American society and eventually would force the United States to capitulate. (Whenever local news reporters came to interview Zeitlin in Madison, he was far more circumspect. Zeitlin positioned himself as a political progressive deeply committed to nonviolence and American democracy.)

Literary critic Dwight Macdonald endorsed the black power movement in 1967 and demanded that New York City fire Jewish teachers and replace them with minorities. Jews who opposed their removal from the public schools, Macdonald thundered, were "racist demagogues." Earlier Macdonald had informed a congressional committee that the Vietnam War was an "absurd anti-Communist crusade" and represented nothing less than "global McCarthyism." Like most members of the intellectual set, Macdonald felt nothing but contempt for the earthy, blue-collar style of Lyndon Johnson. The president, after all, had been a Texas schoolteacher, not an Oxford don.

In 1968 Macdonald participated in the SDS occupation of campus buildings at Columbia University. Having been an anti-Stalinist Marxist himself during the Great Depression—albeit a revolutionary with an annual income equal to $100,000 in 2000—Macdonald relived the "exhilaration" and "joyous excitement" of his youth. (Critics called Macdonald an "aging intellectual camp follower of the Youth Cult.") Crossing swords with Columbia faculty members who complained that SDSers were urinating out the office windows of university president Grayson Kirk, Macdonald retorted, that "If anybody's windows can be peed out of, it's his windows." Kirk, Macdonald said, "was a big stuffed shirt" while the SDSers were "the best generation I have known in this country, the cleverest and the most serious and decent." He also contended that students learned more at the barricades than they did in their classrooms.

While a number of America's major magazines, elite newspapers, and television reporters condemned student and faculty insurgents, other media outlets and journalists praised the protesters. The balance between the media foes and supporters of campus activism steadily shifted. By the 1970s a generational changing of the guard was occurring in the newsroom as anti-Communist World War II veterans were being displaced by younger reporters who often rejected the cold war. In terms of class background and politics, members of the prestige press closely resembled the activists of the 1960s. The majority of elite reporters came from secularized upper-middle-class families; graduated from Columbia, the University of Chicago, and Northwestern; and detested cold war Democrats.

Jack Newfield, a *Village Voice* reporter and author of a glowing book on the New Left—*The New Radicals: A Prophetic Minority*—advocated an alliance of "campus, ghetto, and suburb." Although the *Village Voice* was certainly more leftist than the *New York Times*, even reporters employed by mainstream media organizations took sides against cold war Democrats. During the clashes between Chicago police officers and radicals at the 1968 Democratic National Convention, CBS Evening News anchor Walter Cronkite, a regular frequenter of Martha's Vineyard, denounced the Chicago police as "thugs." Hugh Downs of NBC's "Today Show" used the word "pig" to describe the police officers. Tom Wicker of the *New York Times* followed suit, as did *Newsweek* and the *Washington Post*. The media elite also condemned Chicago mayor Richard Daley for his rough handling of the anti-war demonstrators. Daley, in turn, angrily retorted that "The television industry is part of the violence and creating it all over the country."

Ordinary Americans, who were angered that the national media ignored assaults against the Chicago police, endorsed Daley. Seventy-four thousand people wrote letters of support to the Chicago mayor, and public opinion polls showed that supporters of Daley outnumbered critics two to one. Wilting under a public backlash, CBS News admitted that some radicals may have tried to provoke a violent response from police officers. Chicago police officers demanded that the networks show them being pelted with rocks and bottles. Invariably camera crews filmed the police as they clubbed students, giving a misleading impression that the Chicago cops were always the aggressors. Wynston Jones, a Bay Area student who had participated in the 1968 Chicago protest, later admitted that police officers had fallen into a media-SDS trap:

> It was a lot of fun for a lot of people to do something that would cause the cops to lose it. Calling them pigs, saying little things in their ear, giving them gestures. The cops had no training in resisting people taunting them like that. They would lose it entirely and start swinging their clubs, knocking people. There were enough clever people around who understood the media, and understood that you could get publicity by showing the cops out of control.

Like their counterparts in the elite news media, Hollywood actors, directors, and producers enthusiastically embraced the "youth revolution" and the anti-war movement. Actress Shirley MacLaine was a McGovern delegate from California at the 1972 Democratic National Convention and a crusader for the legalization of abortion. (MacLaine later claimed that she could talk to the spirits of the dead.) Her brother, actor Warren Beatty, served as a liaison between McGovern campaign manager Gary Hart and film and music industry people eager to stage fund-raising events for the anti-anti-Communists who had taken control of the Democratic party.

Among the hundreds of Hollywood personalities who endorsed radical change in the 1960s and early 1970s, few achieved the notoriety of actress Jane Fonda. The daughter of legendary actor and New Deal Democrat Henry Fonda, Jane Fonda's most political act before her return to the United States from France in 1969 had been to star as a super "sex kitten" in the film *Barbarella*. Upon arriving in America, she threw herself into the causes of the New Left. She performed near military bases with actor Donald Sutherland in what they described as "Fuck the Army" tours.

Most famously, Fonda went to Hanoi in 1972 where she

posed in an anti-aircraft gun turret and made several broadcasts over Radio Hanoi to American troops in South Vietnam. Fonda denounced "U.S. imperialism" and said of the Vietnamese Communists, "Never in my life have I been in a country of people that are so loving and so nonalienated." Pointing to the U.S. military officers in South Vietnam, she all but invited GIs to shoot their commanders, since "in the past, in Germany and Japan," war criminals had been "tried and executed." When American prisoners of war in the "Hanoi Hilton" later claimed they had been tortured, Fonda called them "liars and hypocrites" and said their exposure to Vietnamese culture should have made them "better citizens than when they left." Eventually Fonda admitted that some torture might have occurred—but it had been justified because the American soldiers had "misbehaved and treated their guards in a racist fashion."

In January and February 1971, Jane Fonda and her future husband, SDS founder Tom Hayden, helped stage the "Winter Soldier Investigation." Claiming they were forging a link with Vietnam veterans, Fonda, Hayden, and CALCAV convened a "war crimes" trial in Detroit. If veterans were willing to confess their crimes against the Vietnamese people, the anti-war movement was prepared to offer absolution. Just one hundred Vietnam veterans out of two million came to Detroit. They provided the news media with dramatic tales about the torture of Viet Cong prisoners and the murder of innocent civilians. Skeptics discounted such horror stories and questioned whether the men who testified had actually been in South Vietnam. (The overwhelming majority of Vietnam veterans resented their depiction as "baby killers." Anti-war activists failed miserably in drawing Boomer veterans and campus activists together.)

Aside from the Vietnam War, sexual freedom, and SDS, Jane Fonda and the 1960s cultural elite embraced another cause: black power. Norman Mailer, who had written *The Armies of the Night*, a romanticized "history/novel" of the 1967 March on the Pentagon, celebrated the sexual promiscuity and lawlessness of the black underclass. Unrestrained sex and violent rioting among urban blacks, Mailer believed, represented a revolt against capitalism. (For that matter, Mailer regarded the orgasm as the ultimate human experience.) Author Susan Sontag—a celebrant of the Viet Cong—went further than Mailer, insisting that "The white race is the cancer of human history."

Journalist Murray Kempton, in the *New York Times Book Review*, praised Panther founder Huey Newton as a nonviolent leader for his times who came "not as avenger but as healer." Historian and journalist Garry Wills similarly defended the Panthers. "Never, it would seem, have people [the Panthers] threatened more and been guilty of less.... And in the end there is a sense of the almost incredible ability of men [like Huey Newton and Eldridge Cleaver] to find dignity in resisting the viciousness of other men—like lifting a 500-pound weight with one hand while stooped under a 1,000-pound weight kept on one's back."

Historian Robert Starobin effusively praised the Black Panthers. Starobin claimed that the cold-blooded murder of innocent black militants by capitalist-sponsored law enforcement agencies was proof "of the depths of racial oppression in the United States." He dedicated a 1970 history of slavery to Bobby Seale and the "martyred" Panther Fred Hampton. Starobin became extremely depressed when black militants told him they did not want Jews—even secularized leftist Jews—associating with them. He later committed suicide.

Leftist academics and writers asserted that black crime was an understandable consequence of white male oppression. Urban riots were, as Mailer described them, revolts against a racist capitalist system. When the urban poor stole automobiles and television sets—they seldom took food—the academic and literary left said, Why not? Why should inner-city blacks not take what was rightfully theirs? Since capitalism thrived upon the exploitation of the poor, there could be no such thing as legitimate property ownership. Given that the democratic electoral system could never respond to the plight of the underclass because American corporations profited from exploitation and enjoyed the support of white working-class racists, urban rioting was the only effective way for poor blacks to seek redress.

A handful of intellectuals—most of whom were cold war Democrats—spoke out against the New Left's view on race relations, sexual freedom, and American foreign policy. They were, however, outnumbered in academia and less and less able to find forums where they could present their point of view. Harvard professor Edward Banfield, in his 1968 book *The Unheavenly City*, argued that the poor did not plan for the future, failed to delay gratification, and indulged themselves in self-destructive vices. Mounting illegitimacy, on top of a propensity to spend whatever money they acquired rather than saving it, prevented the urban poor from furthering their education and acquiring the job skills necessary to lift themselves out of poverty. Worse, this cycle of counterproductive behavior perpetuated itself generation after generation as the poor passed along their habits to their children.

Banfield came under fire by various activist groups, chiefly the National Welfare Rights Organization, the National Organization of Social Workers, and the National Council of Churches. Leftist academics, social workers, and clerics argued that it was white racism and capitalist exploitation that created poverty. Illegitimacy was an inconsequential side effect of the liberated sexuality of underclass men and women. Welfare rights advocates also demanded increased federal and state payments to the urban poor. (The spokesmen for the underclass ignored the fact that impoverished whites outnumbered poor blacks by a factor of 5 to 1. Given that reality, how could racism be blamed for creating poverty?)

Student and faculty militants called Banfield a racist and denounced him for "blaming the victim." SDSers disrupted his classes at Harvard and threatened him with physical harm. Most university administrators, fearing campus riots, refused to allow him to lecture at their institutions. Marcuse's philosophy won the day in the university in the 1960s as academic freedom became a one-way street.

Journalist Tom Wolfe, who had received a doctorate in American studies from Yale, coined the term "radical chic" to describe those who excused the excesses of the black and white left. In 1969 Wolfe ridiculed the cocktail soirees held for the benefit of the Black Panthers and hosted by symphony conductor Leonard Bernstein and others in their Park Avenue and Soho residences. (It was not unusual for the partisans of radical chic to spend $1 million just on decorations for their lofts and townhouses.) The Panthers received over $7 million in financial support from such cultural elites as "Today Show" host and NBC reporter Barbara Walters; heiress Marion Rockefeller; Random House editor John Simon; former Sarah Lawrence College president Harold Taylor; actors Donald Sutherland, Marlon Brando, Jane Fonda, and Harry Belafonte; and directors Otto Preminger, Sidney Lumet, and Bert Schneider.

(Schneider produced the 1974 Academy Award–winning documentary *Hearts and Minds,* which depicted the Vietnam War as the product of America's racist, militaristic, football-playing culture. The producer also purchased "safe houses" around the country for fugitive Panthers and SDSers.)

Hosting leftist militants became so popular among a certain elite in the 1960s that Wolfe predicted that a "Rent-a-Panther" franchise would have to be founded to help meet the demand. The *New York Review of Books*, Wolfe noted, turned over its pages to touting the Panthers, the New Left, and revolutionary violence. According to Wolfe, the *New York Review,* America's premier literary magazine, was "the chief theoretical organ of Radical Chic." (In 1971 the astute academic journal *Public Opinion Quarterly* described the *New York Review* as the "most influential magazine read by the nation's intellectual elite.")

Many of New York's elite eventually wilted under public ridicule for supporting the Panthers and, as Wolfe observed, "turned their attention toward [saving] the sables, cheetahs, and leopards" from extinction. The political style of radical chic, Wolfe wrote, favored "radicals who seem primitive, exotic, and romantic." Most important of all, such militants were not likely to be found "underfoot" at inopportune times, or doing things like burning down the Park Avenue homes of the cultural elite. Radical chic also contained a strong element of cosmopolitan contempt for the moral values of the white working and middle classes. Paradoxically, though the Panthers were anti-Semitic, most of the adherents of radical chic were Jews who employed black servants. Luckily for the New York left, the Bernsteins managed to secure white Chilean servants whom they shared with their friends when they hosted the Panthers and Puerto Rican radicals. Cynics called the Bernsteins "the Spic and Span Employment Agency."

Other exceptional intellectuals rejected radical chic while clinging to an increasingly divided Democratic party. The Georgetown political scientist Jeane Kirkpatrick provided a damning analysis of the anti–cold war intellectuals and their student foot soldiers. Kirkpatrick believed that such people constituted a "New Class" in America. The problem with this New Class, she wrote after the 1972 presidential election, "lies in believing that their intelligence and exemplary motives equip them to reorder the institutions, the lives, and even the characters of almost everyone—this is the totalitarian temptation."

Michael Novak would not have disagreed with Kirkpatrick. The son of working-class Slovaks from Johnstown, Pennsylvania, Novak had grown up during the Great Depression. When he was four years old, the Bethlehem Steel Corporation brutally suppressed a strike for union recognition. All the union officers and organizers were pious Catholics. No stranger to social injustice, Novak had little sympathy for conservative Catholic intellectual William F. Buckley, Jr.'s anti–New Deal politics. To this former seminary student, Buckley's "Anglo-Saxon" style and privileged background made him ill-suited to speak to working-class Catholics. As Novak confessed in later years,

"Like many young Catholics and Jews, I had imbibed from an early age a set of suspicions concerning big business, capitalism, Marlboro man individualism, and Anglo-Saxon ethnic superiority." Buckley seemed to be one of *them*, rather than one of us.

In the 1960s Novak became a reporter for the "progressive" Catholic magazine *Commonweal*, promoted the anti-war cause through the Catholic Peace Fellowship, and taught religion at Stanford and the Old Westbury campus of the State University of New York. Novak's disenchantment with campus activism grew dramatically at Old Westbury. "Most students" at Old Westbury, Novak recounted, "wanted total liberty, meaning no standards, no restrictions, no differentiations, no authorities, no requirements." When Novak and university president and anti-war stalwart Harris Wofford insisted on nonviolent social protest as well as academic standards, they were publicly identified as "fascists." Then the student activists, annoyed with Novak's pacifism and embrace of the Catholic Peace Fellowship, threatened to bomb his house.

Faculty colleagues at Old Westbury, Novak observed, were scarcely more mature than their students. One professor broke into a "bourgeois" bookstore and gave away texts to student looters. Another faculty member, wishing to prove "his thoroughgoing egalitarianism," conducted a seminar while sitting *beneath* a desk. "Think of this as childish vulgar Marxism," Novak said of his Old Westbury experience. "The grown-up version has uncannily repeated itself in every Communist Party victory."

Novak concluded that there was not just one despicable "Establishment" but two. The first Establishment governed from Wall Street and coldly dropped bombs on hapless peasants in Vietnam. A second, and equally obnoxious Establishment, was based on the nation's campuses. These elitist, secularized intellectuals disdained working Americans and sought control over the Wall Street Establishment.

Dismayed by the mounting violence of the campus left, and disturbed by what he saw as an anti-Catholic bias in the news media, Novak reached his breaking point during the 1972 presidential campaign. When college professors and students complained about Nixon's "Silent Majority" of socially conservative Catholics, Novak became exasperated. "Anti-personnel bombs were not invented by men on a construction gang," he replied. "Guys on beer trucks did not dream up napalm. Ph.D.'s from universities, who abhor bloodshed, thought them up." His experiences as an adviser to vice presidential candidate Sargent Shriver led to his disavowal of the Democratic party. While arranging campaign stops in 1972 for Shriver, Novak noticed how coldly his fellow Catholics were receiving them:

> Shriver was greeted with scarcely veiled disdain, I thought, by workers at the gates of the Homestead [Pennsylvania] Steel mills—my own kind of folks, who would normally be with us by upwards of 89 percent. In Joliet, Illinois, on a factory floor where I encountered dozens of Slovak faces that made me think of my cousins in Johnstown, workers did not want to shake McGovern-Shriver hands. Trying to find out why, I met with our "advance person"—a young woman wearing a miniskirt, high white boots, and a see-through blouse, with a large pro-abortion button on her collar. On that factory floor in 1972, the clash of social classes and cultural politics could scarcely have been more discordant.

Other professors and writers also reacted against the peace movement. Andrew Greeley, a sociologist and Catholic priest, emerged as one of the most vocal academic critics of the New Left—even while he opposed the Vietnam War. Greeley argued in 1971 that both the secular and the *religious* left had made Americans less willing to open peace negotiations with Hanoi because they might appear to be endorsing the anti-war movement. Moreover, the New Left had helped elect Richard Nixon president in 1968 by provoking an anti-protest backlash vote. As for the anti-war activists who wrote Catholic peace homilies for the *Commonweal*, such people were "intellectual crooks and elitist poseurs." Addressing himself to Garry Wills, who disparaged socially conservative Catholics, Greeley contended that

> Catholic intellectuals like Mr. Wills are interested only in talking about themselves and their little coterie of friends on the evident assumption that their own religious doubts and attitudes are somehow closer to the truth about Catholicism in the Sixties than what has been happening to 55 million American Catholics. In this view, Jesuits from Woodstock [Seminary] who are working on stage design are more important than the priests and nuns who are staffing the only available alternative school system in the inner cities of the country, and protesters in front of the Harrisburg [Pennsylvania] federal courthouse are of greater interest than graduate students trying to articulate the Polish-American experience to an academic world that is not quite sure that Poles are capable of experience. It used to be that only bishops counted, now only intellectuals count.
>
> The American-Catholic community has finally succeeded in producing an intelligentsia so taken with itself that it either does not know anything about the Catholic community as a whole or simply thinks that the masses are too dull to bother with.

Norman Podhoretz, a member of the misnamed "Silent Generation," grew to feel similarly repelled by the cultural elite. Podhoretz had begun the decade of the 1960s as a rebel of sorts. As the editor of *Commentary* magazine, published by the American Jewish Committee, Podhoretz had "discovered" Paul Goodman and helped arrange for the publication of *Growing Up Absurd.* He had also printed Staughton Lynd's essays on American politics and foreign policy, belonged to SANE, and opposed the Vietnam War because he thought it "unwinnable."

Even when he identified with New York's intellectual set in the early 1960s, however, Podhoretz remained somewhat out of step. His essay "My Negro Problem" enraged civil rights activists. In it Podhoretz committed the unpardonable sin of discussing the pathologies of the ghetto. He noted that as a child, black youths would beat him up and refer to Jews as "Christ killers." Podhoretz never accepted the intellectual legitimacy of the New Left. He dismissed SDS's Port Huron Statement as a self-righteous document lacking "complexity" and "nuance."

Once Staughton Lynd identified himself with the Viet Cong in 1965, Podhoretz concluded that "Lynd and his friends and allies in the peace movement were not interested in creating a new radicalism that would be free of the old illusions about Communism." Looking at the family ties of the national SDS leaders, Podhoretz observed with disdain that they were the "scions of what could be called the First Families of American Stalinism." Podhoretz believed that the New Left was just as much of an enemy of independent intellectual thought and of the democratic process as the Communist party had been in the 1930s.

Irving Kristol, a World War II combat veteran and compatriot of Podhoretz's, published an essay in *Foreign Affairs* (1967) which attempted to explain the motivations and insecurities of the cultural elite. In "American Intellectuals and Foreign Policy," Kristol observed that the critics of American society believed that they alone possessed sufficient "moral authority" to guide the nation. To the professorial left, President Johnson and his advisers were "stupid," "wicked" "war criminals" and "mass murderers." Kristol thought university faculty were particularly vocal and alienated because they felt underpaid, unappreciated, ignored, and bored with their teaching and scholarly duties. The professors, and other members of the cultural elite, wanted excitement and a role in molding American values and government policies in their own image. The leftist intellectuals had "dreams of power," Kristol concluded, but no practical solutions to offer the nation. What the cultural elite offered, Kristol implied, were pithy slogans that could easily fit on picket signs and automobile bumpers.

For all of their barbs, as well as their efforts to be heard,

Kristol, Podhoretz, Wolfe, and others like them were a minority among their peers. They swam against a tide of anti-anti-communism and radical chic that increasingly dominated liberal arts departments, the national media, and Hollywood. Yet while the cultural elite persuaded millions of disillusioned Boomers to turn against the Vietnam War and lose faith in democracy, they also alienated millions of other Americans and helped widen the class and values gap between the "producers of culture" and the general public.

5

The Escalation, 1964–1967

THE INITIAL IMPETUS to campus activism arose not from foreign policy concerns but over the issue of *in loco parentis*. According to a 1964–1965 survey of undergraduates at 850 colleges, students claimed that the most important issues in their lives were university dress codes and curfews. One-quarter of America's college campuses in 1964 and 1965 reported some kind of student protest against *in loco parentis*. Just 9 percent of the nation's students, however, participated in such demonstrations.

At Michigan State the handful of students who belonged to the Committee for Student Rights did not promote a political agenda. They simply wanted the requirement that male students wear neckties in the dining halls be lifted. That, however, did not stop university president John Hannah from suspending the organization's leader, whom he regarded as a dangerous subversive. Despite the modest ambitions of most students, several hundred radicals at Berkeley in 1964 managed to capture national media attention and set the tone for future campus clashes over *in loco parentis—and* American foreign policy.

Berkeley's Free Speech Movement (FSM) was born on October 1, 1964. Jack Weinberg, a mathematics graduate student and veteran of Mississippi Freedom Summer, had set up a table stacked with political literature on a strip of land in front of the Sather Gate campus entrance. Believing that Weinberg was on university property illegally distributing political materials, a police officer attempted to arrest him. A few hundred students surrounded the police car and held the officer at bay for thirty-two hours. Some students decided to use the trapped car as a lecture podium, eventually crushing its roof under their weight. Other students set up makeshift tents around the squad car, with many taking the opportunity to have sex on the street and sidewalk.

Although Weinberg would soon fade from view as other more flamboyant activists came to the fore, he coined a phrase that became the clarion call of Boomer radicals: "Don't trust anyone over thirty." (In the 1980s Weinberg resurfaced to express his scorn for the young Americans who voted in droves for Ronald Reagan: "Don't trust anyone *under* thirty.")

Mario Savio quickly emerged as the most eloquent spokesman of Berkeley's Free Speech Movement. Like Weinberg, Savio had spent the previous summer in Mississippi. He equated the Free Speech Movement with the civil rights crusade. "Last summer I went to Mississippi to join the struggle there for civil rights," Savio recounted. "This fall I am engaged in another phase of the same struggle, this time in Berkeley." Believing that Berkeley's middle-class white student body had much in common with impoverished Southern blacks, Savio declared, "Asking why [the revolt] happened in Berkeley first is like asking why Negroes, and not Americans generally, are involved in securing access for all the good which America could provide for all her people."

(Savio's effort to equate the Free Speech Movement with the civil rights struggle greatly amused his faculty critics. He was equating Mississippi blacks, who lived in an environment of segregation and disfranchisement, with Berkeley students who had to endure large classes that were often taught by graduate students.)

Warming to his topic, Savio compared the campus and city police officers to Nazis and, in the same breath, ridiculed the traditional family. "They're *family* men, you know," Savio sneered at the police. "They have a job to do! Like [Nazi war criminal] Adolf Eichmann." Savio also called Berkeley's administrators, who had thus far declined to use force to disperse the crowd, "a bunch of bastards." Inspired by David Horowitz's 1962 book *Student*, Savio then decried Berkeley for turning youths into conformist cogs in the corporate machine. Reaching a fevered pitch, Savio shifted his attack from the campus to the entire American political system, arguing that Washington manufactured fear of domestic and foreign communism in order to destroy progressive movements.

Although Savio had been raised in a Catholic household, he had abandoned his religion in favor of a more cosmopolitan faith. The same could be said for a number of Free Speech Movement activists. They too had thrown aside any remnants of their religious upbringing. Many Berkeley militants came from affluent, upper-middle-class, secular Jewish households. Their fathers were lawyers and academics whose own politics ranged from Democratic to Communist.

Jackie Goldberg's background was typical. A red diaper baby who had gone to Moscow in 1963 as part of an American Communist delegation, Goldberg became a member of the Free Speech Movement's executive committee. She was one of 814 people who occupied Sproul Hall in December 1964 to protest university "repression" of the Free Speech Movement. (Two hundred and twenty-four of the 814 sit-in participants were not Berkeley students.) After students roughly tossed a police officer out of the building while screaming "Get the cops! Kill the cops!", 733 were arrested for trespassing—including Jackie Goldberg. The police, at the urging of the local prosecutor, Edwin Meese III (later the U.S. attorney general in Ronald Reagan's administration), wanted to interrogate Goldberg, but they could not identify her because they did not have her first name. Four female Goldbergs were arrested at the Sproul Hall sit-in.

Clark Kerr, academic chief of the University of California system and a cold war Democrat, floundered in his efforts to deal with the Free Speech Movement. In part Kerr's difficulty stemmed from his philosophical opposition to the use of force and his belief that all disputes could be arbitrated. Too, university administrators had to fear legal retribution from irate parents if they treated their offspring harshly. The local community also proved to be a bastion of anti-Kerr sentiment. Folk singers Joan Baez and Malvina Reynolds became bards of the Free Speech Movement, giving the Berkeley uprising a sympathetic spin in student coffeehouses from coast to coast.

Reynolds, the daughter of a founder of the American Communist party, had earlier received a doctorate in English from Berkeley. Her songs praised the Free Speech Movement and ridiculed the white working-class opponents of the Berkeley left. She believed that white workers had only one ambition in life: to live in "ticky tacky boxes" that they called suburban homes.

To add to Kerr's difficulties, he lacked the support of the majority of his faculty, particularly those in the liberal arts and social sciences. Only a handful of faculty criticized the Berkeley Free Speech Movement. Sociologist Lewis Feuer, for instance, called the Free Speech Movement a "magnet for the morally corrupt." Drawing upon his scholarship on social movements, Feuer concluded that the FSM was an anti-intellectual organization that advocated drug abuse, group sex, and nihilism. Similarly, Seymour Martin Lipset, also a sociologist, regarded the Free Speech Movement activists as totalitarians. For Savio and Goldberg, Lipset insisted, the real issue was not free speech but the power to do whatever they wanted.

Although Feuer and Lipset were much mocked at the time (and to this very day) for their characterization of the Free Speech Movement as a hotbed of hedonism, they had a point. Few sympathetic accounts of the Berkeley uprising have noted the close relationship of the FSM to the emerging drug and sex culture. As with the initial October 1964 sit-in around the police car, later demonstrations provided ample opportunity for the consumption of narcotics and for vigorous sexual experimentation. At the December 1964 Sproul Hall sit-in, female students roamed the corridors looking for birth-control pills so they could stay overnight. Others dropped acid and smoked hashish.

It seemed as if the pursuit of sex and drugs took precedence over the struggle for free speech. During the executive committee meetings for the FSM, which were held at the Hillel Jewish student center, Savio, Goldberg, and others coupled with wild abandonment. As FSM steering committee member David Lance Goines put it, the free speech crusade represented a great opportunity to have intercourse. "What I wanted was sex," Goines recounted, "and I resolved to cut as wide a swath through the ranks of Berkeley's maidenhood as I possibly could." Berkeley, Goines continued without any sense of irony, provided "good weather and lots of happy sex" as students carried on their struggle "to become adults, to throw off the benign parental authority and become full, responsible citizens."

Not surprisingly, sexually transmitted diseases, as well as incidents of rape, mounted in the wake of the Free Speech Movement. In 1960 Berkeley had reported 150 cases of gonorrhea. By 1965, 560 students admitted to having contracted gonorrhea. These developments, however, did not hold the attention of America's college students. Instead, activist students at other campuses worked to catch up with Berkeley. The military escalation of the Vietnam War in 1965 made their catch-up efforts that much easier.

President Lyndon Johnson's decision in February 1965 to commence "Operation Rolling Thunder," the first sustained U.S. aerial bombing of North Vietnam, prompted ten thousand University of Wisconsin students and faculty to stage an antiwar rally. By March 1965 it became obvious to the White House that selective bombing alone of North Vietnam would not win the ground war in South Vietnam. American combat troops were needed. The president argued that the United States had to defend South Vietnam from Viet Cong terrorism. If Washington backed down now, Johnson warned, the Communists would launch guerrilla wars throughout Asia, Africa, and Latin America.

Seeking a way to mobilize campus opinion against America's expanding military commitment to the Saigon regime, anti-war faculty and SDSers at the University of Michigan organized the first teach-in. Over the course of March 24 and 25, 1965, three thousand Michigan professors, students, and community activists participated in a marathon round of discussion and lectures about Vietnam. Thirty-five other universities followed suit, with Berkeley's thirty-six-hour teach-in drawing an audience of twenty thousand. Only two speakers braved a hostile crowd at Berkeley to speak in favor of the Vietnam War. They were vigorously booed by the veterans of the Free Speech Movement.

Ann Arbor SDS leader Carl Oglesby set the left-of-center tone of the Michigan teach-in. Later teach-ins at Michigan become even more radical, with faculty and SDSers endorsing Communist revolution in the third world. Leftist Michigan professors also began revising the curriculum, offering courses on revolution in the American cities and "Marxist Anthropology," as well as requiring undergraduates to read Che Guevara's manual *On Guerrilla Warfare*. Ann Arbor activists made little effort at their teach-ins, and in their classrooms, to present the anti-Communist point of view in an objective manner.

The campus opponents of America's Indochina policy proceeded from two interrelated contentions. First, America was a racist nation seeking to turn the world into "Mississippi." Second, a counterrevolutionary, anti-democratic ideology animated U.S. foreign policy. One white female veteran of Mississippi Freedom Summer succinctly linked the Vietnam War to racial discrimination in the United States. "The people we're killing in Vietnam," she contended, "are the same people whom we've been killing for years in Mississippi."

Seeking to respond directly to his campus critics on April 7,

1965, President Johnson delivered a major speech on American foreign policy at Baltimore's Johns Hopkins University. Johnson tried to make it clear why America was in Vietnam:

> Our objective is the independence of South Vietnam, and its freedom from attack. We want nothing for ourselves. . . . The first reality is that North Vietnam has attacked the independent nation of South Vietnam. Its objective is total conquest. . . . And it is a war of unparalleled brutality. Simple farmers are the targets of assassination and kidnapping. Women and children are strangled in the night because their men are loyal to their government. . . . Over this war, and all Asia, is another reality: the deepening shadow of Communist China. . . . The contest in Vietnam is part of a wider pattern of aggressive purpose.

Unfortunately for Johnson, press reports coming out of South Vietnam focused on the suffering caused by American bombing. The media largely ignored Communist terrorism. *New York Times* reporter Charles Mohr graphically related the story of a Vietnamese civilian disfigured by napalm:

> . . . there is a woman who has both arms burned off by napalm and her eyelids so badly burned that she cannot close them. When it is time for her to sleep her family puts a blanket over her head. The woman had two of her children killed in the air strike which maimed her . . . and she saw five other children die.

Young anti-war activists saw no reason to accept Johnson's defense of American foreign policy. At the first national anti–Vietnam War rally in Washington in April 1965, SDS president Paul Potter, a onetime student at Oberlin College, pointed to the undemocratic nature of American foreign policy. He then denounced the United States as the "greatest threat to peace in the world today" and implied that the American government was made up of sociopaths:

The president mocks freedom if he insists that the war in Vietnam is a defense of American freedom. Perhaps the only freedom that this war protects is the freedom of the war hawks in the Pentagon and the State Department to "experiment" with "counter-insurgency" and guerrilla warfare in Vietnam.

Meanwhile in the San Francisco Bay Area, graduate student Jerry Rubin and mathematics professor Stephen Smale organized the Berkeley Vietnam Day Committee. Rubin had dropped out of Berkeley's sociology program—having been enrolled for just six weeks—to devote himself to full-time activism. He could draw on a trust fund and did not have to work for a living.

Committed to "action," the Vietnam Day Committee invaded the Berkeley city council chambers. Berkeley's radicals demanded that the city council order the federal government to cease moving troops bound for Indochina through the nearby Oakland Army Terminal. In October 1965 a few hundred people massed outside the Oakland terminal to block incoming troop trains. They were about to clash with three hundred police officers when Hell's Angels bikers tried to attack the Berkeley students. The Oakland police suffered a few broken bones but managed to keep the campus activists from harm. Dejected, Rubin and the students marched back to the campus.

Having grown up in a prosperous Cincinnati, Ohio, family, Rubin had little real-life experience with white workers. That may have been, in part, why he thought white workers were not worth the effort to educate them about American "imperialism." In any event, as C. Wright Mills and Herbert Marcuse had concluded, working people were racist and reactionary.

Instead of a working-class uprising, Rubin envisioned a revolution based on such lifestyle issues as the legalization of abortion and drugs, and the abolition of the draft and community ordinances that infringed on sexual freedom. According to Rubin, "Lifestyle determines politics." Ultimately that meant middle-class youths would choose the New Left over cold war Democrats and Republican conservatives "because we had excitement and they had boredom." Of course, Rubin realized, to maintain the level of excitement that Boomer students were coming to expect from their political activism, each successive confrontation had to be more violent.

Plenty of Bay Area activists shared Rubin's contempt for conventional morality and white workers. Free Speech Movement participant and anti-war stalwart Marvin Garson was so irked when labor unions criticized the New Left for championing Hanoi that he fumed, "The next time some $3.00 an hour AFL-type workers go on strike for a 50 cent raise, I'll remember the day they chanted 'Burn Hanoi, not our flag,' and so help me I'll cross their fucking picket line."

While Berkeley radicals set the tone of student protest, activists at other campuses sought to mobilize their constituencies. In Ann Arbor in the fall of 1965, thirty-eight Michigan students were arrested for trying to disrupt the operations of a local draft board. Among those taken into custody were Diana Oughton, a Bryn Mawr graduate who had been raised by a nanny, and Bill Ayers, the son of a millionaire business executive. Threats by Selective Service to draft Ayers and the other privileged Michigan militants were mysteriously and rapidly withdrawn.

At a November 1965 anti-war march on Washington, SANE, which had boycotted the April rally in the capital, reluctantly agreed that SDS could share its podium. Sanford Gottlieb, SANE's protest coordinator, vowed that his more moderate, "respectable," and grown-up peace group would keep the SDS "kooks, Communists or draft dodgers" in line. To SANE's horror, SDSers waved Viet Cong flags and carried placards demanding an immediate U.S. withdrawal from South Vietnam.

Unlike SDS, SANE hoped for a negotiated settlement of the war and believed that an independent South Vietnamese republic could co-exist with North Vietnam. SDS, in contrast, idolized Ho Chi Minh. Gottlieb thought the New Left's support for the Communist insurgency in Vietnam would alienate the American people and harden attitudes toward the peace movement. In talking with several Philadelphia SDSers who had affiliated with the student SANE chapter, Gottlieb had warned them to sever their ties to the Communist party. He also thought they should venture out from their sheltered environment at the University of Pennsylvania and talk to the city's white workers about the Vietnam War. But Gottlieb's efforts in Philadelphia—and in Washington—were for naught.

Addressing fifty thousand demonstrators in Washington, newly installed SDS president Carl Oglesby gave a rousing speech. Oglesby—who regarded SANE as a "pro-war" organization—hailed third-world revolution, sang the praises of the Viet Cong, and took aim at the cold war Democrats who had started the Vietnam War. Oglesby also asserted that anticommunism served as a cover for capitalist exploitation of the third world:

> Far from helping Americans deal with . . . truth, the anti-Communist ideology merely tries to disguise it so that things may stay the way they are. Thus, it depicts our presence in other lands not as a coercion, but a protection. It allows us even to say that the napalm in Vietnam is only another aspect of our humanitarian love—like those exorcisms in the Middle Ages that so often killed the patient. So we say to the Vietnamese peasant, the Cuban intellectual, the Peruvian workers: "You are better dead than red. If it hurts or if you don't understand why—sorry about that."
>
> This is the action of *corporate liberalism*. It performs for the corporate state a function quite like what the [Catholic] Church once performed for the feudal state. It seeks to justify its burdens and protect it from change.

SDS subsequently printed thousands of copies of Oglesby's speech, which were distributed on college campuses.

A month later, in December 1965, while 184,000 American

soldiers battled the Viet Cong and Hanoi's forces, SDS held a national conference to discuss its future. Lee Webb, a onetime SDS national secretary, had recently complained that the New Left was abandoning thought in favor of action. "Calls to fight the draft, stop a troop train, burn a draft card, avoid all forms of liberalism, have become," Webb moaned, "the substitute for intellectual analysis and understanding." (Webb's lament occurred *two years before* sympathetic historians of the New Left marked the shift of SDS from an intellectual organization of elite college students to an irrational group of less-well-educated Midwestern militants.) Paying no heed to Webb, the SDS delegates proclaimed to the world that "We have slogans which take the place of thought: 'There's a change gonna come' is our substitute for social theory. . . . What sociology, what psychology, what history do we need to know the answers?"

SDSers may have had the answers, but they still needed to persuade larger numbers of students to look to them for political guidance. An early 1966 Gallup public opinion poll revealed that 47 percent of college youths endorsed President Johnson's conduct of the war. An additional 23 percent of student respondents, frustrated with Johnson's unwillingness to invade North Vietnam and bomb Communist sanctuaries in Laos and Cambodia, called for further military escalation. Earlier, 16,000 students at Michigan State, 6,500 at the University of Minnesota, and 4,000 at the University of Texas had signed petitions circulated by collegiate Republicans and the Young Americans for Freedom endorsing Johnson's Vietnam policy.

Anti-Communist sentiment thrived at campuses where the overwhelming majority of students came from culturally conservative and middle-class—not upper-middle-class—backgrounds. One Penn State student, in a letter to his campus newspaper, the *Daily Collegian*, set forth the majority hawk point of view:

South Vietnam is the present battlefield of the Cold War. Korea, Laos, and Cuba are former battlefields. America has never had a decisive victory over Communism on any of the battlefields because of self-restraint. . . .

It is time for the United States to show its strength to the world by turning South Vietnam into a place of victory. America is capable of winning in South Vietnam and I sincerely hope that it does not restrain itself here.

Nothing would please me more than to know that the war has been carried into North Vietnam. Even though this runs the risk of another world war, what good is living if one doesn't have something that is worth dying for?

Penn State SDS had just sixty members in 1966, compared to five hundred in the Wisconsin chapter. Moreover, where the Madison and Ann Arbor left could count on attracting additional participants once a sit-in began, that did not hold true at Penn State. To make matters worse, the "Happy Valley" SDS crippled itself with poorly considered actions and statements. Brushing aside the objections of SDSer Leverett Millen, who contended that the New Left should be making overtures to religious "progressives," agnostic Penn State SDSers disrupted a Mass. Hoping to illustrate that the Catholic church had a long history of supporting right-wing regimes, Penn State radicals distributed copies of an article describing the ideological harmony between Nazism and Catholicism.

Having thoroughly alienated religiously observant students, Penn State SDSers decided to cast an even wider net. They publicly denounced the "Pennsylvania primitives from the backwoods and small towns" who debased the university's cultural and intellectual life. For an organization disproportionately represented by secular Jews and Philadelphians, and operating in an environment that was heavily Protestant and small-town, such tactics were not at all conducive to expanding SDS's following.

Fortunately for the proponents of the New Left, their lack of success at Penn State could be balanced by advances elsewhere. Berkeley students physically intimidated on-campus navy re-

cruiters. Harvard SDSers ambushed Secretary of Defense
Robert McNamara's car. They refused to let McNamara leave
until they had subjected him to an intense session of jeering and
cursing. When president John Hannah fired a Michigan State
faculty member for editing the pornographic student literary
journal *Zeitgeist*, a thousand students occupied a campus building. This event represented the first time Michigan State students had staged a sit-in. The leaders of the *Zeitgeist* action
belonged to the campus SDS chapter.

At the University of Chicago four hundred SDSers staged a
three-day sit-in of the administration building. Chicago SDSers
were protesting the university's decision to give their grades
and class rankings to Selective Service. (A grade point average
below a "C" and a mediocre class ranking might endanger a
male student's draft deferment if the university informed Selective Service.) The university administration proved reluctant to
call in city police officers to remove the students. One university
official later admitted, "We were prepared to lose that building
or any other building by occupation or by arson" rather than resort to force. During the sit-in a radical feminist faction of the
Chicago SDS—WITCH, or the Women's International Terrorist Conspiracy from Hell—placed a curse on the sociology
department and made magical incantations.

Wisconsin SDSers seized their administration building over
the same issue of providing academic information to Selective
Service. The Wisconsin SDS chapter also took aim at Massachusetts senator Ted Kennedy, who came to Madison to give a
speech. Regarding him as a lackey of corporate imperialism,
SDSers heckled Kennedy and tried to prevent him from speaking. (Two years earlier, Madison radicals had disrupted an
appearance by Republican presidential candidate Barry Goldwater. To SDS, Barry Goldwater and Ted Kennedy were ideological twins—a position that would have horrified both
politicians.)

The growing militancy of the Wisconsin SDS, according to
James Gilbert, a radical graduate history student, had three

sources. First, Gilbert recounted, "We learned from the students at Berkeley and Michigan." Second, Madison radicals "copied some of the tactics of the civil rights movement." And third, putting his finger on what he believed was the most significant reason why protest at Wisconsin swelled in the mid-sixties, Gilbert observed that "we learned the exhilaration of action."

Wisconsin administrators took note of the student left's "exhilaration of action." They became so concerned that a visit by Lady Bird Johnson would provoke demonstrations that the First Lady was not permitted on campus. The Madison left had successfully given notice in 1966 that the right to free speech did not extend to anyone who took Lyndon Johnson's side. Although it appeared as if the university's leaders had caved in to the radicals, it just so happened that their interests and those of SDS coincided. University president Fred Harvey Harrington opposed the Vietnam War—but not so loudly as to endanger the state appropriations he needed to continue his building spree. Harrington had recruited SDS "guru" Harvey Goldberg to the university and was the intellectual godfather of the radical "Wisconsin School of history."

Harrington and Madison's anti-war activists also had the support of the state's Democratic party establishment. Democratic congressmen Gaylord Nelson, William Kastenmeier, and William Proxmire were vocal critics of the cold war in general and of Johnson in particular. Both Nelson and Proxmire had worked with the Madison left in the 1950s to unseat Senator Joseph McCarthy.

1967 saw unrest mount on many of the nation's campuses and in the cities. Former Student Nonviolent Coordinating Committee chairman Stokely Carmichael spent part of 1967 in Cuba, North Vietnam, and China. Carmichael met with North Vietnamese government officials and discussed strategies to defeat American imperialism. In a tidy summation of American foreign policy and history, Carmichael described the Vietnam War as "white people sending black people to make war on yel-

low people in order to defend the land they stole from red people."

Carmichael's 1967 speaking tours of the nation's historically
black colleges were lively events. After Carmichael roused an
audience at Fisk University in Nashville, black students rioted.
Ten police officers and one black student were wounded and 50
youths arrested. Carmichael's Mississippi lecture series inspired
rioting at Jackson State and led to the death of one white man.
(Three years later, when white police officers killed two Jackson State students, black power sympathizers in academia and
the media denounced "white racism," neglecting to mention
the behavior of Jackson State's students in the 1967 riot.)
Carmichael's appearance at Texas Southern was memorable.
After he called on blacks to "fight for liberation by any means
necessary," Texas Southern students killed one policeman and
wounded three others. Once law enforcement officials restored
order, 488 students received expulsion notices.

While Carmichael inflamed passions at black colleges, the
"long hot summer" of 1967 began. In Newark, New Jersey, police officers arrested a black cab driver for a traffic violation.
Unfounded rumors spread through the ghetto that the cab
driver had been beaten to death. A five-day riot ensued, with
black looters, arsonists, and snipers fighting the police. The rioters were responsible for the deaths of twenty-five people and
$10 million in property damage.

A black anti-poverty official in Newark hailed the rioters,
arguing that "Complete chaos will have to prevail in the streets
of America and blood will have to flow like water before the
black man will become an accepted citizen of this society." SDS
founder Tom Hayden, who had been living in the area as a
community organizer, declared that the Newark riot had raised
the revolutionary consciousness of black people. Hayden called
for the formation of an army of white and black "urban guerrillas."

SNCC chairman H. Rap Brown gloated that Newark was a
"dress rehearsal for revolution." This was the same man who

called President Johnson a "white honky cracker" and warmed up his audiences by asking, "How many white folks did you kill today?" Brown's response to critics who charged him with inciting blacks to murder whites was straightforward: "Fuck a muthafucka who hates me, because if I ever get him on the wrong end of my gun he's in trouble." (In March 2000 Brown, who had renamed himself Abdullah Al-Amin, allegedly shot two Fulton County, Georgia, deputies, killing one—a black man. Brown, an alleged drug and gun dealer, had been sought by authorities for impersonating a police officer and receiving stolen property.)

Newark, though not a "dress rehearsal for revolution" as Brown believed, was a warm-up for a worse riot in Detroit. An attempt by Detroit police officers to confiscate illegal moonshine at a homecoming party for two black soldiers who had just returned from Vietnam led to a riot that left forty-three dead and $250 million worth of property in charred ruin. It took the 101st Airborne Division to quell what Carmichael hoped to be "the beginning of urban guerrilla warfare" in the United States. The Detroit "insurrection" inspired rioting in Minneapolis, Cincinnati, Kansas City, Des Moines, Milwaukee, Philadelphia, and a hundred other cities.

Hoping to make common cause with the growing numbers of campus and urban black power adherents, white leftists in September 1967 promoted the Chicago "New Politics Conference." More than 2,000 delegates from 372 groups met to explore the possibilities of creating a radical third party to challenge President Johnson. The conference did not go well. H. Rap Brown refused to address white delegates; comedian and black militant Dick Gregory justified anti-Semitism; and SNCC members booed Martin Luther King, Jr., and threatened him. (By 1967 SNCC had become known among wry observers as "the Non-Student Violent Disintegrating Committee.") Militants formed a black caucus which demanded half the total convention votes, even though they represented barely 15 percent of the overall number of delegates. Amid chants of

"Kill whitey! Kill whitey!", black radicals got their way and quickly pushed through a resolution denouncing "Zionist imperialism." SDS financial angel Martin Peretz—an ardent friend of Israel and later the publisher of the *New Republic* magazine—stalked out of the convention.

White radicals tried to put the best light on the New Politics Conference. Rennie Davis, an SDS "elder" and national anti-war coordinator, explained that a formal coalition between black militants and the white New Left really made "no sense." After all, Davis explained, "We are a movement of people with radically different needs." Taking a different stance, Michigan State psychology professor Bert Garskoff observed that white radicals were "just a little tail on the end of a very powerful Black Panther." Garskoff, who lived in Ann Arbor and was a member of the University of Michigan SDS chapter, hoped that he could "be on that tail"—if Carmichael and Rap Brown would let him.

Like the black militants, many SDSers rejected electoral politics. Making peace with President Johnson, who had done so much to advance the cause of civil rights, was out of the question. SDSers equated Johnson with American Nazi party leader George Lincoln Rockwell and, in demonstrations outside the White House, chanted, "Hey, hey, LBJ, how many kids did you kill today?" Although New York senator Robert Kennedy had been critical of the Vietnam War and was contemplating a primary run against Johnson for the Democratic presidential nomination, SDS would have nothing to do with him either. SDSers ridiculed Kennedy in session after session of the New Politics Conference. Among friends, Tom Hayden delighted in calling Kennedy "a little fascist."

At the same time black militants were garnering headlines in 1967, campus anti-war demonstrations grew ever more provocative and confrontational—even though just 35 percent of students favored a gradual U.S. withdrawal from Vietnam. (Forty-nine percent of students favored *escalating* the war.) The waving of Viet Cong banners at campus and national protests, accompanied by the burning of American flags, became commonplace. National SDS president Greg Calvert, a former Iowa State instructor, boasted in the spring of 1967 that "We are working to build a guerrilla force in an urban environment. We are actively organizing sedition." At Berkeley, SDSer Frank Bardacke asserted that the campus left could focus on disruption since it was no longer necessary to waste time educating students about American foreign policy. "Everyone knew the war was the shits," Bardacke said. "We didn't have to educate anybody anymore."

SDS secretary Carl Davidson, a former Penn State radical and writer for the *National Guardian*, a Communist-line newspaper dedicated to the "denazifying" of the United States, believed that student activists could not permit representatives of the military and capitalist corporations to recruit on campus. Recruiters from the Dow Chemical Corporation, which manufactured napalm for the war in Vietnam, were to bear the brunt of the SDS attack. As Davidson argued, "Since they [the Dow recruiters] are without legitimacy in our eyes, they are without rights."

SDSers across the nation heeded Davidson's call to action. The SDS chapter of the State University of New York at Buffalo launched its offensive against campus recruiters from Dow, the CIA, and other "imperialist" organizations. Although some of the SUNY-Buffalo SDSers were not comfortable with the idea of preventing students from going to job interviews with Dow, the firebrands—mostly those associated with the Youth Against War and Fascism—brushed them aside. Taking aim at university president Martin Meyerson, an anti-war Democrat who believed that leftist dissent could "become a form of minority tyranny," SUNY-Buffalo SDSers informed him:

> We feel that you cannot take the bourgeois liberal position that you are against the napalming of children, but you defend Dow Chemical's right to recruit people to napalm. Or that you are against the CIA's murdering of thousands of

people around the globe daily, but that you defend their right to come on campus and coerce people into doing the murdering.

This is not a matter of free speech. We are not talking about the CIA coming on campus to explain their philosophy or policy. We're talking about them coming on campus and holding secret meetings with a few potential murderers in the basement of the Placement Center.

Several hundred student demonstrators, many of them dressed for battle in khaki green dungarees and helmets, later chased the "war criminals" from Dow around the campus, preventing them from interviewing any "potential murderers."

Although Canisius College stood just a few miles from SUNY-Buffalo, its students existed in a markedly different political universe. Canisius College was an academically respectable Jesuit institution of higher education which catered to local youths. Many students were the first in their family to attend college and came largely from lower-middle-class backgrounds. Canisius students were well behaved and, by their lights, patriotic.

In 1965 after David Miller, a member of the pacifist Catholic Worker Movement, burned his draft card outside the Manhattan Army Induction Center, the Canisius student government rallied in support of Lyndon Johnson's Vietnam policy. To underscore their disdain for Miller, Buffalo's Catholic students laminated their Selective Service registration cards to protect them from inadvertent damage. The editors of the Canisius student newspaper, *The Griffin*, endorsed the Vietnam War. At any given time between 1965 and 1967, one could find just thirty Irish Catholic students (out of almost four thousand enrolled) holding peace vigils. No more than a dozen faculty supported the campus peace activists. Many of the anti-war professors were adjunct faculty—largely graduate students from SUNY-Buffalo.

As Canisius students championed the cold war crusade in Vietnam, and the SUNY-Buffalo SDS flexed its muscles, the

Wisconsin SDS initiated a dramatic campaign against Dow. In the spring of 1967, at the first SDS sit-in to disrupt campus recruiting by Dow, Wisconsin chancellor Robben Fleming put up the bail money for the students who were jailed. After parents complained that their children had been treated harshly by law enforcement officers, the Wisconsin attorney general castigated the police for using excessive force. Wisconsin students repaid the university administration and the state attorney general for their consideration by firebombing the office of the associate dean for academic affairs.

In the fall of 1967, Wisconsin's new chancellor, William Sewell, reluctantly permitted Dow and the CIA to continue their campus recruiting. (Fleming had departed Madison of his own accord for the chief administrative position at Michigan.) Sewell had been personally opposed to allowing either the CIA or Dow on campus. His own son was a Berkeley anti-war activist with a police record. But the majority of faculty had earlier reaffirmed the right of students to have access to recruiters from institutions that were on the SDS blacklist.

Calling on students to "move from protest to resistance," the Wisconsin SDS tried again to drive Dow representatives from the campus. Campus policemen, not wishing to give SDS a pretext to riot, disarmed. They removed the bullets from their guns and left their billy clubs at home. Unilateral disarmament, however, seemed only to encourage the militants. Three hundred SDSers grabbed and choked the students who were trying to get to the interviewers. Campus police officers attempted to rescue them but were beaten back by SDS. At that point the city police arrived. They were immediately hit with bricks and stomped on. One Madison officer was so severely wounded that he lost his trachea. Enraged, the Madison police fought back, injuring 175 SDSers and arresting anyone they could catch. Among the students arrested at the SDS-Dow confrontation was the son of the vice president of Wisconsin's Stevens Point campus. After the Dow protest, SDS vowed to "destroy" the University of Wisconsin.

Stuart Ewen, a veteran of Mississippi Freedom Summer whose parents had been 1930s-era radicals, praised his SDS comrades. "Doing something moral," Ewen insisted, "meant going against the law." SDSer Paul Buhle found the confrontation exciting and noted that he had "lost his fear." Buhle claimed that the campus and city police had tried to force their way in, thus provoking the clash. Dow sit-in participant Paul Breines called the Dow demonstration "the Madison police riot." (A 1986 PBS documentary on Wisconsin in the 1960s, "The War at Home," accepted Buhle's and Breines's version of this affair, neglecting to mention that SDSers had assaulted campus police and students on their way to job interviews. The makers of "The War at Home" also failed to inform viewers that their documentary originated as a fund-raiser for Karl Armstrong, one of the 1967 SDS-Dow veterans who later headed up his own terrorist group, the "New Year's Gang.")

During the Dow clash, most of Wisconsin's radical professors, SDS leader Evan Stark observed with some disgust, sat on the sidelines cheering the students as they rumbled with the police. Only the leftist sociologist Maurice Zeitlin had been fool-hardy enough to order the police to desist. His answer was a whack from a billy club. New Left historian William Appleman Williams urged the administration and faculty to ban Dow and CIA recruiters. But Williams warned SDSers that they were provoking a backlash off campus. The anti-war movement, Williams contended, had to solidify public opinion against America's cold war foreign policy. Angered, Marxist historian Harvey Goldberg told Williams that violence could never be politically counterproductive. Goldberg may have had a point—at least as far as campus politics were concerned. The university administration suspended future campus interviews with Dow representatives.

The violent struggle between student militants and law enforcement agents was not confined to Madison. At an October 1967 "Stop the Draft Week" protest outside the Oakland Army Induction Center, ten thousand Bay Area students fought two thousand police officers. The battle spread to a twenty-block area. Berkeley radicals attacked a draft board office with rocks, bottles, and bricks. Then they slashed tires and moved cars to block traffic. The white militants, however, failed to mobilize the black ghetto. The few blacks who turned out to protest the war held their own segregated rally away from the Berkeley students and their professors.

Elated at the damage he and his followers had wrought, Jerry Rubin declared victory and later boasted that "We were fucking obnoxious, and dug every moment of it." Frank Bardacke of the Berkeley SDS later enthused, "We finally had ourselves a white riot. . . . We had the streets. When it came to street battles now, we felt real confidence—and with good reason." Bardacke also noted that he intended to "cause chaos in this country as long as the war continues." (Bardacke and six other SDSers later stood trial for conspiracy to riot. Before their trial, Bardacke and the "Oakland Seven" insisted that "We did not loot or shoot," or "do anything so grand as 'move from dissent to resistance.'")

While dramatic, the "Stop the Draft Week" protest on the West Coast lacked the symbolic power of the October 1967 "Confront the Warmakers" demonstration in Washington, which attracted 100,000 youths. David Dellinger, a radical pacifist who had spent World War II in jail as a conscientious objector, recruited Jerry Rubin to the National Mobilization Committee to End the War in Vietnam. With the help of Abbie Hoffman, Rubin planned a dramatic assault on the Pentagon. Hundreds of students smoked dope and had sex on the Pentagon lawn as Hoffman recited magical incantations to make the building levitate. (Hoffman, who dismissed anti-war pacifists as "fucking prudes," had a great sense of self-dramatization. He claimed—falsely—that he had participated in the 1964 Mississippi Freedom Summer and had been threatened with lynching "by a redneck deputy.")

While intellectuals such as Paul Goodman, Dwight Macdonald, and Norman Mailer watched approvingly, hundreds of youths tried to breach the Pentagon, much like Russian revolutionaries in 1917 had stormed the Winter Palace. With Viet Cong flags flapping in the breeze, youths threw rocks at the military police and urinated on the Pentagon walls.

Jeff Jones, a former member of the Antioch College SDS in Ohio, and now a New York regional SDS organizer, took his place among the initial assault wave on the Pentagon. Jones, a lapsed Quaker, described the rush against soldiers as "exciting, powerful, intense." Some 683 protesters were arrested—either during the first scuffle between students and soldiers, or later in the evening as U.S. marshals proceeded to detain demonstrators who had sat down outside the Pentagon. One female demonstrator from Ann Arbor felt uncomfortable with SDS's "cop-baiting" and efforts to provoke violence. Fellow Michigan SDSer Robert Meeropol, though, had no such regrets. The event, Meeropol happily recalled, was like a family reunion. Throughout the day Meeropol kept running into red diaper babies and Communist party elders he had not seen since his childhood.

A month later, in New York City, several hundred SDSers, along with the ubiquitous Abbie Hoffman, blocked the intersections outside a Foreign Policy Association dinner for Secretary of State Dean Rusk. The white militants, led by Jeff Jones, heaved trash cans at the police and melted into a crowd of bystanders—all but inviting the police to club innocent people and cause a human stampede. SDS, Jones said, deliberately set out to provoke law enforcement officers in order "to reveal the violence of the State" to American youths. Jones and his band also threw red paint at Rusk and made cold war Democrats "run the gauntlet of hatred."

While radicals at elite universities escalated the level of violence and then depicted themselves as victims of a repressive "police state," an obscure college in Ohio was experiencing unprecedented political activism. A traditional teacher-training school with a large portion of students who were the first in their families to attend college, Kent State University was destined to become *the* symbol of campus unrest in the 1960s.

After a visit to Kent State in the fall of 1964 by a State Department representative who defended President Johnson's Indochina policy, Anthony Walsh of the campus CORE chapter helped found the Kent Committee to End the War in Vietnam. (Walsh, an Irish Catholic student who had served in the military before enrolling at Kent State, had been raised by a radical depression-era CIO organizer who had also been a "soldier" in the Irish Republican Army.) The Kent Committee had fewer than a dozen members. In its early days, few faculty supported the peace group; many professors felt anxious lest they appear to be sympathetic to the organization. As late as April 1967 just thirty-five faculty members signed an anti-war advertisement in the *Cleveland Plain Dealer.* This represented a mere 4 percent of the faculty, a strikingly low figure in comparison to the 25 percent of Michigan State's faculty endorsing a similar anti-war petition in February 1967.

The Kent Committee launched its attack against American involvement in the Vietnam War in February 1965 as Walsh and eleven other students participated in a campus peace picket. One hundred pro-war students mobbed the activists and threw one woman to the ground, kicking her in the face. Passions inflamed, the hawks confiscated and burned the anti-war signs and literature that the committee had brought to the demonstration. Shocked, one campus police officer, a friend of Walsh's, acted on his own to rope off the protesters in order to prevent further assaults. But the crowd simply retreated a few dozen yards and then launched rocks and other projectiles at the "Communists."

Kent State president Robert White—a former high school principal who, unlike SUNY-Buffalo's Martin Meyerson, had no acquaintance with Jeffersonian defenses of free speech—declined to take disciplinary action against the assailants. Instead White described the Kent Committee's organizers as publicity-seeking "martyrs" and suggested that the anti-war movement's goals "are distasteful to the overwhelming majority of us. Similarly, the mass of students within a true university process will come to see the shallowness of its arguments." White's response made further assaults on Kent Committee members inevitable, though the campus newspaper, the *Daily Kent Stater*, advised pro-war students to refrain from violence since this only made the anti-war activists appear "mature," "respectable," and "sympathetic."

Kent State's peace activists continued their weekly vigils, gradually converting some students to their side. The Kent Committee, however, remained small—attracting thirty-six members, just large enough to fend off attacks. Kent activists also began to take the precaution of traveling in small groups rather than alone, both on and off the campus. Thanks to their dedication and to the escalating war in Vietnam, by the spring of 1966 the Kent Committee had attracted two hundred sympathetic students to its rallies. Actual membership, however, stood at no more than three dozen. Among the new recruits to the Kent Committee were Howie Emmer, the son of middle-class Ohio Communist party organizers, and Rick Erickson, whose father, a former Democratic mayor of Akron, was still politically influential.

Anti-war activists found an outlet for their energies in Kent's developing countercultural arena. The city's proximity to the Ohio Turnpike and other major highways made it a convenient way station from points east to Cleveland, Detroit, and Chicago. With the burgeoning resident student population, the city of Kent provided youth-oriented recreational establishments. (Kent State had 21,000 students by 1966, compared to 5,000 in 1954.) Easy access and the youth market attracted rock-and-roll and jazz bands from as far away as Chicago; they found in Kent's remarkable number of bars a place to work on their acts before breaking into the big time. Throughout the 1960s the fame of Kent's bar and musical scene spread throughout the Midwest, making the city a magnet for student revelers, teenage runaways, and activists. (Perhaps one of the reasons why Penn State's countercultural and leftist scene remained so small had something to do with the fact that the campus was, in the words of a past university president, "equally inaccessible from all parts of the state.")

Meanwhile Kent's anti-war ranks grew larger. In the spring of 1967, 150 Kent State students participated in an anti-war rally in New York City. In October 1967, 200 Kent State students took part in the march on the Pentagon. Kent Committee members Howie Emmer and Jim Powrie, whose father was a Hoosier postman, came away from the Washington confrontation with vastly different perspectives. Powrie found the night he spent on the Pentagon grounds to be both "romantic and terrifying." He was sympathetic toward the soldiers who surrounded the demonstrators, perceiving that they were, like him, "scared working-class youths hoping to avoid violence." Reconciliation, not confrontation, Powrie believed, would end the Vietnam War. Emmer, on the other hand, had charged into the soldiers and, exhilarated, thereafter championed active resistance against the nation's civil and military leaders.

A month later, in November 1967, seventy-five Kent State students spent two hours peacefully demonstrating against a Dow representative who was conducting campus interviews. The Kent Committee made no attempt to prevent students from meeting with the Dow recruiter. Spectators flung mud at Kent Committee members and torched several of their "Dow Burns Babies" placards. Yet again, president Robert White stood by in what students could only conclude was tacit approval of the violence directed against the Kent Committee.

Disgusted with the Kent Committee's nonviolent philosophy, Emmer and Erickson hoped to build a more militant and "masculine" organization. They planned to go on the offensive against pro-war students, President White, and American society at large. As moderates in the Kent Committee either graduated and left the area, or remained and lost ground to the new, more radical members, Emmer and Erickson made plans to establish an SDS chapter worthy of its counterparts in Ann Arbor, Berkeley, and Madison.

Even as Kent State's anti-war movement grew and fragmented, and many inner cities seethed with revolt, working- and lower-middle-class whites were becoming restless. It was *their* children, after all, who by the end of 1967 were among the nearly half-million U.S. troops fighting in Vietnam. *Their* children did not riot, drop acid, and champion the Viet Cong. Weary of the apparent inability of cold war Democrats to quell campus and ghetto, voters fell in line behind Ronald Reagan's 1966 California gubernatorial campaign. Reagan, who won the governorship with a million-vote margin, pledged to restore law and order and crack down on the Panthers and the Berkeley militants. To great applause, Reagan instigated Clark Kerr's dismissal from the University of California. Reagan knew he was on firm ground. Three-quarters of California's voters had expressed disapproval of the 1964 Free Speech Movement while national polls in 1966 and 1967 showed that 40 percent of the public did not believe citizens had the right to protest against the Vietnam War.

Meanwhile the ranks of the Young Americans for Freedom had risen to 28,000. An even more impressive display of the growing backlash was the grassroots campaign to place George Wallace of Alabama on the 1968 presidential ballot in all 50 states. To accomplish that goal, Wallace's army of working-class youths and middle-aged "steelworkers and beauticians" had to begin in 1967. California Democrats and Republicans, fearful that Wallace might be putting together a successful independent political party, required the Southerner to get 66,000 signatures on a petition—with each person who signed having to fill out a two-page form. Wallace got *100,000* California residents to jump through the legal hoops to support his as yet undeclared campaign. In Ohio, Wallace had to collect 433,000 signatures on a petition in just 10 weeks. Even though he surpassed that goal by 100,000, the Ohio Supreme Court ruled that his petitions were out of order since he led a "fictional party."

(The U.S. Supreme Court overturned the Ohio court's decision.)

Wallace's growing popularity and national appeal would not have been possible without the New Left and black militants. *Village Voice* writer Jim Sleeper and Saul Alinsky, an Old Left–style organizer, skewered the 1960s radicals. Focusing on the racial ideology of the campus militants, Sleeper contended that the New Left's "obsession with" racial justice "deflected . . . attention from the real problem, which is poverty, and the real need, which is jobs. To 'expose' racism without addressing that problem and that need is to invite responses from one's opponents that only deepen racism itself." Addressing himself to the class biases of the New Left, Alinsky observed that the inability of privileged student activists to recognize "the legitimate self-interest" of working-class whites who felt threatened by campus and ghetto disorder ultimately denied the left mass support as well as any claim to moral superiority.

Conservative columnist George Will noted in 1999 that SDS and anti–cold war Democrats had viewed themselves as foot soldiers in the greatest grassroots political movement in modern history. They were mistaken, Will thought. In the rise of Ronald Reagan and George Wallace one could find an authentic mass political movement. America's greatest social revolution, so Will believed, had not taken place on the campus and in the ghetto. The revolution—or as unsympathetic academic and media commentators called it, the "backlash"—had taken place in blue-collar communities such as Buffalo. At the beginning of the 1960s no one would have dreamed that resurgent Republicans had any chance of breaching this bastion of the New Deal Democratic party. By 1967, however, SUNY-Buffalo students and inner-city militants like Martin Sostre, who called himself a "black Viet Cong," were producing a Republican counter-reaction in the city and its suburbs.

In an attempt to raise its academic profile and become the "Berkeley of the East," SUNY-Buffalo aggressively recruited faculty with scholarly potential. A number of these people were anti-war activists and black power supporters. Most faculty did not plan to stay in Buffalo; several commuted weekly from New York City. Faculty activists, largely employed in the growing liberal arts and social science departments, were outsiders. Many professorial leftists also experimented with drugs, communal living, and group sex. This was not Buffalo's vision of the teacher-scholar. Tellingly, Leslie Fiedler, a SUNY-Buffalo English professor who was destined to be arrested for marijuana possession, observed that he "had never known a single family that had lost a son in Vietnam, or indeed, one with a son wounded, missing in action, or held prisoner of war."

As SUNY-Buffalo's increasingly cosmopolitan faculty grew by 42 percent between 1962 and 1966, the size and social characteristics of the student body changed. From 1962 to 1966, student enrollment increased from 7,350 to 20,000. Once newly installed president Martin Meyerson in 1966 raised admissions standards, the university enrolled a larger proportion of WASP and Jewish students. Fewer working- and lower-middle-class whites from the area were able to gain admittance to SUNY-Buffalo. Black students with lower standardized test scores and high school grade point averages, however, received preferential admission.

Since SUNY-Buffalo had built few dormitories, Jewish and WASP students and faculty moved into the neighboring Catholic wards. They steadily flowed down Main Street, establishing at least a hundred communes and transforming Delaware Park into a preserve for drug consumption. Locals could no longer allow their children to play in their neighborhood park. Students also penetrated farther south on Main Street, creating in the Allentown district an SDS "liberated zone" of the "Free Republic of Buffalo."

The SUNY-Buffalo administrators soon heard community criticism of campus activism, countercultural lifestyles, and student-faculty disruption of Catholic neighborhoods. One Polish-American councilman in 1966 sponsored a resolution demanding that the university president investigate campus activists. The resolution passed 12 to 1.

By the spring of 1967, SUNY-Buffalo activists had founded a group called LEMAR—Legalize Marijuana. (Leslie Fiedler served as its faculty adviser.) LEMAR subsequently sponsored a "Taurian Festival of the Druids," at which two thousand students gathered in Delaware Park to drop acid. Meyerson doggedly defended his radical students and faculty from community censure—even as they ridiculed him. The president of the alumni association resigned in protest over SUNY-Buffalo's new admissions standards, which he felt discriminated against local working-class Catholic youths. Buffalo residents, noting the high proportion of secular New York Jews among the ranks of the student and faculty left, began to call SUNY-Buffalo "Tel-Aviv Tech."

The gulf between Buffalo's locals and the university's cosmopolitans grew even greater following June 1967 rioting in the black wards. Activist SUNY-Buffalo students and faculty posted bail for the rioters, who had been arrested for arson and looting. Frank Felicetta, Buffalo's irate police commissioner, angrily blamed SDS and the Youth Against War and Fascism for fomenting racial unrest in the city. In turn, campus militants laid plans to bring "the war home" to what they regarded as Buffalo's racist, uneducated citizenry. For SUNY-Buffalo, as well as Kent State and the nation's more elite campuses, the years from 1964 to 1967 were a prelude to a period of even greater social division, student radicalization, and urban unrest.

6

The Explosion, 1968–1970

ON JANUARY 31, 1968, the North Vietnamese Army and the Viet Cong launched the Tet Offensive. Provincial capitals in South Vietnam fell rapidly to the Communist forces; thousands of supporters of the South Vietnamese government were executed in the city of Hue; and Viet Cong guerrillas blasted their way into the U.S. embassy compound in Saigon. Over the course of February and into March, American troops regained the momentum and annihilated the Viet Cong. In the process of killing forty thousand Viet Cong, however, the United States sustained its worst combat casualties since 1944. The *Christian Science Monitor* reported, "The Communists' three-day blitz war ... has opened up the possibility of the United States losing its first major war in history." When CBS Evening News anchor Walter Cronkite reported from Vietnam that he thought there was little hope of victory, President Johnson felt even more isolated and under siege.

To make matters worse for Johnson, Senator Eugene McCarthy of Minnesota had entered the Democratic primaries in 1968, winning 42 percent of the vote in New Hampshire. McCarthy's strong showing against an incumbent president encouraged New York senator Robert Kennedy to declare his own candidacy. Kennedy argued that "No matter how many Viet Cong and North Vietnamese we claim to kill, through some miraculous effort of will, enemy strength remains the same." On March 31, 1968, Johnson announced that he would not seek reelection and threw his support to Vice President Hubert Humphrey. Johnson also said he would initiate peace negotiations with Hanoi.

Johnson overreacted to the political situation. He also failed to wait for a clearer picture to emerge—much like the *Christian Science Monitor*, Walter Cronkite, and Robert Kennedy had done in their analysis of the U.S. military situation in Vietnam. McCarthy was not a popular peace candidate. The bulk of his New Hampshire voters were anti-Communist hawks who wanted to pressure Johnson into *escalating* the war. The majority of Americans—61 percent—had rallied behind Johnson during the Tet Offensive. Once the president all but said that victory was impossible and that there was little sense in continuing the fight, most citizens turned against the war. Although Hanoi had sacrificed its guerrilla arm and could not hope to carry on a successful conventional war with the United States, Johnson's loss of confidence rescued North Vietnam's political fortunes.

Four days after Johnson stunned his supporters, James Earl Ray assassinated Martin Luther King, Jr., in Memphis. Rioting broke out in 125 cities across 28 states. In Kansas City, Missouri, rioters torched fire engines and shot police officers and National Guardsmen. Although no more than 10 percent of Kansas City's 112,000 blacks participated in the riot, 40 percent later informed pollsters that they believed violence furthered the cause of racial equality. Many Kansas City whites, unaware that the majority of blacks did not support the rioters, expressed disgust. "The Negroes are getting out of hand," one young white woman told newspaper reporters. "Half of them are just rioting to riot, and they should be stopped just like other law-breakers."

On the West Coast, Panther leader Eldridge Cleaver issued an "executive order" for the assassination of police officers. Cleaver himself ambushed a patrol car, injuring two policemen. When other police officers arrived on the scene, Cleaver and his entourage fled into a house. After a shoot-out, Panther Bobby Hutton died in a hail of gunfire. Hutton became a New Left martyr—the supposedly innocent victim of police brutality and white racism.

In Washington, Stokely Carmichael worked behind the scenes to keep the riot going, encouraging black youths to burn and loot for three days. Although Carmichael and SNCC had earlier ridiculed King as an Uncle Tom, race traitor, and Jewish puppet, he was now a beloved hero. As Carmichael said, King was "the one man of our race that this country's older generations, the militants and the revolutionaries and the masses of black people would still listen to."

Seeing an opportunity to play on "liberal guilt," James Forman, minister of foreign affairs for the Black Panthers, informed white clerics that they had to atone for their sins. Forman demanded $500 million in "reparations" and went as far as to raid church services to get at the collection plates. The Episcopal church gave Forman $200,000.

In 1968 irrationality and violence held sway on numerous college campuses as well as in the inner city. Thirty-nine thousand students engaged in two hundred major demonstrations on one hundred campuses. Ann Arbor SDSer Rayna Rapp and other members of the Women's International Terrorist Conspiracy from Hell (WITCH) placed a hex on the state legislature when it refused to liberalize Michigan's abortion laws. Rapp, a future anthropology professor at the New School for Social Research, vowed that the "old men" in the legislature who opposed abortion on religious grounds "were going to die." Meanwhile, national New Left leaders such as Tom Hayden argued that students and blacks had to make the domestic cost of continuing the Vietnam War so high that the government would have to end it, even if it meant alienating the majority of Americans.

In an attempt to "bring the war home" and inspire students at other universities to follow their example, SDSers at Columbia provoked the most famous campus confrontation of 1968. Staging a "revolutionary action" in the backyard of the nation's broadcasting networks, and at a university whose alumni filled the ranks of the media elite, guaranteed enormous publicity for the Columbia SDS.

Mark Rudd, leader of the Columbia SDS, came from an upper-middle-class, secular Jewish family. He had been enormously impressed with a band of Lower East Side anarchists who called themselves "Up Against the Wall, Motherfucker." The "Motherfuckers" advocated the trashing of property and enjoyed ridiculing liberals. They also had an interesting way of expressing their point of view. For instance, one of them, the stepson of philosopher Herbert Marcuse, urged the grim-faced SDS followers of Mao to go home and have sex. Marcuse's stepson then dropped his pants to show the Maoists which part to use. He also criticized them for wasting their time denouncing the Vietnam War. The problem with America was not capitalist imperialism but that "The fucking society won't let you smoke your dope, ball your woman, and wear your hair the way you want to."

Although Rudd and the Columbia SDS leaders did not agree with the Motherfuckers' inattention to U.S. imperialism, they had no problem embracing violence, the counterculture, and overwrought "street theater." Before the Columbia uprising, Rudd had gained local notoriety for assaulting a Selective Service official with a pie. Once the seizure of campus buildings began on April 23, 1968, Rudd dramatically said to university president Grayson Kirk, "Up against the wall, motherfucker, this is a stick-up." Columbia SDSers regarded themselves as revolutionaries who would radicalize millions of students and inner-city blacks. Their unrealistic expectations and intense energy were fueled by the massive consumption of Black Beauty amphetamines.

At first glance it seemed improbable that anyone like Rudd could bring one of America's most prestigious universities to its knees. Columbia, after all, was primarily a graduate-oriented university with only three thousand undergraduates—of which five hundred belonged to SDS. Rudd and the SDS leaders, however, pursued a shrewd strategy. First, SDS cited Columbia's affiliation with the Institute for Defense Analysis as an example of university complicity with the "war machine." Since most liberal arts and social science faculty at Columbia opposed the Vietnam War and military-sponsored research, they could be expected to side with SDS against President Kirk. Second, SDS argued that Columbia's plans to construct a gymnasium in Morningside Park were "racist." In truth, Columbia did view the Morningside Park project as a way to buffer the campus from Harlem's underclass. Coming just weeks after King's assassination, many black New Yorkers were in an unsettled mood. SDS hoped to forge an alliance with Harlem blacks—an alliance that would intimidate Columbia's and the city's nervous white leadership.

(Rudd later admitted that SDS "manufactured the issues. The Institute for Defense Analysis is nothing at Columbia. And the gym issue is bull. It doesn't mean anything to anybody. I had never been to the gym site before the demonstration began. I didn't even know how to get there.")

The week-long seizure of university buildings (April 23–30, 1968) did not go as Rudd had planned. Shortly after SDS and the Columbia Student Afro-American Society occupied Hamilton Hall, the black militants expelled their white, mostly Jewish allies. Armed members of the Harlem CORE and SNCC chapters joined seventy-five black radicals in Hamilton Hall. They took three white administrators hostage. The black Manhattan borough president announced his support for the Afro-American Society, as did Stokely Carmichael and H. Rap Brown—both of whom enlisted in the occupation of Hamilton Hall. Brown informed the media, "If the university doesn't deal with our brothers in there, they're going to have to deal with the brothers out on the streets." As Rudd predicted, city and university officials were terrified of sparking a riot in Harlem.

The Afro-American Society ultimately succeeded in getting Columbia to halt construction in Morningside Park.

Meanwhile Columbia SDSers, caught off guard by their expulsion from Hamilton Hall, decided they should seize their own campus building. SDS set its sights on Low Library, which housed numerous administrative offices. When police officers tried to clear Low of SDSers, a legion of liberal arts faculty— just as Rudd had hoped—intervened. The professors booed the police and then blocked their entrance into the building. Unwilling to stand up against the faculty militants, President Kirk backed down. Soon white radicals took over Mathematics Hall, and Pete Seeger and the Grateful Dead arrived to provide free concerts. Tom Hayden and intellectual gadfly Dwight Macdonald also came to man the barricades.

Two-thirds of Columbia's undergraduates opposed the SDS and Afro-American Society sit-ins and supported the efforts of the Young Americans for Freedom to oust the radicals. This should have come as no surprise since an overwhelming majority of undergraduates at Columbia had earlier endorsed the right of Dow Chemical to recruit on the campus. Chagrined, Columbia SDSers—and their subsequent sympathizers in the media and the academy—asserted that their student foes represented little more than a minority of racist "jocks." In truth, the white and black militants were the minority. Moreover, Columbia was hardly an athletic powerhouse: of jocks there may have been a handful.

Unfortunately for Kirk, his initial vacillation had made him appear weak to students, university trustees, and angry blue-collar New Yorkers whose own children could not afford to go to Columbia. The children of the working class had to settle for community college—or Vietnam. Once Kirk finally called in the police at the end of April to deal with the *white* radicals, he only succeeded in annoying the faculty. He also won no praise from his exasperated critics, and soon resigned. The new president sought to make amends with the liberal arts faculty by dropping charges against the six hundred whites who had been arrested. Mark Rudd was not among those arrested since he had fled at the first approach of the police. He believed that the success of "the revolution" required him to remain at large.

While the Columbia sit-ins did, as SDS had hoped, inspire building seizures on campuses across the country, a few New Leftists expressed alarm over the attitudes and antics of their peers. Columbia SDSer Paul Berman lamented years later, "Somehow intellect got identified with war, napalm, and reaction, and to be against all evil things was to be against book-cracking too." Berman sadly concluded that "'Abolish brains' was practically a slogan, though no one put it that way. Even left-wing brains came under suspicion."

With the end of the Columbia affair, radicals focused their attention on the approaching Democratic National Convention in Chicago. On New Year's Day 1968, Jerry Rubin and Abbie Hoffman were already mapping their attack on Chicago. Under the influence of alcohol and narcotics, Rubin and Hoffman formed an anarchist, countercultural organization that would be their political vehicle for the Chicago protest: the Youth International Party (Yippie). Desiring some warm-up actions before Chicago, the Yippies in February 1968 destroyed property on the Stony Brook campus of the State University of New York. Rubin and Hoffman knew exactly which slogans to employ to gain media attention and attract student followers. "We believe," Rubin and Hoffman proclaimed, "that people should fuck all the time, any time, whomever they want."

Later scholarly accounts of the events that transpired in Chicago, as well as a 1995 PBS documentary, "Chicago, 1968," tended to put the New Left in a favorable light. (The producers of "Chicago, 1968" used unflattering photographs of Mayor Richard Daley, accompanied by ominous background music, to emphasize that he was a bloated, ugly party boss.) Many historians of the 1960s, and the veterans of SDS themselves, argued that the New Left had no intention of engaging in violent protest. SDSers had placed their hopes on anti-war Democrats

Eugene McCarthy and Robert Kennedy, only to see the former bulldozed by Hubert Humphrey's behind-the-scenes operatives and the latter assassinated. Anti-war radicals simply wanted to come to Chicago in August 1968 to register their dismay with Humphrey and the Vietnam War. It was Mayor Daley and an out-of-control police department that provoked violence. Only then, under bloody assault, did activists fight back.

In truth, Rubin had envisioned turning the Democratic Convention into a violent spectacle a full year and a half before the event. "We wanted to create a situation," Rubin recalled, "in which the Chicago police and the Daley administration and the federal government and the United States would self-destruct." Similarly, Abbie Hoffman wrote to a confidant in December 1967, "We plan to bring 250,000 people to the Democratic Convention. We expect about 100,000 of them to be committed to disruption or sabotage. Both are worthwhile." To a *Village Voice* reporter, Hoffman added,

> We have two alternatives in Chicago, both of them ok. The opposition determines what will happen, they're living actors in our theater. Suppose they choose to tolerate us. Then we'll . . . present a vision of a new lifestyle that will be projected across the country. Suppose they don't tolerate us? Then they'll face a bloody scene. We'll have to adopt guerrilla techniques for dealing with them.

As for being demoralized by the murder of Robert Kennedy by Sirhan Sirhan on June 6, 1968, Rubin had joyfully exclaimed, "Sirhan Sirhan is a Yippie." Eugene McCarthy rated no more favor within the ranks of the New Left. Michigan SDSer Robert Meeropol scornfully called McCarthy "naive." The Minnesota senator, Meeropol groused, was just a "reformer." Former national SDS president Carl Oglesby decried the McCarthy campaign as an "attempt to emasculate" radical protest. Oglesby believed that McCarthy, though he wanted to end the Vietnam War, was fundamentally an anti-Communist

Democrat who did not embrace third-world revolution and black power. For his part, Abbie Hoffman had heckled Eugene McCarthy in Washington.

The hostility that Rubin, Oglesby, and Meeropol felt toward Kennedy and McCarthy was understandable. Both the radicals and the anti-war Democrats were competing for the same constituency. Leftists realized that they were not about to convert great numbers of anti-Communist Catholics, Southern whites, and workers—not that they wanted such people in their ranks in the first place. Consequently SDS had to go after the middle-class WASPs and Jews who had fallen in line behind McCarthy and Kennedy.

McCarthy in particular had drawn thousands of restless college students away from SDS. Angered, the militants sought to radicalize McCarthy's young followers by getting them in the way of Chicago police clubs. SDS vowed to make a revolution in Chicago. Toward that end, SDS organizer Jeff Jones urged students to attack police officers and knock "those motherfuckers on their ass." SDS founder Rennie Davis exhorted crowds to become a "National Liberation Front for America."

In Chicago, Tom Hayden shouted, "Let us make sure that if blood is going to flow let it flow all over this city." David Farber, the historian interviewed in "Chicago, 1968," insisted that the police beating of Rennie Davis had pushed Hayden over the edge. Hayden made the same claim. But such claims were inaccurate.

Before the 1968 Democratic Convention, Hayden and a group of American leftists had journeyed to Bratislava, Czechoslovakia, where they met with a Vietnamese Communist delegation. They discussed ways in which to undermine America's military effort in Vietnam. Returning to the United States, Hayden had announced, "We are coming to Chicago to vomit on [Democratic presidential nominee Hubert Humphrey's] 'politics of joy,' to expose the secret decisions, upset the night-club orgies, and face the Democratic Party with its illegitimacy and criminality. . . . The government of the United

States is an outlaw institution under the control of war criminals." These were not the words of a nonviolent moderate thrown momentarily off balance by police brutality. Likewise, moderates did not, as Hayden had done before the 1968 Democratic Convention, hail the Black Panthers as "America's Viet Cong" and tell friends that "it might be useful if someone were to fire-bomb police cars."

Despite having called Robert Kennedy "a little fascist," Hayden attended his funeral after his assassination and, to the disgust of activists Peter Collier and David Horowitz, shed some tears for the television cameras. Radical historian Staughton Lynd marveled at Hayden's political gymnastics: "On Monday, Wednesday, and Friday [Hayden] was a National Liberation Front guerrilla, and on Tuesday, Thursday, and Saturday, he . . . was on the left wing of the Democratic Party."

Some ten thousand rioters followed Hayden, Davis, Rubin, and Hoffman into battle against the Chicago police. Equipped with helmets and improvised gas masks made of bandannas covered with petroleum jelly, the student rioters flung bottles, eggs, and rocks at the police. (The "Chicago, 1968" documentary did not account for how the radicals, who allegedly had no intention of provoking violence, managed to come to Chicago laden with such "combat gear.") Taking up Jeff Jones's suggestion, the rioters, after stoning a few police officers, mixed in with citizens on the sidewalks. Radicals hoped the police would charge into innocent bystanders, create panic, and further escalate the conflict. To ensure that the police were thoroughly riled, SDSers and Yippies called them "pigs," "fascists," and "cocksuckers." Leftists also chanted, "Kill the pigs!" and "Fuck the pigs!"

Increasingly tired and testy, the 12,000 police officers fought back. One hundred and ninety-two policemen were wounded and 668 rioters arrested. Just 41 percent of the Chicago rioters were residents of the city. Eighty percent tested positive for LSD, marijuana, and hashish. Ed Sanders, a radical musician and publisher, was so stoned that he thought Chicago's Lincoln

Park had turned into "a giant frothing trough of mutant spinach egg noodles." A Chicago police officer assigned to tail Sanders had to help him back to his hotel. (The Chicago police also rescued Abbie Hoffman after a deranged gunman tried to break into his apartment. Far from being grateful, Hoffman dismissed Chicago as "just another dumb Southern town" full of redneck cops.)

Meanwhile, on the convention floor, efforts by McCarthy's supporters to place an anti-war plank in the Democratic party platform failed by 500 votes of the 2,600 cast. Televised scenes of violence in the streets of Chicago made voters wonder how Hubert Humphrey could restore law and order in America if he could not maintain peace at his own convention. Humphrey had won a virtually worthless presidential nomination. The Chicago convention, in addition to undermining Humphrey's candidacy, also marked the beginning of a takeover of the Democratic party by anti-war liberals and the New Left. Indeed, Senator George McGovern, who tried to rally anti-war forces on the convention floor, denounced the Chicago police as "sons of bitches."

Inevitably the Vietnam War was bound to divide the party of Hubert Humphrey more than the party of Richard Nixon. After all, 95 percent of America's peace activists were either Democrats or the children of Democrats and leftists. Just 5 percent of the Republican party's rank and file protested against the war. It was extremely rare to see an anti-war Republican student activist like Wellesley College's Hillary Rodham. The future wife of President Bill Clinton, however, would not remain a Republican for much longer. Rodham concluded that by joining the Democrats, radicalized middle-class students like herself could change the party's anti-Communist foreign policy and promote "lifestyle liberation."

As anti-war activists and anti-Communist politicians fought for the soul of the Democratic party, the SUNY-Buffalo SDS and the Youth Against War and Fascism (YAWF) staged a dramatic off-campus protest. Bruce Beyer, a WASPish SDSer, refused military induction and took sanctuary inside the Elmwood Unitarian-Universalist Church. Members of the newly formed Buffalo Draft Resistance Union (BDRU) joined Beyer. Soon two hundred students and faculty were participating. While Judy Collins sang folk songs and long-haired youths smoked dope on the church lawn, Catholic high school students picketed the church, carrying placards that read, "Keep Marx out of the Church." The church's minister, Rev. J. D. White, received arson threats from residents while SDS leader Robert Cohen warned that "if the authorities come to the church" to get the draft resisters, "they have to do so over our dead bodies." (Cohen had cut his political teeth as a member of the Wisconsin SDS.) After a standoff of nearly two weeks, FBI agents, Buffalo police, and federal marshals stormed the church, arresting nine individuals for draft evasion and assault. They became known as the Buffalo Nine.

SUNY-Buffalo's student newspaper conveyed campus attitudes toward Buffalo by featuring illustrations of armed soldiers with swastikas. Its editors also savaged the university's president Martin Meyerson for not taking what they thought were sufficiently strong stands against racism, police repression, and military recruiting on the campus. Taking advantage of the fact that all undergraduates who showed up for a student government meeting could vote, the SDS and YAWF packed the galleries in order to grant themselves money from the student activities fund and to pass resolutions condemning racism in Buffalo.

Claiming five hundred members by the fall of 1968, the SUNY-Buffalo SDS entered an intense phase of protest. Shouting down a few SDSers leery of further antagonizing Buffalo's blue-collar citizens, YAWF let it be known that "We cast our lot with those who want to fight fascism, not those who bow down before it." In early October four hundred SUNY-Buffalo students—chanting "Two, four, six, eight, we don't want a fascist state"—entered the city's War Memorial Auditorium to disrupt an appearance by Republican presidential candidate

Richard Nixon. The subsequent battle between police and demonstrators spilled outside the auditorium and into city streets. A few days later SUNY-Buffalo students shouted "soowie" at police officer Gerald Donovan as he walked by the off-campus headquarters of the Buffalo Nine Defense Committee. The irate Irish cop returned with a tactical squad which took six students prisoner, including Buffalo Nine defendant Carl Kronberg. Voicing the sentiments of many area Catholics, Buffalo Bishop James McNulty characterized the SUNY-Buffalo activists as "abusive, violent, and non-Christian."

The SUNY-Buffalo SDS was not the only chapter outside New York City making an impression on student and off-campus constituencies. In Ohio, leaders of the Kent Committee to End the War in Vietnam were determined to keep the organization and its nonviolent principles alive even as more of the membership drifted into SDS. In late April 1968 the Kent Committee organized a peaceful anti-war rally on the commons, featuring local folk singers and speeches by clergy. As a few hundred students reclined on Blanket Hill, pro-war youths, armed with high-powered air rifles, fired on the visiting ministers. After the Kent Committee complained, the university administration arrested a leader of the peace group for violating a decree not to publicize the rally on the campus. The campus radio director praised the shooters for "turning the tables" on the Kent Committee while President White made no effort to track down the students who had shot and wounded the clerics.

Howie Emmer and Rick Erickson pointed to White's indirect encouragement of right-wing violence on the campus as a compelling argument for abandoning the Kent Committee in favor of a more militant organization. Both radicals lost no time in demonstrating that SDS represented the future of campus protest at Kent State. In May 1968, 150 Kent State SDSers and members of the Black United Students (BUS), a black power organization, disrupted a campus speech by Hubert Humphrey and then led a noisy walkout. Emmer and Erickson believed in silencing liberals such as Humphrey and anyone else who disagreed with them. Feeling jubilant, in June 1968 they attended the national SDS convention at Michigan State. They were immediately attracted to SDSer Bernardine Dohrn, a University of Chicago Law School graduate who favored leather miniskirts and wore political buttons with messages such as "Cunnilingus is Cool, Fellatio is Fun."

Emmer and Erickson met with Michigan SDSers Bill Ayers, the son of the chairman of Commonwealth Edison of Chicago, and Jim Mellen, a onetime professor of political science at Drew University in New Jersey who had left his wife and two children in favor of revolutionary politics. Erickson also reestablished contact with Mark Rudd. (He had met Rudd that spring during the Columbia uprising.) Emmer and Erikson joined with Ayers and Mellen to create a network of Michigan-Ohio SDS travelers.

Lured to Kent by Emmer as well as by the city's counterculture, Terry Robbins, a Kenyon College dropout and Ann Arbor SDSer, made the campus his base of operations. Robbins and Ayers donated a printing press that enabled Kent State and the Northeast Ohio SDS to publish their own newspaper, *Maggie's Farm*. (The title was lifted from a Bob Dylan song.) Further assistance to Kent State SDS came from Emmer's parents and members of the Ohio Communist party whose children belonged to the campus chapter. Armed with Black Panther and third-world revolutionary principles, as well as with the collected works of Bob Dylan, Emmer and Erikson set out in the fall of 1968 to intensify the struggle at Kent State.

At the first fall meeting of the Kent State SDS, 250 students showed up. In October 200 Kent State SDSers went to the University of Akron to disrupt a speech by Nixon. Kent State SDSers chanted "Seig Heil!" and "Ho, Ho, Ho Chi Minh, NLF is Gonna Win!" at Nixon. They also called Nixon a "fucking asshole." *Time* magazine noted that the Kent militants had staged "the most successful disruption" of a Nixon speech since the beginning of the fall campaign.

Emmer described "the American empire [as] *institutionally* racist and violent" and argued that "the black community in America is in fact a colony within the mother country and is *excluded* as such." It was up to white students, Emmer continued, "to build a *white* radical movement," which, aligned with the Black Panthers and the Kent Black United Students, would overthrow the power structure.

Having urged Kent State SDS "to get our white shit together," Emmer's followers in November 1968 blockaded campus recruiters from the Oakland (California) Police Department. The West Coast police officers, Emmer argued, persecuted and murdered innocent Black Panthers. The 150 SDSers and 150 BUS members let it be known that any white student in the placement office who tried to interview with the Oakland police would be dealt with in an appropriate revolutionary manner. Such threats, however, were premature. A few hundred hostile students, some armed with motorcycle chains, charged the demonstrators. The campus police and the university administration stood aside, making no attempt to halt the beatings.

At the University of Wisconsin, student radicals firebombed South Hall, a campus building, as well as the state headquarters of Selective Service. The first Wisconsin SDS meeting of the fall of 1968 drew 3,000 students—or more than 10 times the number who participated in the Kent State SDS protests and meetings. (Nationally, SDS by the fall of 1968 had 100,000 members in 300 chapters. One in eight Princeton freshmen joined SDS.)

Militant Wisconsin SDSers tried to waylay police officer George Croal and break his arms. (Madison leftists had despised Croal when he was an anti-Communist graduate student. Now that he had joined the city police department he had become an official "enemy of the people.") Given their dismissal of marriage as a "bourgeois institution of patriarchal oppression," Wisconsin SDSers believed that anyone who showed up at their meetings wearing a wedding ring had to be a police spy in need of a beating.

The increasing militancy of the New Left was met with scorn from the student right. In New York City in 1968, the Young Americans for Freedom staged counter sit-ins at the regional headquarters of SDS as well as at the head office of the National Mobilization Committee to End the War in Vietnam. YAF's student cadres also occupied the Boston headquarters of a draft resistance organization and raised the South Vietnamese flag. (The New Right had learned its political theater from the New *and* Old Left. YAF founder Marvin Liebman had been a 1930s-era Communist.) At Purdue University in Indiana, YAF and SDS faced off over the issue of campus recruiting by the CIA. Four hundred Purdue students helped YAF stage anti-SDS demonstrations. In stark contrast to Columbia University, Purdue administrators offered no concessions to SDS. And Purdue's faculty, dominated by engineers and agriculturists, did not defend the radicals.

Purdue's lack of sympathy for the New Left, while placing the campus out of step with the Ivy League and the elite Big Ten schools, was nonetheless in line with national sentiment. A Louis Harris public opinion poll conducted in September 1968 revealed that 81 percent of the electorate believed that law and order had broken down, with the majority of whites holding blacks, students, and anti-war Democrats responsible. Nixon and third-party candidate George Wallace proved to be the beneficiaries of this reaction to unrest on the campus and in the city. (Wallace knew where his votes were coming from, which is why he made a point of answering his hecklers instead of ignoring them as was Humphrey's practice. "You young people seem to know a lot of four-letter words," Wallace would grin in his folksy yet menacing way. "But I have two four-letter words you don't know: S-O-A-P and W-O-R-K.")

Having spent his post-1960 exile cultivating liberal and conservative Republicans, Nixon had little problem securing key endorsements and breezing through the party primaries. A late challenge by California governor Ronald Reagan proved ineffectual. Although conservative activists liked Reagan's anti–big government rhetoric, most Republicans feared his earlier attacks on Social Security would alienate disaffected traditional Democrats. Nixon, on the other hand, made distinctions between Great Society and New Deal programs, with the former embodying all the evils of contemporary liberalism while the latter represented truth, justice, and the American Way. (It was a shrewd position: 40 percent of Nixon's supporters in the general election were people who had voted Democratic in 1964.) On the issue of Vietnam, Nixon told voters he had a plan to end the war. Of course, if he were to spell out his plan during the election, it would tip off Hanoi.

For all of Nixon's efforts, he defeated Humphrey by only 1 percentage point in the popular vote. The AFL-CIO rallied enough of its rank and file behind Humphrey to tighten the race but ultimately fell short. To organized labor's chagrin, Wallace had cut deeply into the Democratic tally. In Italian South Philadelphia, Wallace won 12 percent of the vote, enough to make Humphrey the first Democrat in forty years to lose the district. South Philadelphia had been the scene of increased muggings and militant black demonstrations. Ignoring political directives from the AFL-CIO, New Jersey and Illinois United Automobile Workers locals gave Wallace more than 80 percent of their vote. In the crucible of industrial unionism and the New Deal, Pittsburgh steelworkers served as Wallace volunteers. Those Catholic precincts in Buffalo that bordered on black neighborhoods, or had seen the sprouting of radical student communes, turned out for Nixon or Wallace. The Southerner also picked up Catholic votes in Cleveland and from those Appalachians who had migrated to Akron and Columbus. As a consequence, Ohio went to Nixon.

Wallace cut most deeply into the Democratic party's Southern front. The governor carried Alabama, Georgia, Louisiana, Mississippi, and Arkansas. *Wallace ran second to Nixon* in Tennessee, North Carolina, and South Carolina. The governor scored best in those Southern precincts that favored closing down bars. In the blue-collar suburbs of Richmond, Wallace did well among white voters who opposed welfare and tax levies to support community colleges. Such people felt that welfare benefited the lazy and that their children would never attend college. So why fund higher education? Wallace received nearly half the Southern Baptist vote. Indeed, the governor did best among Baptists and Methodists and scored poorly with Episcopalians and Jews. In a development that foreshadowed the shape of things to come for the Democrats, Wallace strongly appealed to working-class voters under the age of thirty who were not about to follow their parents into the party of liberalism. Worse, just 35 percent of whites voted for Humphrey, compared to 97 percent of blacks.

President-elect Nixon, however, could not rest easy. He faced a badly polarized nation, weary of the Vietnam War and social unrest at home. Nixon had no choice but to continue peace negotiations with Hanoi while shoring up the Saigon government. North Vietnam, however, had little incentive to expedite negotiations since the U.S. government had committed itself to withdrawing its forces without further delay. Worse, now that Lyndon Johnson no longer sat in the White House, larger numbers of congressional Democrats embraced the anti-war cause. They felt little loyalty to Nixon.

First the children of America's governing class had rejected the cold war and conventional morality. Now many of their parents followed their lead. When Nixon identified Ivy League professors, the elite media, and congressional doves as his enemies, he was being indiscreet, not paranoid. Nixon's, and the country's, social divisions were far from over.

In the first six months of 1969 students at 232 campuses engaged in 9,000 separate protests. One of every five campus protests involved bombing, arson, and the destruction of property. Violent off-campus protests took place as well—including the attempted bombing of 27 high schools. Near the Santa Bar-

bara campus of the University of California, students torched a
Bank of America building. According to the campus left, the
Bank of America was a symbol of imperialist finance capitalism. Santa Barbara militants also bombed a university faculty
club, killing a janitor.

On the East Coast, Jane Alpert, a Columbia SDSer, acquired
a measure of notoriety. Born to secular Jewish parents in affluent Forest Hills, New York, Alpert, like Jerry Rubin and other
radicals, had grown up with black servants. While at Swarthmore, she took part in the 1967 Pentagon siege and fell under
the spell of libertarian author Ayn Rand. Although she rejected
Rand's economic theories, Alpert liked her contention that
blowing up buildings was a legitimate method of social protest.
So Alpert initiated the bombing of the Whitehall Induction
Center, the Marine Midland Bank, Chase Manhattan, and five
other government and corporate buildings in New York City.
She did not lack for supporters. Columbia SDS had already
adopted two battle slogans before Alpert began her bombing
spree: "Pick, pick, pick up the gun, the revolution has begun,"
and "Open up a [Viet Cong] front in the United States."

At Penn State, one SDSer from Philadelphia—taking aim at
anti-war religious activists—insisted that political terrorism
was less violent than pacifism:

> What the pacifistic and nonviolent position assumes is that if
> you don't act, you have not committed a violent act. Violence
> is committed every day in our society—in the ghettoes as
> well as in Vietnam. . . . Just because one doesn't pull the trig-
> ger doesn't absolve one of the guilt of compliance. . . .
>
> Therefore, I take the position that an individual is *less* vio-
> lent if he takes part in a violent demonstration either against
> the war in Vietnam or against racism than if he remains apa-
> thetic. For the first person's violent action, while it may have
> hospitalized a few policemen, may have caused his govern-
> ment to cease its war one day sooner, thereby saving twenty
> lives. In this situation, then, the first person through his vio-
> lent actions actually saved several individuals' lives. The sec-

ond person by his apathy was demonstrating compliance with the policies of his government, and thereby participating implicitly in the slaughtering of many people.

The American public, and most college students, had little patience for such intellectual rationalizations of campus violence. In 1969 eight in ten Americans favored a crackdown on student protesters. Americans despised both the Vietnam War and the peace movement. To make matters worse for the New Left and the Democratic doves, though 60 percent of the population now regarded the war as a mistake, just 20 percent wanted an immediate withdrawal. Americans did not like the idea of turning South Vietnam over to the Communists. Nixon knew this and in 1969 tried to rally a "silent majority" of Americans behind his Vietnam policy: "North Vietnam cannot defeat or humiliate the United States," Nixon said. "Only Americans can do that." With one stroke Nixon had associated dovish Democrats more closely in the public mind with SDS.

Even at Berkeley, which had an international reputation as a hotbed of radicalism, in 1969 nearly two-thirds of the students supported the right of ROTC to exist on campus. Nationally, 60 percent of students said they were tired of campus unrest. Just 30 percent of students participated in demonstrations—though their numbers were more than sufficient to plunge a campus into turmoil.

Frustrated in their efforts to expand further, SDSers bickered over ideology and tactics. One faction of SDS, grouped around supporters of the Maoist Progressive Labor party (PL), embraced a two-track program of revolution. On the campus, the PL wanted to continue the tradition of occupying, instead of bombing, buildings. Toward that end, three hundred members of the Harvard SDS-PL faction seized University Hall—the campus administration building—and dared authorities to bring in outside force.

Harvard, wishing to avoid Columbia's 1968 example, moved quickly to bring in city police to clear the building. Seven police officers were injured and 196 SDSers arrested in the ensuing melee. But, as had happened at Columbia, the liberal arts faculty intervened, joining in a campus strike against "police brutality." Ten thousand Harvard students and faculty, shocked that administrators would use even limited force to restore order, participated in the protest.

The second track of the PL's program for revolution looked to building an off-campus constituency of white workers. PL argued that the New Left had failed to win over working-class whites for at least two reasons. First, workers resented student radicals for exempting themselves from a draft that fell hardest on blue-collar males. To correct that problem, PL insisted, students should no longer accept draft deferments. Instead SDSers needed to join the military and subvert the armed forces from within. This was not a popular strategy among college students since most protested the war because they did not care to fight in it. (Once Nixon began withdrawing American troops from Vietnam and created the Selective Service "lottery" in 1969, students with high numbers knew they would never be drafted. Many college students thereafter lost interest in the Vietnam War.)

Second, PL felt that workers hated SDS because of its embrace of the Black Panthers and the counterculture. Therefore SDSers should keep black militants at arm's length and get haircuts, avoid narcotics, and not sleep around. PL did not understand that it was sex and drugs—not Marx and Marcuse—that had drawn many students to radical politics. As Jerry Rubin had noted, Boomer college students wanted excitement, not Maoist lectures on self-denial.

Another faction of SDS (Revolutionary Youth Movement II) followed red diaper baby Mike Klonsky and Berkeley SDSer Bob Avakian. (Avakian's father was a Berkeley judge.) Klonsky detested Progressive Labor's "puritanical Maoism"; Avakian, who wrote for the *Black Panther* newspaper, took his lead from the *Peking Review*. Although they differed on the righteousness of Mao's China, Klonsky and Avakian were both fans of Soviet dictator Joseph Stalin. Neither Klonsky nor Avakian wished to launch a full-scale guerrilla war. They felt that societal disruption short of systematic bombing and assassination would be sufficient to undermine an imperialist, racist America. Avakian went on to found the Maoist Revolutionary Communist party while Klonsky headed up the rival Communist Party Marxist-Leninist. Former SDS national secretary and Penn State activist Carl Davidson joined Avakian's group.

A third faction of SDS, the Weathermen (or Revolutionary Youth Movement I), took its name from the lyrics in the Bob Dylan song "Subterranean Homesick Blues" ("You don't need a weatherman to know which way the wind blows"). One of the Weathermen founders, Jeff Jones, saw the need to create a revolutionary "Leninist party" like the Black Panthers and the Viet Cong. David Gilbert of the Columbia SDS agreed that students had to create "a well-organized, disciplined, combat party" that would engage in guerrilla warfare and completely shatter traditional "bourgeois" mores. Hence the Weathermen would, when not fighting police officers, "smash monogamy" through enforced gay and straight group sex.

Weathermen theorist and Michigan SDSer Jim Mellen considered the United States to be "the fascist center with all the rest of the world" on the road to liberation. Belonging to the Michigan SDS faction loyal to Bill Ayers and Diana Oughton, Mellen dismissed the white working class as greedy and racist. Like Herbert Marcuse and C. Wright Mills, Mellen felt no "obligation to support American white workers who wanted to make fifteen times, instead of twelve times, as much as other workers of the world."

The Weathermen founders proclaimed their goal as "the destruction of U.S. imperialism and the achievement of a classless world; world communism." They also hailed the Black Panthers as "the vanguard force" of revolutionary liberation. National SDS officer Bernardine Dohrn saw the Panthers as authentic revolutionaries. Since 1967 the Panthers had killed 9 police officers and wounded 56 more. The Panthers had lost 10 of their soldiers to "police repression." (In 1969 alone, 348 Panthers had committed murder, armed robbery, rape, and burglary. The Panthers had also taken over vice operations in Oakland, extorting pimps, drug dealers, and shopkeepers to fund their guerrilla operations.)

At the June 1969 SDS convention in Chicago, where the Weathermen officially were born, national council member Mike James threw down the gauntlet. "The time will come when we'll have to use guns," James argued. "Don't let it hang you up. Some of you say violence isn't human. . . . Violence, when directed at the oppressor, is human as well as necessary." Looking askance at the emerging women's liberation movement, which diverted energies from the struggle against racism and imperialism, the Black Panthers' minister of information for Illinois, Rufus "Chaka" Walls, mockingly informed the SDS convention-goers that "We believe in pussy power." When jeered at by the Maoists and those SDSers who had not affiliated with any of the factions, "Chaka" inexplicably retorted, "Superman was a punk because he never tried to fuck Lois Lane."

The several hundred followers of the Weathermen vanguard set out after the 1969 SDS convention to "Bring the War Home." They invaded blue-collar Macomb County Community College in Detroit where they assaulted students and faculty. The young guerrillas also prepared for the 1969 "Days of Rage," which were to coincide with the Chicago Seven Conspiracy Trial. (Rennie Davis, Tom Hayden, Abbie Hoffman, Jerry Rubin, and three other leftists went on trial in October 1969 for their role in the violent protests at the 1968 Democratic National Convention.) They intended to "trash" the city of Chicago.

Before SDS's rematch with the Chicago police, Hayden exhorted the Weathermen to fight American imperialism. Hayden, however, did not participate in the subsequent attack on cars and buildings in Chicago's Gold Coast neighborhood. Although on one level targeting the Gold Coast as a locus of conspicuous capitalism made sense, on another level it seemed Freudian. The Gold Coast was the city's most liberal-to-radical, secular Jewish preserve. Weathermen, at least figuratively and sometimes literally, were trashing their parents' homes.

In the "Second Battle for Chicago," SDSers wounded 75 police officers while 250 of their own number went briefly to jail before posting bail. Most of the Weathermen avoided arrest by fleeing to the campus of Northwestern University, where sympathetic faculty and administrators gave them sanctuary. Weatherwoman Susan Stern, who urged students to become the "Americong," proclaimed the Days of Rage to be a great victory. "We had injured hundreds of pigs," Stern exalted. "Greatest of all, one of Richard Daley's chief counsels [who had thrown himself into the battle] . . . was paralyzed from the waist down." For his part, Jim Mellen had ducked out of the Days of Rage battle to avoid being injured by police.

A month later in November 1969, during the anti-war "New Mobilization" march on Washington, Bill Ayers rallied an army of 3,000 guerrillas. They went around Washington smashing windows and stoning the South Vietnamese embassy and the U.S. Justice Department. One hundred and fifty SDSers were arrested. When anti-war senators Eugene McCarthy and George McGovern attempted to address 250,000 peace activists who had gathered at the Washington Monument, SDSers waved Viet Cong flags and booed the dovish Democrats. As the University of California–Los Angeles chapter of SDS had said of the Democratic doves and their fall peace offensive, "The ruling class [is trying] to take over the anti-war movement and divert it away from the real struggle against the war. . . . Any serious attack on the war in Vietnam must also be an attack on the whole apparatus of imperialism."

(Nixon insisted that he had ignored the November 1969 protest in Washington, but his advisers later admitted that the president realized that any future escalation of the war would inspire America's "vocal minority" to even greater acts of social disruption. Knowing this, however, did not make Nixon more circumspect, as Americans would learn in the spring of 1970.)

At the December 1969 SDS conference in Flint, Michigan, when the Weathermen decided to go underground, Columbia's Mark Rudd enthused, "It's a wonderful feeling to hit a pig. It must be a really wonderful feeling to kill a pig or blow up a building." For her part, Bernardine Dohrn praised the mass murderer Charles Manson: "Dig! First they killed those pigs, then they ate dinner in the same room with them, they even shoved a fork into a victim's stomach. Wild!" Tom Hayden showed up to lead the troops in a few guerrilla aerobics exercises but quickly departed when Dohrn dressed him down for lacking sufficient revolutionary vigor.

Even on the campuses, radical tactics sparked a counterreaction. By 1969 the Young Americans for Freedom claimed 51,000 members at 600 campuses. Taking a leaf from the SDS playbook, collegiate conservatives at the University of Minnesota burned a North Vietnamese flag at an anti-Communist rally. At Washington State University in Pullman, YAF protested the November 1969 New Mobilization against the war by selling 500 red, white, and blue armbands to students to counter the black mourning bands worn by anti-war students. Barely 10 percent of Washington State students expressed opposition to the university's ROTC program; a majority endorsed the presence of military and corporate recruiters on the campus.

Despite its apparent strength and latent student support, the YAF itself suffered internal strife. In 1969 the organization split into competing, irreconcilable factions. Radical libertarians, primarily from California and Pennsylvania, waved placards at the 1969 National YAF convention which read, "Fuck the Draft" and "No More Vietnams." (Tellingly, 22 percent of anti-war student demonstrators in 1969 identified themselves as anarchist-libertarians.)

California YAF activist Ron Kimberling, endorsing the SDS

view of American foreign policy and President Nixon, announced that he rejected "the U.S. imperialist venture in Vietnam, which is being conducted in a manner that seriously undermines freedom for the Vietnamese and for citizens in our own country, who are being subjected to fascism in the name of freedom." Perhaps the greatest moment of radical libertarian street theater took place at the YAF convention when Dave Schumacher of Princeton held his draft card "aloft like the torch of liberty—YAF's official symbol"—and burned it. YAF's more socially conservative members were appalled, as were older figures such as William F. Buckley, Jr.

When one radical libertarian YAF chapter received antiabortion literature from a Catholic group, the student conservatives mailed back used condoms. At the University of Kansas in Lawrence, the libertarian chair of YAF, Gus DiZerega, also led the campus SDS chapter. Libertarians, in addition to opposing the Vietnam draft, endorsed the legalization of prostitution, pornography, and narcotics. No longer willing to abide the right-wing radicals, YAF's moral traditionalists purged the libertarians.

The action at the local or campus level fully reflected the chaos and irrationality that consumed the New Right and the New Left on the national stage. In Madison, black militants invaded the bedroom of Wisconsin chancellor Edwin Young. They demanded minority hiring quotas for faculty and decried academic standards as "racist." The Milwaukee chapter of the Black Panthers joined the subsequent campus protest, disrupting classes and blocking entrance to campus buildings throughout February 1969. Tom Hayden took a break from his Chicago trial to encourage the Wisconsin demonstrators.

Members of the Wisconsin YAF expressed disapproval of the black power protest. One conservative who berated blacks and SDSers for preventing students from attending classes was thrown down a flight of stairs. Initially two thousand students, faculty, and "community people" went on strike. After the administration reluctantly brought in the Wisconsin National

Guard to protect campus property and student bystanders, an additional eight thousand youths and professors enlisted in the strike. In short order the striking black militants received an African-American studies program and faculty hiring quotas, and the university adopted a policy of preferential admission of minority students—with less emphasis placed on academic merit.

By 1969 Madison's Mifflin Street neighborhood had become a "liberated zone" where leftist students and hippies smoked dope and purchased food at co-ops that displayed pictures of Ho Chi Minh in their shop windows. The district elected SDSer Paul Soglin to the city council. Mifflin Street was, in the words of its friends, "an armed camp." When city police officers decided to arrest a young man there for disturbing the peace, a riot ensued. The Madison cops had to duck burning couches that students heaved off the roofs of their porches. All the while, the Madison militants blasted "Street Fighting Man"—the Rolling Stones' anthem of violence—on their stereos.

The Mifflin Street riot marked a new, even more intense period of confrontation at the University of Wisconsin. SDSers stoned the car of former Secretary of State Dean Rusk when he arrived in Madison for a speech to area bankers. Preparing for an October 1969 assault on the campus-based Army Mathematics Research Center, national SDS leader Jeff Jones informed a crowd of several hundred students and faculty, "You don't see no motherfucking students at no motherfucking university. Everybody up here on this stage is a stone Communist revolutionary!" Addressing an audience of fifteen thousand at an October anti-war rally, SDS leader and campus newspaper editor Jim Rowen called on students to take on the "warmakers and their cohorts on this campus." (As Senator George McGovern's son-in-law, Rowen used his government connections to collect congressional reports on the Vietnam War and gain information on military-sponsored university research.)

While one of America's premier public institutions of higher education tore itself apart, a far less prestigious college on the West Coast attracted national notice. San Francisco State's woes began in late 1968 when the administration fired an instructor, who was a Black Panther, for making anti-white statements and urging blacks to bring guns to the campus. Administrators soon found themselves under attack by students and faculty.

At the start of 1969, San Francisco State militants were threatening white faculty who opposed hiring and admissions quotas. Apprised by SDS, the Black Students Union, and the Third World Liberation Front that "We'll get your ass on Monday," John Bunzel, a political science professor and former campaign organizer for Robert Kennedy, became a target of special abuse. Radicals invaded his classroom and screamed obscenities at him. Bunzel also found a homemade bomb in his office. Although he escaped harm, others were not as fortunate. The white student editor of the campus newspaper received a beating when the Black Students Union determined that he did not sufficiently support the revolution. Seeking to intimidate other campus critics, SDSers and the black militants carried guns and made much of their alliance with the Panthers and Stokely Carmichael.

For 134 days San Francisco State radicals, with the support of some faculty, carried on a strike—complete with picket lines and threats against "scabs." University president S. I. Hayakawa took a well-publicized hard line against the strikers, having 450 students arrested at a January 1969 confrontation. Once the media went home, however, the administration, having declared victory, caved in. Administrators established a radical black studies department and agreed to admissions quotas for "Third World Students." (One-third of incoming freshmen had to be "people of color.") University officials also declined to prosecute students and faculty who had run afoul of the law.

During the San Francisco State battle, Berkeley radicals launched a sympathy strike. SDSers and the San Francisco Third World Liberation Front set fire to Berkeley's Wheeler Auditorium and blocked the Sather Gate campus entrance.

Any white student who attempted to enter campus through Sather Gate was beaten by blacks who chanted, "Get your asses out of classes—join the masses."

Inspired by the militancy of the San Francisco State and Berkeley student left, Tom Hayden decided to make the West Coast his base of operations. In 1969 Hayden praised the Bay Area Panthers as "our NLF" and hoped that Berkeley would be the launchpad for a Marxist revolution that would spread to the heartland. Hayden became so caught up in his revolutionary fantasies that he approached interim Panther leader David Hilliard about shooting down a police helicopter. Hilliard was said to have responded, "Just like you, Tom. Get a nigger to pull the trigger."

A handful of black and white activists at rural, conservative Kansas State sought to emulate their West and East Coast counterparts. In December 1968, just as San Francisco State's troubles began, unknown persons firebombed the Nichols Gymnasium. Administrators speculated that the arsonists had mistaken the fortresslike gymnasium for an armory. After the fire, Kansas City, Kansas, native Andy Rollins and New York Black Panther Frank Cleveland, both of whom had enrolled as students thanks to the university's new minority recruitment program, launched their offensive. Rollins denounced his fellow black students as "Uncle Toms" and, hoping to acquire the support of the white SDSers, ridiculed the faculty as "the most bigoted, racist, imperialist minded people; motherfuckers who'd never seen blackness let alone know anything about the Vietnam War." Impressed, the thirty members of the Manhattan, Kansas, chapter of SDS embraced Rollins and Cleveland as their leaders.

From December 1968 into the first months of 1969, Rollins, Cleveland, and the Kansas State SDS goaded campus and local law enforcement officers, chanting, "San Francisco State, here we come!" Attempts were made to set fire to other campus buildings. Rollins confronted a military recruiter at the student union and dramatically took an oath of allegiance to the Marine Corps:

> I swear to kill them dirty gooks in Vietnam cause a gook is a gook is a gook. I swear, swear to kill all them black . . . all them niggers, cause a nigger is a nigger is a nigger. I swear to beat little white kids to death in Chicago who just want peace in Vietnam, cause you know they're crazy. I swear to be a cold-blooded murderer.

After Rollins, Cleveland, and other SDSers interrupted a class and pushed aside the instructor, the faculty and administration took action. The faculty passed a resolution condemning the handful of professors who supported SDS, blaming them for trying to "encourage and precipitate violence and destruction." University president James McCain, who had led the campus since 1950, expelled Rollins and Cleveland. McCain defended his minority recruitment program, insisting that he did not object to having a "ghetto person" at Kansas State. But McCain would not tolerate having anyone "[bringing] the ghetto—or obscenities from the ghetto—on this campus."

Just a few faculty members and students sided with SDS. Tellingly, the Kansas State student newspaper, *The Collegian*, ridiculed the "irrelevant youngsters copying Big Brother [Columbia University] on the East Coast." Unlike the Columbia and San Francisco State militants who could draw upon a vast reservoir of sympathizers, Kansas State's grossly outnumbered radicals had no faculty or community pool of support. The campus left quickly disappeared, with only the gutted Nichols Gymnasium as evidence that the Panthers and SDS had made an appearance in Manhattan, Kansas.

A 1969 survey by the Urban Research Corporation of Chicago showed that protesting black students were twice as likely to get their demands met than were white radicals. And the more violent black student protest became, the more likely a university administration would surrender. Events at Cornell

University in Ithaca, New York, bore out the results of the Urban Research Corporation's study.

Cornell president James Perkins had deliberately recruited black students with significantly lower Scholastic Aptitude Test scores than was the case for whites. To Perkins's astonishment, instead of being grateful for an opportunity to acquire an Ivy League education and avoid the draft, many of Cornell's black students were angry. Blaming "racist" white faculty for giving them failing grades, Cornell's black militants wanted them replaced with sympathetic minority professors. One of the people the students wanted hired to teach black studies was a college dropout and former SNCC activist. They also demanded "black only" classes and living quarters. Black students who began the 1960s demonstrating *against* racial segregation, by the end of the decade were embracing it.

Dramatically, Cornell's black radicals took the chairman of the economics department hostage, seized control of the sociology department, trashed the library, and brandished guns in front of the television cameras. Protest leader Thomas Jones, with gun in hand, warned that Cornell University had "three hours to live." Jones also vowed that "racist" white professors would be "dealt with." In response, the dean of the College of Arts and Sciences admitted that all white professors were "institutional racists" who probably should not be teaching blacks. President Perkins agreed, then praised the student militants for creating "probably one of the most constructive, positive forces that have been set in motion in the history of Cornell."

Disgusted with Perkins and his professorial colleagues, philosophy professor Allan Bloom groused that "A few students discovered that pompous teachers who catechized them about academic freedom could, with a little shove, be made into dancing bears." (Years later Thomas Jones, who became president of the largest private pension fund in the world, joined the Cornell board of trustees. After fleeing Cornell, Bloom wrote a best-selling polemic about the anti-intellectual culture of the post-1960s university, *The Closing of the American Mind*.)

With the national media camped out at Cornell, few reporters took notice of the events transpiring just hours away in Buffalo. As 1969 dawned, black students at SUNY-Buffalo had already assaulted councilman and law-and-order advocate Raymond Lewandowski. When the Buffalo Nine trial began in early 1969, the university's radical draft resisters informed the court that they were "of the working class; our acts were in opposition to the capitalist class because we want an end to capitalist rule and the building of socialism." Although they claimed to be working class, the SUNY-Buffalo defendants had graduated from some of the nation's most elite preparatory and suburban high schools. Judge John Curtin, an Irish Catholic jurist who remembered all too well the hardships of the Great Depression, despised the affluent student radicals. Curtin gave one defendant—who soon fled to Sweden—a three-year prison sentence.

Campus support for the Buffalo Nine fed a mounting wave of protest against ROTC and Project Themis, a military-funded research undertaking at SUNY-Buffalo. (The Navy Department had awarded grants to medical school faculty to explore the physiological problems of constructing underwater submarine bases.) Throughout 1969, bands of as many as seven hundred students sacked ROTC offices and firebombed Themis research facilities. President Martin Meyerson pleaded for reason and warned yet again of a community backlash against the university. The radicals compared Meyerson to Hitler; denounced Buffalo's hostile working-class whites as "fascists," "imperialists," and "racists"; and escalated the violence. Angered, the city's common council demanded Meyerson's resignation.

Council representative Alfreda Slominski was disgusted with SUNY-Buffalo's activists. She could not understand why Meyerson seemed unwilling to punish them for destroying public property. "The police," Slominski stated to the editors of the Canisius College newspaper *The Griffin,* "should have the right to go on campus. I can't understand it. Where else in Buf-

falo can you take over buildings. . . . I can't see a double stan-
dard of laws for college students and citizens."

SUNY-Buffalo students and faculty further outraged
Slominski and her Polish-Catholic constituents by publishing
the *Buffalo Marijuana Review* and a second alternative newspaper, the *Undercurrent*, which carried photographs of homosexuals engaged in anal intercourse. Mounting a vigorous campaign
for mayor in 1969, Slominski won 42 percent of the general vote
and 70 percent of the ethnic Polish vote. Her Democratic oppo-
nent, Frank Sedita, a law-and-order candidate, owed his victory to ethnic Italians and blacks; Italians voted for one of their
own while blacks chose what they perceived to be the lesser of
two evils, given Slominski's claims that the racial integration of
public schools lowered educational standards.

Slominski had expressed the anger felt by many of Buffalo's
citizens and political leaders. Canisius College president James
Demske, a Jesuit priest, signed a petition in October 1969 endorsing Nixon's Vietnam policy and later chided Meyerson for
lowering admissions standards to educate blacks "on a quota
system." Republican councilman William Lyman lashed out
against SUNY-Buffalo students, exclaiming: "Those creeps,
every goddamn one of them, should be put on a boat and taken
back to Russia. They're nothing but a bunch of draft
dodgers. . . . Those kind of people should have no rights."
Other citizens expressed their feelings in hate letters. "Why kid
yourself or any other of the law abiding people about the scum
attending your school?" wrote one citizen to Meyerson. "Only
way to treat the BASTARDS, crack down and throw the scum
out. There isn't any way you can deal with this type but to get
tough."

While SUNY-Buffalo's radicals and an irate citizenry moved
toward all-out war, the Kent State SDS was well on its way to
making history. Wanting to underscore their commitment to
action, Rick Erikson, Howie Emmer, and Terry Robbins organized a 50-member Kent State SDS contingent that went to
Washington in January 1969 to protest Nixon's inauguration.

SDSers threw a bottle at Nixon's car, leading to a rumble with police and the arrest of four Kent State radicals. This was just a prelude to the Kent State SDS Spring Offensive as Emmer directed his attention to the campus ROTC program and the university's various military research contracts. In April 1969, 250 SDSers marched on the administration building where they confronted 700 pro-war students. Fistfights broke out. Kent State president Robert White ordered the arrest and suspension of Emmer and Erikson. He also banned SDS from the campus.

Michigan SDSer Jim Mellen, standing on top of an overturned trash can, rallied Kent State SDS, warning jeering students:

> I know that there are some pigs out there who still think we should occupy Vietnam. And there are some pigs out there who still think they can go into the ghettoes and push people around. Well, what we're telling you is that you can't do it anymore! We are no longer asking you to come and help us make a revolution. We're telling you that the revolution has begun, and the only choice you have to make is which side you're on. And we're also telling you that if you get in the way of that revolution, it's going to run right over you.

Two hundred Kent State SDSers then marched on the Music and Speech Building where Emmer and Erickson's suspension hearings were being held. Their decision to occupy the building and disrupt the hearings, however, was unwise. President White had stationed a large number of Ohio Highway Patrol officers in the basement of the building, preparing to trap and arrest the entire campus SDS chapter. Only the help of a sympathetic faculty member enabled most of the SDSers to find an unguarded escape route out of the building. Although White managed to expel a number of SDSers, he had overplayed his hand. Several hundred normally silent students now rallied to the defense of SDS. An unprecedented number of students had been galvanized into taking part in anti-war and anti-university administration protests. Soon Viet Cong flags could be seen flying from the marijuana-filled Tri-Towers dormitory complex. Pro-war students began to refer to the Tri-Towers as "Hanoi, Ohio."

At the June 1969 national SDS convention, Kent State radicals made their presence felt. The majority of SDSers who followed Bernardine Dohrn and Mark Rudd into the Weathermen were from Michigan and Kent State. Several Kent State SDSers became national Weathermen leaders, including Emmer and Erikson. Although banned from Kent State, the SDS-Weathermen continued to make the city their base of operations. Meanwhile Emmer and Erikson, along with Terry Robbins, established radical communes in Akron, Cleveland, and Columbus. The first national SDS orgy took place in 1969 at the Columbus collective. Bodies were so thick on the floor that the youths rolled over one another. As Terry Robbins said, "People who fuck together, fight together." Another participant—a woman—observed the morning after that, "I'm sure they have to do it this way in Vietnam."

The beginning of 1970 saw no letup in the intensity of campus violence. Nationally, between January 1969 and April 1970, five thousand terrorist bombings occurred in the United States. Most of the bombs were planted by campus-based leftists, spurring the Nixon White House to widen its surveillance and infiltration of the anti-war movement.

In Ann Arbor the Michigan SDS had perfected the hit-and-run trashing of ROTC offices and other campus facilities. Deploying lookouts, Michigan SDSers usually fled the scene before the arrival of the campus or city police. Michigan SDSer Robert Meeropol, who supported his graduate studies with a Ford Foundation grant, proclaimed that nonviolent protest was pointless. The Michigan SDS, Meeropol insisted, had to increase the cost of the Vietnam War to America through violent disruption and the destruction of property.

Over the winter of 1970, Michigan SDSers attempted to drive military recruiters from the campus. Every day SDSers blocked the rooms where recruiters had set up shop and attacked students who came for interviews. To avoid identification, as well as to appear more menacing, the Ann Arbor radicals wore ski masks. During one protest against a General Electric recruiter, SDSers stormed the engineering building. The Michigan SDS fought outraged engineering students and broke down classroom doors to flush out the corporate recruiters. When police officers finally arrived, SDS stood its ground. Meeropol recounted that the Michigan SDS "singled out officers who made an arrest" and beat them.

When a jury convicted the Chicago Seven defendants in February 1970, Meeropol recalled, the Michigan "SDS vowed to make the State pay for a guilty verdict." Five thousand Michigan students and campus hangers-on marched to the Ann Arbor city hall, breaking the windows of downtown businesses and wrecking a police car along the way. A month later the Michigan SDS rallied behind the campus Black Action Movement (BAM) in its "do or die" struggle to lower admissions standards for blacks and establish faculty hiring quotas. BAM and SDS won.

While the Ann Arbor police and the university administration often appeared as if they were trying to avoid getting into the path of the campus demonstrators, there was no mistaking the new order that had arrived in Buffalo. Wearied by militant students and a hostile community, President Meyerson resigned in early 1970. Acting President Peter Regan, with the consent of conservative faculty, alumni, and the community, cracked down on protest. His decision to summon Buffalo police on February 24, 1970, to prevent the disruption of a basketball game angered campus militants. The next night forty students stoned Regan's office. To their surprise, a Buffalo police squad appeared. The students fled into the Norton Union with the police close behind. As the officers dragged youths from the union, eight hundred students attacked. Retreating to the Sixteenth Precinct station house, the police surveyed their eighteen prisoners and allegedly muttered that America "should have let Hitler win, he'd have known how to take care of [Jewish] fuckers."

The next day one thousand SUNY-Buffalo students attacked ROTC offices, demolished Project Themis construction sheds, and set fire to a university police car. Two hundred Buffalo police officers, equipped with riot guns and gas-grenade launchers, arrived on the scene. The crowd, now swollen to fifteen hundred, chanted, "Pigs go home!" before disbanding. For several days, thousands of students marched through the campus and blocked entrances to university buildings.

On the night of March 12, 1970, hundreds of SUNY-Buffalo students engaged in a running battle with the police, screaming, "Ho, Ho, Ho Chi Minh, NLF is Gonna Win!" They also lobbed Molotov cocktails at faculty peace marshals trying to keep students and police apart. Frenzied, policemen clubbed the faculty marshals and pursued students down Main Street, beating press photographers and dragging innocent students from restaurants and stomping them into the pavement. Forty-five faculty, outraged with Peter Regan for bringing police to the campus and wishing to end the violence that ultimately hospitalized 125 and caused $200,000 in property damage, occupied his office. They were promptly arrested—the largest number of American faculty ever jailed at one time.

A week before the Buffalo riot, on March 6, 1970, a Weathermen bomb factory in New York City blew up. The demolished townhouse belonged to Cathy Wilkerson's father—a media magnate who was vacationing in the Caribbean. The leftist terrorists were preparing to plant an anti-personnel bomb at Fort Dix, New Jersey, intending to kill as many enlisted men as possible. Wilkerson and Kathy Boudin—the daughter of Communist party attorney Leonard Boudin—escaped. Michigan SDSer Diana Oughton, Columbia SDSer Ted Gold, and Kent State's Terry Robbins died. *Washington Post* columnist Nicholas von Hoffman—an anti-war Democrat who had little patience with the New Left—wrote that the Weathermen were spoiled children "who grew up accustomed to being obeyed, to having their own way." Such elites, von Hoffman argued, "can afford moral sensibility," for they had "the resources to buy a social conscience."

Just before his death, Terry Robbins had successfully bombed the home of the judge presiding over the New Haven murder trial of twenty-one Black Panthers. Bobby Seale and the "Panther 21" stood accused of killing a black radical whom they incorrectly believed was a police informant. Yale University president Kingman Brewster nonetheless invited the Panthers and SDS to take part in a May Day, 1970, protest rally. Brewster informed the media, "I am skeptical of the ability of black revolutionaries to achieve a fair trial anywhere in the U.S." The Panther trial, Brewster insisted, was "one more inheritance from centuries of racial discrimination and oppression." (In the 1930s Brewster had himself been a student activist. He was a leader of America First, an organization opposed to Franklin Roosevelt's efforts to help Great Britain fight Nazi Germany.)

Brewster's embrace of the Panthers and SDS was no aberration on the Yale campus. The Yale Law School, for instance, provided numerous student volunteers to the Panther 21's defense team, including anti-war activist Hillary Rodham. Radical law students also published the *Yale Review of Law and Social Action*. Its editors and contributors included Rodham and two future members of the Clinton administration, Mickey Kantor and Robert Reich. Amidst its scholarly articles on American imperialism, racism, and fascism, the *Yale Review* contained illustrations of policemen who were depicted as racist pigs. Other illustrations showed bleeding and decapitated pigs who had been defeated by the Panthers and their white student allies. Hillary Rodham's classmate and boyfriend, Bill Clinton, though he made much of organizing an anti-war rally in 1969 while studying at Oxford, put a lot of distance between himself and the *Yale Review*.

Some twenty thousand Panthers and white militants descended on New Haven to take advantage of Brewster's offer of free lodging and food. Jerry Rubin and Abbie Hoffman—still at large pending appeal of their Chicago conspiracy convictions—led students in chanting, "Fuck Kingman Brewster!" and "Fuck Nixon!" Brewster, Rubin and Hoffman charged, by condemning the Panther trial was merely trying to co-opt the left. Tom Hayden—also out on bail—called on the activists to take more revolutionary action. Someone must have been listening, for Yale's hockey rink was soon dynamited. Brewster charged that *right-wingers* were the culprits.

The events transpiring in New Haven from late April to May Day, 1970, were soon overshadowed by other developments. On April 30, 1970, President Nixon announced to a stunned nation that he had authorized American troops to invade Cambodia in order to halt North Vietnamese infiltration into South Vietnam. The Vietnam War, which many students had thought was all but over, now seemed in danger of escalating anew. And this time around, with the creation of the lottery and related reforms in Selective Service, there would be no student deferments. If the Indochinese war expanded into Cambodia, troop calls would rise and even students with high lottery numbers would be caught in the draft.

Enraged students firebombed ROTC buildings at Michigan State and Wisconsin. At Kent State on May 1, five hundred students gathered on the commons to bury the Constitution of the United States, which they felt Nixon had killed. That night, as thousands of students celebrated the first warm spring night of 1970, a fight broke out at a Kent bar. The fight quickly spilled into the streets and turned into a riot after a middle-aged Kent resident tried to run over the student bystanders with his car. A mob of four hundred students and out-of-town revelers then rampaged through downtown Kent, smashing windows. By the early hours of May 2, the mayor of Kent had requested assistance from the Ohio National Guard. Meanwhile city police arrested fourteen students and, with the aid of tear gas, pushed fifteen hundred back to the campus. Weathermen leaders

Howie Emmer and Rick Erikson were spotted among the crowd.

Ohio governor James Rhodes quickly obliged the Kent mayor and even went as far as to visit the city and rally the forces of law and order. For Rhodes, the Kent affair was shaping up as a political windfall. Barred by the state constitution from seeking a third consecutive term as governor, Rhodes had decided to enter the Republican senatorial primary and take on the wealthy and well-known Robert Taft, Jr. As early as December 1969, Rhodes had discovered that bringing the Guard to a restless campus drove up his public approval ratings. When *three* minority students at the University of Akron staged a black power demonstration, Rhodes sent in *seven hundred* Ohio Guardsmen. A tough stand at Kent might just seal a primary victory for Rhodes. If, as some later commentators suspected, the Weathermen viewed Kent State as the perfect tinderbox in which to spark a national white student uprising, Rhodes had played into their hands.

On the night of May 2 rioting again broke out as the campus ROTC building went up in flames and firefighters were assaulted with rocks and had their water hoses cut. Unknown youths beat anyone with a camera who tried to record the scene. Although the fire was finally extinguished, a few individuals later rekindled it. At that point Troop G of the Ohio Guard occupied the campus. Notable Kent State Weathermen fled the area. Nearly the entire black student population of Kent State, worried that the Guard might single out minorities and suspecting that white radicals would not mind seeing a few black "brothers" martyred for the "revolution," had already left Kent. (Black United Students had recently cut off relations with SDS, believing that the white radicals were using them as a "shield." SDSers, Kent's black students thought, wanted "to live their fantasies out. Those cats loved their headlines. They would read the papers to each other about themselves. They wanted to use us to get themselves some big headlines.")

On May 3 several hundred Kent State students staged a sit-in demanding that President White defuse the situation and remove the Guard from the campus. The young Guardsmen, a number of whom had enlisted to avoid combat in Vietnam, were visibly jumpy. With fixed bayonets they charged into the demonstrators, stabbing several and arresting 51. The next day, May 4, the anti-war activists who had remained on campus and in the community proceeded with a peace rally scheduled for 11:30 a.m. at the commons. Events quickly swirled out of control as overwrought students called the troops "motherfucking cocksuckers!" Students also launched rocks, bottles, blocks of wood with nails imbedded in them, and spent tear gas canisters at the Guard. Then it happened: a group of Guardsmen fired 61 rounds into the crowd. Four students were killed and 9 wounded. A teenage girl who had run away from home knelt over the body of a dead student and, arms outstretched, wept. Her anguished face, captured on film for the world to see, brought 4 million students at 1,350 universities into the streets.

The student reaction to the Kent State slayings was quick and violent. In all, 35,000 Guardsmen were called out to 21 universities to quell unrest. Nearly a third of the nation's campuses experienced some form of anti-war protest activity. One hundred and sixty-nine bombs exploded on college campuses. Although Ann Arbor was quiet because the school year had ended before the shootings, several hundred Berkeley students burned cars, broke shop windows, and threw rocks at police officers. California governor Ronald Reagan, having earlier stated that if a "bloodbath" was in the making on his campuses he was ready to let it begin, chose the path of discretion. Reagan closed the University of California and California State systems. In all, 900 universities across the nation shut down until the fall.

In Buffalo the invasion of Cambodia and the Kent State shootings triggered new demonstrations. Councilman Gerald Whalen exclaimed, "The hell with gas, bring out the bullets!" Four hundred Buffalo policemen occupied the SUNY campus and from speeding cruisers fired bird shot into a dozen students. The Erie County grand jury, which had already opened an investigation into campus unrest, subpoenaed the personnel records and transcripts of 91 student and faculty activists. Residents and state legislators cheered the police while community members picketed SUNY-Buffalo, carrying placards that read, "Clean Up UB, Start Here" and "Taxpayers Wake Up!" Meanwhile 433 people, largely from the neighboring working-class towns of Lockport and Niagara Falls, petitioned President Peter Regan to expel the student militants.

Anti-student sentiment did not abate with the end of the school year. Responding to community complaints that SUNY-Buffalo students were flooding blue-collar Catholic wards with drugs, police stormed the Allentown district and gassed hundreds attending a rock concert. Later Erie County sheriff Michael Amico testified before the U.S. Senate Internal Security Subcommittee that SUNY-Buffalo radicals in Allentown were training students and blacks "to kill policemen" and had to be stopped. Amico also informed Canisius College youths that "dirty, filthy, despicable" SUNY-Buffalo students from New York City were responsible for the bulk of drug trafficking in Buffalo.

Following the Kent State shootings, Wisconsin students sought out local merchants whom they suspected of having voted for Nixon and broke their shop windows. The Wisconsin radicals also set fire to garbage and, with faces blackened and armed with two-by-fours, ambushed police officers as they cut through dark alleys. Once again the Mifflin Street district rioted, forcing Madison police officers to dodge flying chairs, couches, and feces.

The *Daily Cardinal,* Wisconsin's student newspaper, weighed in on the spring 1970 riots. James Rowen, an editor, contended that the real terrorists in America were not the students but the U.S. government. Moreover, "Where damage was done in Madison it was against property, not the property of sod walls and thatched roofs housing young women and children. But property that by its existence consolidates and furthers the cause of terror." Rowen repeated his vow "to fight the military on this campus."

Madison's alternative newspaper, the *Kaleidoscope*, which like the *Daily Cardinal* was dominated by SDSers from the East Coast, exhorted students to "Take Up the Gun!" because "No Shittin' That's where it's at now." If the revolution was to succeed, the *Kaleidoscope* concluded, "The community gotta become an armed camp."

At least one Wisconsin student, and a few faithful followers, had taken up the gun months before the Kent State tragedy. Karl Armstrong, a rare working-class youth in the Wisconsin left, had been suspended three times by the university—because of his grades, not for his political activities which included participation in the 1967 Dow recruiting riot. The University of Wisconsin, reluctant to fail a male student and thereby make him eligible for the draft, readmitted Armstrong all three times. Armstrong's only "A" in 1969 came from a course entitled "Social Disintegration."

In December 1969, Karl Armstong and his brother Dwight established the "New Year's Gang." Needing funds to buy explosives, the Armstrongs and a few other Wisconsin students sold drugs. Between December 1969 and August 1970, the New Year's Gang firebombed the campus ROTC offices and the Madison Selective Service headquarters. They even attempted an unsuccessful aerial bombing of a nearby munitions plant.

Since 1969 Wisconsin SDSers had been calling the Army Mathematics Research Center a "real presence of death and killing and genocide in our midst." Picking up on SDS's demand for the closing of Army Math, the New Year's Gang vowed to increase the "level of violence." If the university did not sever its ties to the military, the New Year's Gang informed the campus, "the university physical plant" would be destroyed and Wisconsin shut down. James Rowen and the *Daily Cardinal* endorsed student terrorism, insisting that the Vietnam War justified extreme protest measures. Karl Armstrong credited the *Daily Cardinal* and the *Kaleidoscope* with inspiring his most dramatic bombing.

Fashioning a bomb with 1,700 pounds of ammonium nitrate,

which they set off with fuel oil, in August 1970 the four members of the New Year's Gang hit the Army Math building. Army Math emerged virtually unscathed when the bomb—with the equivalent explosive blast of 3,400 sticks of dynamite—went off. The physics department absorbed much of the blast, resulting in the death of a graduate student and the blinding of a night watchman. Twenty doctoral physics students saw their dissertation research destroyed. The explosion knocked the nearby Old Chemistry Building 8 inches off its foundation. A major cancer research project inside that building was ruined. In all, 26 campus buildings were damaged, costing the university $2.5 million for repairs and requiring 38,000 square feet of plywood to cover broken windows.

The *Kaleidoscope*, edited by an SDSer from New Jersey, applauded the terrorist attack. It argued that the physics student who had been killed deserved to die for having collaborated with the war machine. (In fact, the student had been a critic of the Vietnam War, and his research had no direct value to the military.) The New Year's Gang also received moral support from leftist historian and onetime Madison SDSer Paul Buhle, who reasoned that the death of the physics student was "less than that in any one village in any one day of fighting in Vietnam."

Weighing in on the campus discussion of the bombing, the president of the Wisconsin student body, a New Yorker, warned the national media and state and federal law enforcement agents to keep their distance. Wisconsin students, he said, had stockpiled a thousand guns and were prepared to meet the police and FBI in combat. The Madison left refused to cooperate with the FBI investigation and advised students and faculty to beware of the "pigs." Consequently the New Year's Gang managed to flee—the Armstrongs first going to Minneapolis and then to Canada.

Although many Wisconsin students and faculty rallied behind the New Year's Gang and expressed their loathing of the Ohio National Guard, the general public was of a decidedly

different state of mind. Eighty-two percent of Americans condemned the spring student strikes. Among youths in their
twenties, nearly three-quarters expressed opposition to the
strikes. Overall the majority of citizens—the World War II
generation, the "Silent Generation," *and the Boomers*—endorsed the May 4 actions of the Ohio National Guard.
(Working-class Boomers and business and engineering majors
were the most supportive of the Ohio Guard; middle- and
upper-middle-class liberal arts students tended to be the most
critical.)

In Ohio, Governor Rhodes's popularity soared. Before the
shootings, Rhodes had trailed Robert Taft in the senatorial primary by several percentage points. The Kent State slayings
helped Rhodes close the gap and nearly brought him the senatorial nomination. Political analysts concluded that if the Republican primary had taken place just a few days later, giving
Ohio residents more time to reflect on the Kent State tragedy,
Rhodes would have won in a landslide.

After the Kent State affair, and in the wake of the Wisconsin
bombing, campus-based protest—which had been on an upward arc since 1965—tapered off dramatically. Even the most
radical members of the student and faculty left realized that the
public temper would now support a wholesale crackdown on
disruptive campus protest. Additionally, most of the 4 million
students who went on strike in May 1970 against the invasion of
Cambodia and the Kent State incident had little reason to continue protesting. The Democratic Congress had cut off funds to
Nixon's Cambodian operation. There would be no danger of a
new escalation of the war and thus no fear that draft calls
would rise. Nixon, facing a hostile Congress and a weary public
that wanted to put the war and the peace movement into "the
dustbin of history," had to keep bringing U.S. troops home. By
1971 the president had reduced the number of American soldiers in Vietnam from 324,000 to 156,000. At the end of 1972
that figure fell to 24,000. The campus anti-war movement had
ended with both a bang and a whimper.

7

Counterculture

IN THE SUMMER of 1969, 400,000 youths gathered at Woodstock, New York. While Boomers tripped on acid and rolled naked in the mud, The Who, Janis Joplin, and Jimi Hendrix performed. "Purple Haze," the title of one of Hendrix's most popular songs, was also the name of a potent brand of LSD. After Woodstock, both Hendrix and Joplin died of drug overdoses. Other rockers soon followed.

LSD, the drug of choice for Boomer youths who enjoyed seeing the world through vibrant day-glo lenses, owed its prominence to two pioneers: Timothy Leary and Augustus Owsley Stanley III. In 1961 Harvard University fired clinical psychologist Timothy Leary for testing LSD on students. Convinced that LSD could "open the doors of perception," Leary became an Apostle of Acid. (Beyond assisting in one's self-discovery, Leary claimed that LSD could enable men and women to sustain hundreds of intense, satisfying orgasms.) Leary acquired thousands of young acolytes who would do anything for him— including breaking him out of jail. He later repaid his SDS liberators by cooperating with the FBI in its efforts to capture them.

In 1965 Augustus Owsley Stanley III, a Berkeley student and grandson of a U.S. senator, opened the nation's first LSD factory. (Stanley went by the name "Owsley" since it seemed more "far out" than Stanley.) With $20,000 in start-up capital drawn from his trust fund, "the Henry Ford of LSD" manufactured 4 million acid tablets which he sold for $2 apiece. One-quarter of his initial LSD batch went to just 10,000 San Francisco youths. Thanks to the fact that state and federal penal codes had nothing to say about the legality of LSD production and consumption, Owsley spent his first year in business unmolested by the police. (The U.S. Congress and the California legislature outlawed LSD only in 1966.)

Owsley soon established a national distribution network for his product. He also underwrote a Bay Area rock-and-roll group that sought to propagate the gospel of acid—The Grateful Dead. By the mid-1960s Owsley had become a renowned figure in the West Coast youth scene. A second rock-and-roll band that he helped along the way—The Jefferson Airplane—nicknamed him "White Rabbit." (The Jefferson Airplane's 1967 hit song "White Rabbit" was an acid-inspired retelling of *Alice in Wonderland*.)

The Haight-Ashbury neighborhood of San Francisco—where Owsley's most loyal customers lived—became, in the words of its sympathizers, "a small psychedelic city-state." Rock and roll entrepreneur Bill Graham wasted no time tapping into the musical and drug subculture. Both of Graham's San Francisco auditoriums, the Fillmore and the Winterland, were regular performance venues for The Jefferson Airplane and Big Brother and the Holding Company. The Fillmore and the Winterland generated $35,000 in ticket sales weekly (or the equivalent of $140,000 in 2000). To help youths get into the proper frame of mind, the dance halls provided free apples laced with LSD.

Haight-Ashbury—"Hashbury" to its denizens—entered the nation's consciousness in June 1967 as a result of the Monterey Pop Festival. The Jefferson Airplane, Big Brother and the Holding Company, and The Grateful Dead, among other Monterey Pop participants, popularized a new style of "psychedelic music." Grace Slick and Janis Joplin seemed to be defining an exciting, liberating lifestyle. Attracted to nearly perfect year-round weather, an abundance of narcotics, a vibrant music scene, and the prospect of frequent sex, 75,000 youths descended on San Francisco during the "Summer of Love." Many hung out in the I/Thou Coffeehouse where they dropped acid, held hands, and tried, as one participant explained, "to absorb vibrations from a flower."

Begging for food and spending their tuition money on drugs, the 1960s "hippies" came into the world. (The term "hippie" evolved from "hipster," which in turn had been urban black slang for someone who lived free of moral constraints.) The hippie movement soon made its way east. In 1967 Ohio State students claimed to be the first youths in the Midwest to stage LSD group-sex parties. In Baltimore, Johns Hopkins University dropouts tried to replicate San Francisco's "hip scene." Underground newspaper reporter P. J. O'Rourke, however, later observed that "A bunch of young people who stayed high all day and weren't working didn't make a huge impression on a city full of unemployed drunks."

If the cause of hipness had far to go in Baltimore, the seemingly unlikely locale of Lawrence, Kansas, could have given San Francisco a few lessons. Home of the University of Kansas, Lawrence had three factors that combined in the 1960s to transform it into a countercultural mecca of the heartland. First there was abundant farmland which proved ideal for the production of low-grade marijuana ("ditchweed"). Second, Lawrence was strategically located along major highways, which permitted distribution of its marijuana crop along all points of the compass. And third, university officials tended to be anti-war, sympathetic to the black power movement, and contemptuous of the conservative rural politicians who condemned student protest and the counterculture.

By the late 1960s Lawrence had more hippie dropouts (thirteen thousand) than students (ten thousand). The city's hippies, however, were not the gentle flower children of media and academic fame. Lawrence's "young punks," as appalled residents called them, vigorously guarded their marijuana fields from law enforcement officers. Kansas hippies, who formed an alliance with campus SDS and local black militants, engaged in numerous attacks against city officials and policemen. They firebombed the home of the county district attorney, threw acid into the home of a county district judge, and made false-alarm calls to firefighters and police. When police and firemen responded to a false alarm, hippies and their allies ambushed them with shotgun and rifle fire. When pursued, the hippies led police officers into dark alleys where they had strung neck-high piano wire. The youths would then find sanctuary on the campus.

Lawrence was in the forefront of a burgeoning counterculture. Nationally by the end of 1967, an estimated 300,000 men and women had adopted the hippie lifestyle. (That figure rose to what was believed to be 3 million by the early 1970s.) In 1969 one-third of students surveyed at 57 campuses had used marijuana. At the elite universities of Michigan and Harvard, the proportion of students who had smoked marijuana was 44 percent and 48 percent, respectively.

Where in the early 1960s just 4 percent of youths eighteen to twenty-five years of age had smoked pot, by 1972 half had done so. Sixty percent of college students were pot smokers. Interestingly, students sometimes expressed more support for the legalization of narcotics than for the peace movement. At UCLA in 1967 a majority of students voted to support the decriminalization of marijuana. Only a minority called for the United States to withdraw from Vietnam and demand that the university ban military contractors from recruiting on the campus.

Marijuana usage—and narcotics consumption overall—steadily filtered down from the upper middle class to the white working class. By 1972 one-quarter of blue-collar youths in Massachusetts had used pot. As subsequent social commentators noted, "Middle-class youths had their 'Sixties' in the Sixties, and working-class youths had their 'Sixties' in the Seventies." 1960s-era rock music, which had not yet fragmented along class lines, helped spread the urban underclass and middle-class drug culture to working-class white youths.

In South Vietnam, where a daily heroin habit could be sustained for $2, compared to $200 in the United States, drug addiction among American soldiers mounted. In 1971, 22 percent of all Vietnam veterans had become addicted to heroin. Seventy percent of such addicts were working-class whites. Paradoxically, by the end of the 1960s the military had also become a conduit for spreading the drug culture into America's blue-collar communities. (Students at one humble college campus—Kansas State—received their drugs from members of the Big Red One infantry division stationed at nearby Fort Riley.)

Although college students in the Midwest and the East tried to surpass the example set by their Berkeley mentors, San Francisco remained, as an admirer wrote, "the Rome of a future world founded on love ... the love-guerrilla training school for drop-outs from mainstream America ... where the new world, a human world of the 21st century is being constructed." Only in San Francisco would a couple entering into matrimony have a wedding cake with the slogan "Smash Monogamy!" inscribed on it. (The new couple had their wedding rings manufactured in North Vietnam from the remnants of an American military plane.)

All but a handful of the 75,000 youths who made Haight-Ashbury their home in 1968 came from prosperous Jewish and WASP families. Yet while San Francisco's hippies copied the lifestyle and drug habits of the urban underclass, they avoided the neighboring black ghetto. According to the frightened hippies, "Spades are programmed for hate." A few hippies regretted this state of affairs, noting that "The spades ... are our spiritual fathers.... They gave us jazz & grass and rock & roll.... If it weren't for the spades, we would all have short hair, neat suits, glazed eyes, steady jobs & gastric ulcers." (The most sinister person living among the hippies, however, was white—future mass murderer Charles Manson. It said much about the culture of Haight-Ashbury that a violent maniac could establish a sex and drug cult and then go virtually unnoticed.)

Wanting to create an alternative newspaper for the San Francisco hippie community in 1967, rock promoter Bill Graham, along with a few drug dealers, helped establish the *Oracle*. One underground reporter succinctly described the *Oracle*'s media function as offering "dope news for dopers." This was not shocking to anyone who read typical *Oracle* fare such as this: "Now in this twentieth of recent centuries a generation, considered by many to be the reincarnation of the American Indian, has been born out of the ashes of World War Two, rising like a Phoenix, in celebration of the slightly psychedelic zeitgeist of this brand-new Aquarian Age." (The editors of the *Berkeley Barb* expressed similar sentiments a little differently: "We defy law and order with our bricks bottles garbage long hair filth obscenity drugs games guns bikes fire fun & fucking—the future of our struggle is the future of crime in the streets.")

Most participants in the 1960s drug scene offered enthusiastic testimony to the benefits of psychedelics. One denizen of "Hashbury"—who later became a Boston bank executive—recalled that drugs made him more aware of his total being: "You got stoned and there were parts of your body that you never knew existed, that you could suddenly concentrate on for hours. You could listen to yourself breathe for an hour, and it was a major event." Another young celebrant of the counterculture, a future artist, believed that narcotics had launched him on his voyage of self-discovery:

> In high school, I was asleep. My intuition was lying dormant, I was living the life that was prescribed for me, externally. With LSD, I had a revelation that there was a whole lot more to who I was than that. My drug experiences taught me what my intuition was. Now my life is guided by my intuition.

The libertarian members of the Young Americans for Freedom were no less effusive about acid and the counterculture.
Sharon Presley, a former Berkeley YAF activist, disdained
"stuffy" conservatives and praised long-haired youths who
were "just being what they wanted to be." Another YAF member and rock fan identified with the counterculture's "free-
spirit philosophy." Rod Manis, the onetime chairman of the
California YAF, argued that "If man is going to be able to enjoy,
even just cope with the fantastically complex society and the
world of the future, he will have to have the help of mind-
expanding drugs." One California YAF leader later recalled
that he preferred LSD to the repressive administrations of Lyndon Johnson and Richard Nixon:

> The whole drug thing really impressed me and gave me lit-
> erally a new way of thinking. And it changed the rules: sud-
> denly I was an enemy of the state. I was doing something
> illegal, and the government could come down and bite my
> ass. I didn't like having to be put in that position for doing
> something I thought was absolutely none of their business
> and was exercising my personal freedom.

Social conservatives in YAF were not impressed with Presley
and Manis. Mary Fisk, an editor of the national YAF newspaper, *New Guard*, explained her distaste for the counterculture in
traditional moral terms: "It goes back to the Catholic foundation of folk beliefs that these people were not living up to being
the best a human being could be. They were typically gratifying
whatever whim or desire or need they had." For her part,
Michigan YAFer Emmy Lewis bemoaned sexually suggestive,
drug-laced rock-and-roll music that "reduces Man to being an
animal. . . . [Countercultural advocates] don't recognize or see
or want to elevate man to his higher natural state."

Lewis and Fisk would have been shocked to learn that at
least one underground newspaper cartoonist had no more en-
thusiasm than they did for the Boomer counterculture. Robert
Crumb, who created the hedonistic feline "Fritz the Cat," al-

lowed that San Francisco in the summer of 1967 was "much more open than any other place."

> But the air was so thick with bullshit you could cut it with a knife. Guys were running around saying, "I'm you and you are me and everything is beautiful, so get down and suck my dick." These young, middle-class kids were just too dumb about it. It was just too silly. It had to be killed. You'd see them skipping through the park with their bamboo flutes and their robes, calling themselves things like Gingerbread Prince. And they had an irritating, smug, superior attitude. If you didn't have long hair, if you didn't have a bamboo flute, they just ignored your existence.

A more sympathetic observer of the counterculture was underground newspaper cartoonist Gilbert Shelton. A former University of Texas student, Shelton was probably read by more rank-and-file student activists than C. Wright Mills, Herbert Marcuse, and Paul Goodman combined. First syndicated by the *Los Angeles Free Press*, Shelton's "Fabulous Furry Freak Brothers" chronicled the adventures of three dope addicts who avoided work, hung out on the fringes of college campuses, collected government welfare checks, and consumed vast quantities of drugs. Their motto said it all: "It is better to live in times of dope and no money, than in times of money and no dope." The Freak Brothers often did battle with the evil, hypocritical "Governor Richpigg" (presumably California chief executive Ronald Reagan) and the banal, sinister "President Nignew" (an amalgam of Richard Nixon and Vice President Spiro Agnew).

The hippies did not lack for support among intellectuals who would not have seen themselves as keeping company with the Freak Brothers. In 1967 Robert McAfee Brown of the Stanford religion department praised the hippies for being "a good deal closer to the early Christian movement than the churches." What Brown, a leader of Clergy and Laymen Concerned About Vietnam, did not note, however, was that if the hippies were reminiscent of the original Apostles, their religious beliefs were Zen Buddhist, Hare Krishna, and Wiccan—not Christian.

A number of New Leftists explicitly linked the counterculture, and particularly drugs, to revolutionary politics. Michael Lerner, a Berkeley SDSer, told David Horowitz, "You *have* to take LSD. Until you've dropped acid, you don't know what socialism is." (Lerner, with funding from his heiress wife, later published the left-leaning magazine *Tikkun*, which featured articles by other SDSers-turned-academics. In Hebrew, *Tikkun* means "to heal and repair the world.")

In 1969 Jerry Rubin argued that "Pot is central to the revolution. It weakens social conditions and helps create a whole new state of mind." Better yet, Rubin asserted, "Marijuana makes each person God." On a similar note, the SDS publication *New Left Notes* insisted, "The only thing that mattered was what you were doing for the revolution. That's why dope was good. Anything that undermined the system contributed to the revolution and was therefore good."

Rubin's partner, Abbie Hoffman, declared during his Chicago conspiracy trial, "I want to be tried not because I support the National Liberation Front—which I do—but because I have long hair. Nor because I support the Black Liberation Movement, but because I smoke dope."

Panther leader Eldridge Cleaver similarly associated political rebellion with drug consumption and the counterculture. "The characteristics of the white rebels which must alarm their elders—," Cleaver wrote, "the long hair, the new dances, their love for Negro music, their use of marijuana, their mystical attitudes toward sex—are all tools of their rebellion."

Other activists, seeking inner peace and insight, praised the beneficial nature of narcotics. As a writer for Atlanta's underground newspaper, the *Great Speckled Bird,* contended: "DOPE turns you on, heightens sensory awareness, sometimes twists them out of shape and you experience that too, gives you vision and clarity, necessary to create life from death." By the end of the 1960s former SDS president Carl Oglesby found contentment after abandoning protest politics in favor of full-time drug consumption. "There were a lot of good, righteous people showing up in places like Vermont and New Hampshire in those days. Lots of parties, great reefer, good acid."

Oglesby's example appealed to more youths than Rubin's efforts to wed the counterculture with social activism. Most dope-smoking youths who jammed to the tunes of Grace Slick, Janis Joplin, and Jerry Garcia wanted to "tune in and drop out," not take over campus buildings. Even though The Jefferson Airplane gave money to Weathermen fugitives Jeff Jones and Bernardine Dohrn, the vast majority of rock singers wanted nothing to do with radical politics. When Abbie Hoffman, at Woodstock, attempted to make a political announcement, Pete Townshend of The Who hit him with his guitar and then drove the activist from the stage. Janis Joplin spoke for a legion of hippies when she said, "My music isn't supposed to make you riot. It's supposed to make you fuck."

(Joplin had a better sense of the nature and history of rock-and-roll than Abbie Hoffman and Jerry Rubin. The term rock-and-roll derived from Southern black slang for sex; such 1950s-era songs as "Shake, Rattle, and Roll," "Rock Around the Clock," and "Sixty Minute Man" were explicitly about intercourse. In order to break into the middle-class white market, the major record companies toned down the lyrics and employed safe white singers to "cover" the rock songs. It was no accident that Baptist ministers Martin Luther King, Jr., and Billy Graham in the 1950s jointly crusaded against what they regarded as the sinful music of an immoral underclass. Although rock-and-roll lost much of its sexual edge when performed by Pat Boone in the 1950s, young British performers like John Lennon and Mick Jagger rediscovered the roots of their favorite music and brought it back to America fully restored. In the 1990s Harvard professor Harvey Mansfield was quite correct in contending that "Rock is sex on parade.")

Sex, like LSD and rock, played a central role in 1960s counterculture and politics. As John Sinclair, the radical leader of the Ann Arbor–based White Panthers, asserted, "There are three essential human activities of the greatest importance to all persons, and that people are . . . healthy in proportion to their involvement in these activities: rock and roll, dope, and fucking in the streets. . . . We suggest the three in combination, all the time." The White Panthers' 1968 manifesto, besides reviling American imperialism and racism, exhorted youths to "Fuck your woman so hard . . . she can't stand up."

In 1965, the same year that Lyndon Johnson sent combat troops to South Vietnam, Jefferson Fuck Poland, a veteran peace and Berkeley Free Speech Movement activist, established the Sexual Freedom League. (Poland had legally changed his middle name to Fuck.) The Sexual Freedom League organized orgies and advocated the legalization of gay sex, pornography, and pedophilia.

Anti-war activist and literary figure Paul Goodman continued to raise his voice on behalf of sexual liberation, contending in 1969 that homosexual promiscuity represented—to paraphrase an SDS slogan—"democracy in the sheets [streets]":

> Queer life . . . can be profoundly democratizing, throwing together every class and group more than heterosexuality does. . . . I myself have cruised rich, poor, middle class, and petit bourgeois; black, white, yellow, and brown; scholars, jocks and dropouts; farmers, seamen, railroad men, heavy industry, light manufacturing, communications, business and finance, civilians, soldiers, and sailors, and once or twice cops. There is a kind of political meaning, I guess, in the fact that there are so many types of attractive human beings.

In contrast to Goodman and Poland, Betty Friedan was more reserved. Her 1963 book, *The Feminine Mystique*, represented an opening shot on behalf of women's liberation and the sexual revolution. *The Feminine Mystique*, which sold one million copies, denounced the "sexual counterrevolution" of the 1950s when legions of middle-class women had chosen to raise a family rather than pursue a career. Calling the lot of the suburban housewife "domestic drudgery," Friedan wanted a fundamental alteration in the economic, sexual, and social relations between men and women. Although she presented herself as a typical, hitherto apolitical suburban housewife, she was less than candid. She had worked as a writer for the Communist-led United Electrical Workers Union. As far as being an ordinary housewife, she was a graduate of Smith College, lived in a mansion, and had a black woman servant.

Friedan, who would go on to help found the National Organization for Women (NOW), could not have timed the publication of her book any better. Millions of young middle-class women who before World War II would have not gone to college and then pursued a career outside the home, were enrolling in the universities. By the late 1960s 40 percent of college students and 10 percent of the faculty were female. The overall proportion of women in the workforce steadily rose, from 38 percent in 1960 to 50 percent by 1980. In the long term, the American economy—and higher education itself—would benefit enormously from the influx of bright youths from a previously untapped pool. But some male authority figures in the university and the business world were not prepared to regard women as equals. At Northwestern University, for instance, one anti-war historian derided female graduate students and accused them of taking the place of males who needed to avoid military service in Vietnam.

Although gender equality formed the core of early feminist thought, most youths—female and male—tended to concentrate on sexual liberation. Rox Baxandall, a red diaper baby and radical graduate history student at Wisconsin in the late 1950s, stood in the forefront of the free sex movement. To Baxandall, sex outside marriage was heroic. "Most women [in the 1950s] pretended to be virgins," Baxandall recounted, "but to me, admitting you fucked was a red badge of courage."

The downside of sexual liberation did not get much media and academic attention in the 1960s. As literary critic Diana Trilling astutely observed, the people who had the most to lose from the arrival of the sexual revolution were women. If the logic of 1960s lifestyle liberation demanded equality between the sexes, women could not complain about men who used them for sex and then discarded them. And if the birth-control pill failed, women, not men, would have to get an illegal abortion or face raising a child by themselves. The late historian Christopher Lasch put it best in his classic 1978 book, *The Culture of Narcissism*, when he wrote that "Sex valued purely for its own sake loses all reference to the future and brings no hope of permanent relationships. Sexual liaisons, including marriage, can be terminated at pleasure."

Sexual liberation had the potential to oppress, or at least dehumanize, women. One woman radical in 1969 complained that "The free sexual revolution has only served to oppress women and especially radical women. If she doesn't want to sleep with men, a woman is 'hung up.' If she does, she's known as someone's wife or girl friend," or, paradoxically, as sexually promiscuous. "The reverse, of course," for men, "is not true."

There were plenty of examples of ways in which leftists treated women as impersonal objects. Ed Sanders, the publisher of the pornographic journal *Fuck You: A Magazine of the Arts,* as well as the leader of a rock group, The Fugs, boasted that he played "horny cunt-hunger blues." At a 1969 anti-Nixon protest in Washington, male radicals repeatedly interrupted Marilyn Webb, a feminist speaker, shouting, "Take her off the stage and fuck her!" Afterward a female SDSer called Webb and warned her that if she ever brought up sexism in the New Left again, "we're going to beat the shit out of you wherever you are."

At Washington University in St. Louis, one campus radical admitted that politics took a backseat to more important concerns. "The class struggle turned into the ass struggle," he said of a typical meeting, "when men tried to figure out how they were going to get laid." SDS leader Bill Ayers bragged that in just three months in 1969 he had sex with one hundred women. Taking no time to learn their names, Ayers grabbed the young women he met at campus SDS meetings and gratified himself in the back of his Chevy van. While organizing the Columbia uprising in 1968, SDS leader Mark Rudd often demanded that someone "get me a chick to do some typing."

Defenders of the New Left emphasized that Ayers and Rudd embodied the SDS spirit of the *late* 1960s. In fact, they represented no dramatic departure from the sexual attitudes of the early 1960s New Left. As one SDS leader in 1962 candidly observed, "The movement hangs together on the head of a penis." Cathy Wilkerson of the Swarthmore SDS claimed that the only way to succeed as a woman in the New Left was by having sex with male radicals whenever they demanded it.

Barbara Haber, the wife of SDS's first president, recalled that "There were a few dozen men who stood out as incarnations of the Revolution, so that to sleep with them was the equivalent of taking political communion." She also observed that male SDSers, including her husband Al Haber, did not treat her as an equal:

> I was brought up to think I was special, to think that I was smart, and to think that I was going to accomplish something. In graduate school . . . I was a good student, had a fellowship, and was treated by my professors as someone with promise. But in SDS I couldn't get no respect. I was constantly being diminished and I often felt all confused and crazy.

The predatory impulses of male leftists became so acute by 1965 that Mary King and Casey Hayden—who was briefly married to Tom Hayden—issued a manifesto, "Sex and Caste: A Kind of Memo." King and Hayden, both of whom had worked long and hard for the Student Nonviolent Coordinating Committee, wondered, "Why is it in SNCC that women who are competent, qualified, and experienced are automatically assigned to the 'female' kinds of jobs such as: typing, desk work, telephone work, filing, library work, cooking . . . but rarely the 'executive'?" Their critique of sexism fell upon deaf ears, though Stokely Carmichael gave them an answer of sorts when he said that the rightful "position of women in SNCC is prone!"

A few female SDSers at Kent State and Penn State mounted ineffectual opposition to New Left sexism. Kent State SDS leader Rick Erickson, for instance, dismissed feminism as an insignificant "pots and pans revolution" when compared to the heroic anti-imperialist struggle of the Viet Cong and the Black Panthers.

At Penn State, SDSers financed the publication of their underground newspaper, the *Water Tunnel*, with advertising from the pornography industry. (Penn State's first alternative newspaper took its name from a navy-sponsored research facility on the campus—the Garfield Thomas Water Tunnel.) The *Water Tunnel* also carried notices from students seeking threesomes, S & M (sadomasochism), and gay sex. This was by no means a unique development. Of the three hundred countercultural newspapers published in the United States in 1969, most kept afloat with support from pornographers who profited from the exploitation of women. At least one underground publication proudly identified itself as "the newspaper you can read with one hand."

Some women radicals tried to turn the tables on male leftists. SDS leader Bernardine Dohrn did not hesitate to engage in sexual intercourse to advance a personal agenda. As SDSer Jim Mellen said of Dohrn, "She used sex to explore and cement political alliances. Sex for her was a form of ideological activity." Dohrn was the only female member of the Weather Underground who exempted herself from the organization's mandatory orgies.

(Dohrn was exceptional. More common were women radicals like Susan Stern. After painting a portrait on her house walls of "an eight-foot-tall nude woman with flowing green blond hair and a burning American flag coming out of her cunt!", Stern admitted that she "painted what I wanted to be somewhere deep in my mind; tall and blond, nude and armed, consuming—or discharging—a burning America.")

In 1969, at an Ann Arbor conference of the Underground Press Syndicate (UPS), feminists exhorted the alternative press to stop running pornographic advertisements and to hire more women reporters. Radical feminism, however, could go too far in its crusade against "male chauvinism" in the New Left. A woman reporter at New York's *Rat*, who had accused a former male colleague of being a "sexist pig," found herself attacked on the grounds that she was insufficiently militant. In 1969 one-time SDS organizer and *Rat* editor Jeff Shero had to agree with a mainstream writer who told him, "I used to envy your freedom. Now I have more freedom than you. You can't offend blacks, women, hippies, anyone except upper-middle-class white men."

Although members of the New Left constituted just a fraction of the Boomer cohort, their lifestyle values—if not their politics—were having an impact on great numbers of youths. By 1969 opinion polls showed that one-third of Boomers rejected marriage and the idea of having children. Fully 40 percent of youths felt that the United States was a "sick society," dedicated to the obsolete values of monogamy, self-sacrifice, and patriotism. Radical folk singer Joan Baez was not alone in calling the national anthem "just so much trash." One married SDS couple who had a child in 1968 earned the scorn of their comrades. "They thought that [the baby] was going to enslave Karen, that I had done this to her," the husband recalled. "That even getting married, having the state sanctify your relationship, was counterrevolutionary."

While President Richard Nixon appealed to his "silent majority" of law-abiding Americans to rally behind traditional moral values, Hollywood, Broadway, Madison Avenue, and the three television networks wasted no time in cashing in on the cultural revolution. The pursuit of the Boomer youth market had preceded the rise of the 1960s counterculture. In the early

1950s the ABC television network had faced imminent bankruptcy. Then, along came the "Mickey Mouse Club," which generated millions in advertising revenues and made ABC commercially viable. ABC's financial resurrection anticipated a future in which more programming would be designed for young Boomer viewers with money to burn.

In the 1960s the Boomer market grew even larger. Having little use for the World War II generation's harsh Aqua Shave–style odors, Boomer *males* spent $500 million annually on fragrant scents and beauty aids. Boomers also transformed the recording industry. In 1964 Columbia Records, a division of CBS, did 15 percent of its business in rock. By 1969 that proportion rose to 60 percent.

Marketers knew that Boomers—the most media- and advertising-saturated generation in American history—would buy any slickly packaged product. First there were Micky Mouse ears and Davy Crockett coonskin hats—just like actor Fess Parker wore in the Disney films—to purchase. Then, when the Boomers arrived in their later teens and began to date, came anti-pimple creams. Entering college, the Boomers swayed to the reefer-drenched, sexually charged airs of Gary "U.S." Bonds and Mick Jagger. Was there any reason why the counterculture could not also be marketed?

For Hollywood studios, which had spent the 1950s watching their patrons abandon movie theaters to take up residence in front of living room television sets, jumping on board the youth culture bandwagon required little soul searching. Half the audience for films in the 1960s was under twenty-four years of age; three-quarters of moviegoers were under forty. The World War II generation tended to watch television. As ticket prices increased, fewer working-class families went to movies; college students and recent university graduates soon became the most regular moviegoers. Culturally sophisticated Boomers demanded sex- and violence-driven film plots.

The 1968 film *Bonnie and Clyde*, a Warren Beatty and Faye Dunaway vehicle that exalted the spirit of lawlessness and featured stylized violence and attractive villains, reaped respectable profits and earned ten Academy Award nominations. In 1969 the inexpensively produced film *Easy Rider* celebrated drugs and sex—and made a great deal of money for actor Peter Fonda. (Peter was the brother of Hollywood activist Jane Fonda.) At the end of the 1960s Disney stood nearly alone in making films suitable for parents who did not want their children seeing blood, dope smoking, and sexual intercourse on the screen.

On Broadway the 1968 theatrical production *Hair*, which billed itself as the "first tribal-love-rock musical," featured nudity, calls for draft resistance, and acid communions. In 1969 *Che* celebrated the life and politics of the Argentinean Communist revolutionary, Che Guevara. *Che*'s cast of characters included a naked Catholic nun as well as a revolutionary who made Marxist political points while waving his penis for emphasis.

Seeking a way to bring a toned-down version of the counterculture to curious middle-class adolescents, NBC in 1966 launched "The Monkees." "The Monkees" imitated the antics of the Beatles' 1965 movie *A Hard Day's Night*. Richard Lester, the film artist behind *A Hard Day's Night*, had interspersed his movie with Beatles' music, stimulating their record sales. NBC's plan was no less ambitious. On its Colgems label, NBC's recording company had captured little of the teen market. To rectify that, NBC brought in Don Kirshner, who had worked with such saccharine performers as Bobby Darin and Neil Sedaka. Kirshner wrote The Monkees' songs and hired the actors to portray the fictitious band members. Although Kirshner chose the actors for their photogenic, as opposed to musical, attributes, "The Monkees" became a popular series from 1966 to 1968, and their songs sold well on the Colgems label.

Emboldened by his success with "The Monkees," Kirshner in 1968 created another rock group, this time in cartoon form, "The Archies." Based on the comic book adventures of several teenagers, "The Archies" became a musical force, with chart-

topping singles and a cardboard-and-wax-coated record available on the back of selected cereal boxes. They could be played a
few times before wearing out, requiring another trip to the
store. "The Archies" inspired other cartoon rockers, notably the
leggy, leopard-skin clad "Josie and the Pussycats." (Before *Play-
boy* became more readily available to adolescent boys in the
1970s, "Josie and the Pussycats" was it—unless one lived near a
college campus or a military base.)

Some television writers and producers wanted to go beyond
the mild youth rebellion of "The Monkees" and the coy sexuality of "Josie and the Pussycats." They wanted to inject counter-
establishment values into their series. Gene Roddenberry,
creator of "Star Trek" (NBC, 1966–1968), hoped to force his
adult audience to confront the issues of war and racism.
Equally politicized, Barney Rosenzweig, as line producer and
script supervisor for "Daniel Boone" (ABC, 1964–1970), tried to
depict the American Revolution as a colonial Vietnam War,
"with the colonials as the Viet Cong and the English as the
Americans." (In the 1980s, when he oversaw the feminist cop
show "Cagney & Lacy," Rosenzweig depicted pro-life Christian
activists as deranged, bomb-throwing terrorists.)

Sensitive to the upsurge of the black power and feminist
movements, the producers of "Batman" (ABC, 1966–1968)
changed the casting of the Catwoman character: black singer
Eartha Kitt replaced white Julie Newmar. In 1967 the series
added a new character, Batgirl. Batman, Robin, and Batgirl
ventured directly into politics by taping a public-service commercial on behalf of civil rights protection for women. The
scene was the office of Police Commissioner Gordon. A telephone call came in concerning super-villain activities in
Gotham City. Batman and Robin began to leave, ordering Batgirl to stay behind since the situation out in the streets could be
dangerous. Outraged, Batgirl rebuked the Dynamic Duo,
pointing out that discrimination was against the law.

By the late 1960s demographics, profits, and politics became
ever more closely linked elements in decisions regarding net-

work programming. In 1968 ABC commissioned sociologists at Columbia to survey the viewing habits, consumption patterns, and ideological orientations of young Americans. Two years later A. C. Nielsen, the company that measured the size of the networks' audience for particular shows to determine the advertising rates that companies were charged, adjusted its reporting system. To assist advertisers in better catering to the expanding youth market, Nielsen divided its youth cohort into two groups: consumers eighteen to twenty-four and twenty-five to thirty-four years of age. These two groups contained the highest proportion of upwardly mobile consumers in the country.

Network executives and mass marketers paid close attention to the 1969 Daniel Yankelovitch poll for *Fortune* magazine that showed American youths simultaneously opposed to radical extremism *and* critical of the Establishment. Convinced that they were tuned into the mind-set of youths, television programmers entered a period of social relevancy and progressive political advocacy. They would go far to bring the counterculture into the mainstream while pursuing enormous potential profits.

ABC in 1969 offered "The Bold Ones," an umbrella title for four rotating series: "The New Doctors," "The Lawyers," "The Protectors," and "The Senator." In the first two shows, wise, older sages inspired and sometimes clashed with idealistic colleagues who identified with unpopular causes. In "The Protectors," a white deputy police chief learned to combat his unconscious racism thanks to the efforts of a black activist district attorney. In "The Senator," an anti-war politician and his activist daughter fought corrupt political bosses who closely resembled Chicago mayor Richard Daley and the anti-Communist AFL-CIO president George Meany.

In 1968 ABC introduced the "Mod Squad," featuring three rebellious youths who became police officers: an affluent WASP, a black ghetto activist, and a liberated yet vulnerable white female. Assigned as undercover officers, the gender- and racially balanced trio tracked down middle-aged criminals who preyed upon innocent countercultural youths in Southern California.

ABC, which had taken the lead in the new youth programming, also broadcast "The Young Lawyers" and "The Young Rebels." In "The Young Lawyers," a wise and understanding law school professor played mentor to three activist students: a Jewish idealist, a streetwise yet vulnerable black woman, and a racially sensitive WASP. Together they operated a legal assistance clinic in the Boston ghetto, defending blacks against racist white landlords and police officers. "The Young Rebels," which was set in the time of the American Revolution, featured four heroes: a liberated yet vulnerable WASP woman, the son of a liberal WASP politician, a WASP intellectual, and a former slave with the style of Black Panther Huey Newton. "The Young Rebels" waged guerrilla war against middle-aged British soldiers and the "system." (Demonstrating that they had not yet figured out how to keep the Boomers tuned in, ABC executives followed "The Young Rebels" and its celebration of armed struggle with "The FBI.")

Not wishing to surrender the youth market to ABC, CBS counterscheduled with its own hip shows, among them the short-lived "Storefront Lawyers." This show detailed the adventures of an activist WASP attorney who provided free legal assistance to minorities in the Los Angeles ghetto. On the rock entertainment front, CBS hired James Fouratt, a hippie and friend of Abbie Hoffman, to coordinate advertising for Columbia Records.

Fouratt was in the forefront of a new generation of advertising executives who smoked marijuana and brought "hip capitalism" to the television networks. In the late 1960s and early 1970s the television audience could watch young black males with ballpoint pens shouting a variation of the Black Panther exclamation "Write On!" while Chrysler trumpeted "The Dodge Rebellion." An Alberto VO5 shampoo commercial showed a young woman who had a peace symbol superimposed over her face. Mary Wells, the forty-year-old creator of the

"Love Power" advertising slogan that associated freedom with consumerism, epitomized the true spirit of capitalist rebellion. Angered by the U.S. surgeon general's ban on televised cigarette advertising, Wells decried the prohibition as "un-American."

By 1971 CBS executives wasted little time in purging their schedule of top-rated rural comedies and faltering social advocacy dramas. The problem with shows such as "The Beverly Hillbillies" and "Green Acres" was that they were popular with grade-school-educated Americans over the age of fifty. Such viewers were not prime consumers and thus were not attractive to most advertisers. To enhance profits, CBS aimed to create new shows that would appeal to young, college-educated professionals who lived in large East or West Coast cities and Chicago. Such viewers were too sophisticated to enjoy the mindless "Beverly Hillbillies" and contemptuous of the overtly crusading "Storefront Lawyers." College-educated viewers in their twenties and thirties tended to be more interested in plots that dealt with abortion and other lifestyle issues. Weekly sermons against war and racism were tiresome.

Into this programming revolution stepped CBS president Robert Wood. A libertarian Republican, Wood had ordered the cancellation of "The Smothers Brothers" show in 1969 after the hosts invited anti-war activist and baby doctor Benjamin Spock to appear as a guest star. The network president, however, gained greater fame for championing seemingly daring shows, notably "All in the Family" (1971–1979) and "M*A*S*H" (1972–1983). Though he had quashed the Smothers Brothers for being too overtly leftist, the shows Wood now programmed featured anti-war, gay, and feminist characters. The creators of these series, Norman Lear and Larry Gelbart, frequently asked such advocacy organizations as the Gay Activist Alliance, the National Organization for Women, and the National Abortion Rights Action League for script ideas.

Although it may have seemed an ideological anomaly for a Republican to promote programs with subtle leftist political agendas, it was not. Wood concluded that feminists, gays, and civil rights and abortion rights supporters were overwhelmingly college educated and upper middle class—precisely the network and advertisers' target market. The network executive also believed that lifestyle issues, in contrast to the Smothers Brothers' polemics against American foreign policy, posed no threat to capitalism. In any event, Norman Lear's depiction of "All in the Family's" anti-hero, Archie Bunker, as a narrowminded bigot and object of ridicule was perfectly in line with the vision most white-collar professionals had of the so-called George Wallace constituency. Neither the partisans of the New Left nor the libertarian New Right had much use for labor union members who drank domestic beer and ate Hostess Twinkies.

Next to Robert Wood, the greatest countercultural entrepreneur of the 1960s had to be Jann Wenner. The Boomer publisher of *Rolling Stone* magazine, Wenner had turned an initial investment of $7,500 into a $250 million media empire. Born the son of a successful California businessman in 1946, Wenner forsook what few Judaic religious beliefs he had been raised with once he enrolled at Berkeley. He associated with the Berkeley activists in the radical student government organization SLATE and positioned himself on the periphery of the Free Speech Movement. But he disdained the bohemian lifestyle that was becoming fashionable in San Francisco. He eschewed roach-infested crash pads in favor of his own penthouse apartment.

As a columnist for the Berkeley campus newspaper, Wenner had written some noteworthy observations, including this one: "One of these days Lyndon Johnson is going to try to find out why the 'leaders of tomorrow' are hung up on LSD instead of LBJ." Wenner then joined the staff of the Sunday supplement of *Ramparts* magazine, which had acquired national fame for attacking the Roman Catholic church, Ronald Reagan, and Barbie dolls. At *Sunday Ramparts*, Wenner hung out with Timothy Leary and Panther leader Eldridge Cleaver, but mostly he watched publisher Warren Hinckle beg money from wealthy anti-war Democrats.

It occurred to Wenner that capitalism, radicalism, and hedonism could be blended into a lucrative mix. His vehicle was *Rolling Stone* magazine. *Rolling Stone* would churn out generally glowing reviews of records and attract advertising dollars from the major labels. As Wenner knew, countercultural Boomers and weekend revelers would flock to a magazine that celebrated rock singers and a lifestyle of good sex and drugs. On the political front (always a secondary consideration), Wenner published Hunter S. Thompson's savage attacks on Richard Nixon and Hubert Humphrey. Most of Thompson's fans, however, did not look to him for political insight. They read Thompson for his alcohol- and drug-induced digressions.

Underground cartoonist Robert Crumb had anticipated the rise of people like Jann Wenner, Robert Wood, and Bill Ayers. In 1972, thanks to director and animator Ralph Bakshi, Crumb's "Fritz the Cat" made it to the big screen—albeit with an "X" rating. Though Fritz reveled in drugs, sex, and violence, Crumb and Bakshi were honest enough to reveal their hero's selfish core. Fritz, a New York University student and SDSer, was a hedonist who did not worry about what happened to others as a result of his violent, self-indulgent acts. Fritz pursued group sex and drugs with a ruthless single-mindedness— while poor blacks lost their lives during a riot that Fritz provoked. Even as police officers and white construction workers were depicted as boorish pigs and cows, the Weathermen appeared as rats and slugs. If there is one source indispensable to understanding the 1960s counterculture, radical politics, and how opportunists found ways to profit from the exploitation of others, "Fritz the Cat" is it.

8

Legacies of the 1960s

FOLLOWING THE BOMBING of Wisconsin's Army Mathematics Research Center in 1970, Karl Armstrong fled to Canada. It took federal and state authorities three years to locate Armstrong, extradite him to the United States, and place him on trial. His attorney, William Kunstler—who had helped turn the Chicago Seven conspiracy trial into "guerrilla theater"—tried to turn Armstrong's defense into an indictment of America's cold war foreign policy. Kunstler insisted that the death of one Wisconsin student at Armstrong's hands was insignificant compared to the millions of Vietnamese orphans created as a result of university-military research projects and the policies of President Richard Nixon.

Armstrong did not lack for high-profile allies in academia and politics. MIT linguist Noam Chomsky regarded New Left terrorism as a necessary response to American war crimes in Indochina. (In a 1967 essay, "The Responsibility of the Intellectuals," which appeared in the *New York Review of Books*, and in later works, Chomsky compared cold war Democrats to Nazis and called the Vietnam War genocidal and imperialist.) Idealists like Armstrong, Chomsky argued, had helped "raise the domestic cost" of the Vietnam War. The U.S. government, being little different from Nazi Germany, Chomsky said, had no right to prosecute Armstrong. Seconding Chomsky, Princeton professor Richard Falk testified that the U.S. war in Vietnam was criminal. Being a man of good conscience, Falk observed, Armstrong had no choice but to strike back against America's Nazi-like foreign policy.

New Left historian Gabriel Kolko also defended Armstrong, contending that "To condemn Karl Armstrong is to condemn an entire anguished generation." Boston University historian Howard Zinn testified that Armstrong had "good and social motives." Activist historian Staughton Lynd compared Armstrong to the abolitionist John Brown, who understood that terrorism and murder were often necessary to achieve social justice. Wisconsin historian Harvey Goldberg, a long-standing champion of revolutionary violence and SDS, also testified on Armstrong's behalf.

Ernest Gruening, who had been one of two U.S. senators to vote against the 1964 Gulf of Tonkin Resolution, which provided Lyndon Johnson with the congressional authorization to bomb North Vietnam, showed up at Armstrong's trial. Gruening told the court that the bombing of the Army Math building had been necessary to stop the Vietnam War.

After a jury convicted Armstrong for causing the unintended death of a student and committing the most destructive terrorist bombing of a college campus in American history, he spent a few years in a state facility before being paroled. He is now a Madison businessman.

The intensive manhunt for Armstrong and his subsequent prosecution took place against a backdrop of escalating domestic terrorism. In the early 1970s left-wing groups were committing eight hundred bombings a year, attacking police stations, military installations, corporate headquarters, and banks. In 1970 the Weathermen bombed a New York City police station, injuring seven people. The SDSers also attacked a Long Island courthouse and San Francisco's Presidio army base. A year later the Weathermen bombed a U.S. Senate restroom. In 1972 they exploded a bomb in the Pentagon.

Having thus far failed to kill any military personnel, the Weathermen redoubled their efforts, forging an alliance with the Black Liberation Army—a group that had evolved from the Panthers. In 1981 the Black Liberation Army and SDSers Kathy Boudin and David Gilbert held up a Brink's armored car in Nyack, New York. They murdered a security guard and two police officers, one of whom was black. Boudin, who is the daughter of radical attorney Leonard Boudin, and Gilbert are currently serving life sentences for murder and armed robbery.

Following the 1969 implosion of SDS, at least twenty leftist groups—from Seattle's Quarter Moon Tribe to California's Symbionese Liberation Army—followed the lead of the Weathermen. In 1970 a group of wealthy Brandeis University students and two paroled criminals who had received federal financial aid to go to college robbed a Brighton, Massachusetts, bank. They killed a Boston police officer. One of the Brandeis terrorists, Katherine Power, successfully eluded federal authorities for two decades. When she was finally tried, Power's supporters in academia and the media pleaded for leniency given her exemplary conduct as a fugitive. The Boston jury, however, did not forget that she had deprived several children of their father and voted for conviction. Luckily for Power, the judge gave her a short prison sentence. She was paroled in 1999.

Three of the most notorious Weathermen leaders, Mark Rudd, Bill Ayers, and Bernardine Dohrn, resurfaced from the underground in the mid-1970s and early 1980s. Arguing that the FBI had tainted its cases against the Weathermen through illegal break-ins and wiretaps, Rudd, Dohrn, and Ayers bargained themselves out of jail time. Dohrn is currently an adjunct faculty member of the Northwestern University Law School.

As Bill Ayers boasted, "Guilty as hell, free as a bird. America is a wonderful country." Before moving to Chicago with Dohrn, Ayers received a Ph.D. in education from Columbia University's Teachers College. He is a professor at the University of Illinois, Chicago—along with fellow SDSer and Communist revolutionary Mike Klonsky. In interviews, Dohrn and Ayers have continued to praise SDS and characterize their vio-

lent past as a justifiable reaction to American racism and oppression.

The successful academic, legal, and media careers that
Dohrn, Ayers, and other Boomer activists have enjoyed under-
lines the importance of class in the 1960s student protest. For
middle- and upper-middle-class white youths—and even for
black militants such as Huey Newton—protest came cost-free.
(Newton died at the hands of a fellow crack dealer, though the
Bay Area left claimed that he had been assassinated by either
the CIA or the FBI.) As early as 1968 Abbie Hoffman realized
that class privilege exempted nearly all of even the most violent
white Boomers from lethal force and imprisonment. "We
couldn't have pulled this shit during the Korean War, during
the Second World War," Hoffman gloated to friends. "I mean
there are people going to Hanoi, collaborating with the enemy,
people carrying the Viet Cong flag."

Hoffman was on to something. The Kent State shootings
and the imprisonment of Weathermen terrorists David Gilbert
and Kathy Boudin were exceptional events. Federal and state
authorities and elite university administrations tried to avoid
violent confrontation with Boomer radicals and their faculty
champions. (The U.S. Justice Department did place Panthers
and SDSers under surveillance. Former activist David
Horowitz has argued that given the thousands of terrorist
bombings taking place in the 1960s and 1970s, the New Left
merited such attention.) Karl Armstrong, despite failing grades
and participation in the bloody 1967 anti-Dow protest, discovered that the University of Wisconsin would not expel him.
Even Jane Fonda, who berated tortured American prisoners of
war in Hanoi, continued to enjoy a successful Hollywood career. She later married media mogul Ted Turner after her di-
vorce from Tom Hayden.

Confronted with 100,000 protesters at the 1967 march on the
Pentagon, President Johnson grew more disheartened. (Even if
all 100,000 demonstrators had been students—and many were
not—they still represented just 1 percent of the college popula-

tion.) Johnson, who worried that China might intervene with troops in the Vietnam War, also feared an escalating "domestic crisis" that would leave the United States without an adequate number of law enforcement officers to police campuses and inner cities. By the time of the Tet Offensive in 1968, Johnson had no stomach to continue as president for another four years.

SDS and other student left groups proved that a few hundred thousand youths could cause enormous social disruption. Campus radicals fed on student fear of the draft. They also promised Boomers that they would usher in a new age of sexual liberation. Hedonism and self-preservation were powerful recruitment tools. The student left provoked police officers, escalated the level of violence, and radicalized larger numbers of youths. But once the threat of the draft disappeared, campus radicalism faded away—its memory kept alive by the 1960s activists who became, in the words of their conservative critics, the "tenured radicals" of the contemporary university. Drugs, sex, and rock-and-roll, however, remained alive and well on the post-1960s campus.

While many SDSers eluded jail and became successful white-collar professionals, the same could not be said for several members of the Nixon administration. Aiming to stem the flow of political information from the White House to a news media that conservatives regarded as treasonous, and wanting to track down leftist terrorists, the Nixon administration threw out the Constitution of the United States. Finding enemies everywhere, the Nixon White House went as far as to tap the phones of the Democratic National Committee's Watergate Hotel offices in Washington.

Given that Senator George McGovern, the 1972 Democratic presidential nominee, had met with North Vietnamese government officials while traveling outside the United States—in addition to his family ties to the Wisconsin SDS—it was difficult for Nixon not to tie anti–cold war Democrats to New Leftists. McGovern even copied the New Left's shrill, uncivil rhetoric when he compared Nixon to Hitler. Nixon's subsequent cover-up of the Watergate break-in, exposed by *Washington Post* reporters Bob Woodward and Carl Bernstein, led to his resignation in 1974. (Bernstein's father had been a Communist lawyer in the 1930s and 1940s. Nixon, perhaps unwilling to be ridiculed by the *Washington Post* as a "red baiter," chose not to mention Bernstein's political lineage.)

Nixon's Indochina policy had a few short-term successes but in the long run turned into an abject failure. The withdrawal of American troops from South Vietnam and the creation of the Selective Service lottery defused campus protest. *Washington Post* writer and anti-war stalwart David Broder noted that where Harvard had been a hotbed of radicalism in 1970, just a year later students who no longer lived under the threat of the draft happily played with their Frisbees.

To get North Vietnam to agree to a truce, Nixon allowed Hanoi to keep 200,000 troops in South Vietnam. He assured the Saigon regime that if Hanoi launched an offensive, the U.S. Navy and Air Force would come to its rescue. The president's secret agreements, though, depended on his remaining in the White House. In the spring of 1975, less than a year after Nixon's resignation and two years after the withdrawal of U.S. combat troops from Indochina, Hanoi overran South Vietnam.

Writing on the twenty-fifth anniversary of the fall of Saigon, historian and Vietnam veteran Walter McDougall complained that the United States had repeatedly "betrayed" the "non-Communist Vietnamese":

> The first [betrayal] was in 1963 when President Kennedy's men sanctioned the overthrow of Diem because he was an authoritarian patriot who refused to play puppet. If they were intent on judging the Saigon regime by different standards than they did South Korea and Taiwan, then they should have pulled out.
>
> Instead, the Johnson Administration not only took over the war, but chose means—search and destroy missions in the South and calibrated bombing in the North, without any

effort to cut the Ho Chi Minh Trail [through neutral Cambodia and Laos]—that were as ineffective as they were destructive. Then Lyndon Johnson just washed his hands of the mess after Tet 1968, when he halted the bombing, begged for peace talks, gave Hanoi time to recoup from the devastating losses suffered by Viet Cong cadres and bequeathed to his successor 540,000 demoralized American troops who knew we "weren't in it to win." That was America's second betrayal of the South Vietnamese.

. . . Instead of blaming the Democrats and "bugging out" in his personal interest, Nixon determined to withdraw gradually. That did him in. He was a war president held to peacetime standards of governance, and when Congress cut off aid to Saigon after the 1973 Paris Accords, it was voting for defeat, not for peace. That was America's third betrayal.

America's longest war cost the lives of 58,000 of its citizens. Five hundred and twenty-five thousand South Vietnamese and 666,000 Viet Cong and North Vietnamese also died. While American radicals called their country genocidal and racist for killing so many Vietnamese, onetime leftist Peter Collier pointed out that more Asians were executed in the first two years of Communist rule in Indochina than had perished between 1965 and 1975. Unwilling to criticize the Vietnamese and Cambodian Communists, intellectuals such as Noam Chomsky claimed that Indochina's "killing fields" were little more than CIA-inspired fantasies. Disillusioned with his comrades, historian and former SDSer Ronald Radosh concluded in 1987 that "The New Left became as much an agent for the Vietnamese and Cubans as had an earlier generation of Communists for the Soviet Union."

Zbigniew Brzezinski, a member of President Jimmy Carter's National Security Council, insightfully called the Vietnam War "the Waterloo of the WASP elite." According to Brzezinski, the dazed and confused Ivy Leaguers in the State Department and the CIA no longer had the will to project American military power overseas. Their lack of resolve invited aggression from Soviet and Arab terrorists. Vietnam, Brzezinski believed, had radicalized and disoriented America's patrician rulers. In this light it is understandable why, by 1971, the majority of Americans informed pollsters that the working-class youths who had gone to Vietnam were "suckers."

Most of the men and women who joined the administrations of Jimmy Carter in the 1970s and Bill Clinton in the 1990s had no use for anti-communism. In the Carter administration, Robert Pastor, head of the National Security Council staff for Latin America, urged the president to embrace the revolutionary Marxist Sandinistas in Nicaragua. To David Horowitz's chagrin, Pastor informed one political science professor that "Horowitz's *Free World Colossus* [written before his disillusion with the left] had a dramatic impact on me and taught me the truth of the radical critique of the Cold War mentality."

Carter's United Nations ambassador, Andrew Young, called Israel a racist nation and defended Fidel Castro's military intervention in Angola. "I don't believe that Cuba is in Africa because it was ordered there by the Russians," the black activist argued. "I believe that Cuba is in Africa because it really has a shared sense of colonial oppression and domination." Outlining his foreign policy objectives in 1977, Carter informed a commencement audience at the University of Notre Dame that anti-communism was a discredited policy of the past. "We are now free of that inordinate fear of Communism which," Carter said, "once led us to embrace any dictator who joined us in our fear."

In the three years following Carter's Notre Dame address, the Soviet Union expanded its nuclear arsenal, acquired military bases in Africa and Southeast Asia, invaded Afghanistan, and supplied weapons to Marxist guerrillas in Nicaragua. Meanwhile Cambodian Communists exterminated 2 million of their fellow citizens. As American prestige fell, anti-American terrorist groups stepped up their assaults. In Iran, Islamic fundamentalists overthrew the shah and seized the American embassy. For 444 days, 52 Americans were prisoners of a regime that had, by the rules of international law, committed an act of war against the United States.

Republican presidential candidate Ronald Reagan pledged in both his successful 1980 and 1984 campaigns to restore America's self-esteem and halt Communist aggression. At a 1988 Veterans Day ceremony in Washington to honor the Americans who had died in Vietnam, Reagan vowed that "Young Americans must never again be sent to fight and die unless we are prepared to let them win." The *Canadian*-born rock-and-roll star Neil Young found inspiration in Reagan's words. Young, whose songs had celebrated Woodstock and mourned Nixon's repression of the anti-war movement at Kent State, shocked reporters and fans in the 1980s when he said,

> I'm tired of feeling like America has to be sorry for the things it's done. . . . Reagan, so what if he's a trigger-happy cowboy? He hasn't pulled the trigger. Don't you think it's better that Russia and all these other countries think he's a trigger-happy cowboy than think it's Jimmy Carter who wants to give them back the Panama Canal?

Young's praise of Reagan's anti-Communist foreign policy in the 1980s might have been too generous. For all his tough rhetoric, Reagan, and later presidents George Bush and Bill Clinton, hesitated to commit American ground forces to protracted, costly wars. Victory had to be quick, with few casualties, and the goals were to be sharply limited—liberate Kuwait (1991) or restore calm in Kosovo (1999). America would not get into a long bloody struggle to capture aggressors in their Iraqi or Serbian lairs.

If American foreign policy had not fully recovered its bearings since the 1960s, the universities—as conservatives from syndicated columnist John Leo to University of Pennsylvania historian Alan Kors have documented—had lost their intellectual moorings. Larger numbers of students, faculty, and even administrators heeded Herbert Marcuse's call to silence campus opponents of the left. Although SDS splintered and the Vietnam War faded as an issue, "political correctness" (PC)—the ideological offspring of Marcuse's philosophy of "repressive tolerance"—became enshrined on the college campus.

Civil rights activist James Meredith, for instance, whose admission to Ole Miss had provoked a bloody riot in 1962, found himself in the 1990s booed and threatened at Mount Holyoke College. Meredith had offended Mount Holyoke's radical student and faculty feminists by trying to speak in favor of traditional family values. (He also earned the scorn of the white left by having served on the staff of North Carolina senator Jesse Helms. Although Helms had recanted his support of segregation in the 1960s, he remained one of the most loathed conservatives in America.)

In the late 1980s and throughout the 1990s, instances of "political correctness" abounded. Arizona State University denied tenure to a theater professor because he required students to read too many plays by William Shakespeare and not enough by women and minorities. Radicals at Cornell, Georgetown, San Francisco State, and the University of Pennsylvania routinely destroyed newspapers published by conservative students. Campus administrators did nothing about it, though at Dartmouth College one university official dismissed conservative student publications as "litter." Feminists at the University of Maryland, claiming that all males were likely rapists, had a unique way of getting across their point of view. The Maryland feminists published "Wanted for Rape" posters that contained the names of all the male students at the university. Maryland administrators, like their Penn counterparts, declined to take disciplinary action.

At Boston College, a Catholic institution of higher education, Mary Daly spent twenty years barring male students from her courses. Daly, a radical feminist, contended that men created an oppressive atmosphere in the classroom and thereby hindered the education of women. She also argued that males were the "lethal organs" of America's "rapist society." In 1999 one male student finally filed discrimination charges. Boston College officials, unable to explain why they would have fired a faculty member for excluding blacks and Jews from their classrooms but ignored Daly, had to force her into retirement.

One Stanford Law School professor in the 1990s vigorously defended campus speech codes that were largely aimed at silencing conservatives. "Freedom of speech should belong mainly to the powerless rather than those in power," he argued. SDSer-turned-sociology-professor Todd Gitlin concurred. Gitlin contended that conservatives exaggerated the extent and negative consequences of campus speech codes and "political correctness" because they had never reconciled themselves to the elevated status of women and minorities at the post-1960s university.

Civil libertarian Nat Hentoff, who had cheered SDS and the Berkeley Free Speech Movement in the 1960s, spent the 1990s criticizing his former allies—some of whom he denounced as "neo-McCarthyites of the righteous left." Hentoff also recounted a tale from Stanford in 1991. Writing in the campus newspaper *The Daily*, a student had bemoaned the double standards that were often present in university speech codes:

A flier for this weekend's Omega Psi Phi Jamm '91 party depicted a black man holding in one hand a sword and in the other the severed head of a white man.

If this situation had been reversed, it is obvious what would have happened. It would have been universally condemned, it would have made the front page of *The Daily* and the fraternity would no doubt have been placed on probation. But here (I am only guessing) it is seen as a very PC expression of rage at white oppressors.

The fact is, however, that racism is racism. Showing a white man killed by a black is hardly constructive.

Upset with the loss of academic freedom that he believed had accompanied the rise of "political correctness," former Yale University president Benno Schmidt sadly observed,

> The most serious problems of freedom of expression in our society today exist on our campuses. On many campuses around the country, perhaps most, there is little resistance to growing pressure to suppress and punish, rather than to answer, speech that offends notions of civility and community. Offensive speech cannot be suppressed under open-ended standards without letting loose an engine of censorship that cannot be controlled. To stifle expression is, apart from the invasion of the rights of others, a disastrous reflection on the idea of a university. A university is a place where people have to have the right to speak the unspeakable and think the unthinkable and challenge the unchallengeable.

Not surprisingly, alumni, taxpayers, and legislators have grown increasingly reluctant to fund state universities. The student violence of the 1960s and the revolt of the liberal arts professors opened a chasm between the public university and the working and middle classes. Soaring tuition costs and the public perception—rightly or wrongly—that "overpaid" faculty spend too much time researching and not enough time teaching, have only widened that chasm.

Higher education has not been the only institution to suffer from declining public support and trust. The news media, both electronic and print, have lost their audiences while becoming fragmented along class and cultural lines. In part the proliferation of cable channels and the national networks' practice, dating from the late 1960s, of "narrowcasting" are to blame. (In narrowcasting, advertisers and programmers place far less emphasis on the size of the viewing audience. Instead they focus on the financial and educational characteristics of the—perhaps fewer—number of people viewing a particular program. Programmers know that one white-collar professional with disposable income is a better audience than fifteen high-school-

educated convenience-store clerks. Consequently, narrowcasting replaced broadcasting.) Today fewer than half of America's
households watch ABC, CBS, and NBC.

A revulsion against what sociologists Stanley Rothman and
S. Robert Lichter call "liberal media bias," however, has also
played a role in creating a credibility gap between viewer and
network. In 1972, while 60 percent of the electorate voted for
Nixon, 80 percent of the media elite supported McGovern. By
1992, as more radicalized Boomers entered the ranks of the national media, 89 percent of prestige journalists supported Bill
Clinton. Such journalists endorsed same-sex marriage, abortion
on demand, and racial hiring quotas—stances that the majority
of Americans reject. Boomer journalist Nicholas Lemann, who
has written extensively on racism, embodies the attitudes of his
class. "Mostly because of Vietnam," Lemann recounted, "I grew
up regarding every American president in my lifetime as a
pathological war criminal" and viewing the United States as "a
force for evil in the world."

Another consequence of the 1960s protest and the counterculture—both friends and foes of the counterculture agree—
has been a sea change in the moral values of many Americans.
(Confronted with the financial costs of enforcing *in loco parentis*
and policing campus morals, by the beginning of the 1970s most
universities threw in the towel.) In 1973 James Reston of the
New York Times had said of the impact of campus protest and
the counterculture, "There has been a sharp decline in respect
for authority in the United States as a result of the war—a decline in respect not only for the civil authority of government,
but also for the moral authority of the schools, the press, the
church, and even the family."

As one Berkeley Boomer leftist observed, "My generation
has learned that what people do is simply what people do.
There is no right or wrong." Such moral relativism, conservative critics have contended, has coarsened American society, undermined the institution of marriage, and led to increased
crime. Liberals counter that repressing one's true self is hypo-

critical and ultimately socially destructive. Why should someone stay in a failing marriage and subject both spouse and children to acrimony and, possibly, domestic violence? Why
pretend that teenagers will not become sexually active if they do
not watch MTV or learn about condom usage in the classroom?

To these propositions, moral traditionalists like to cite a few
statistics. In 1960, for instance, the overall American illegitimacy rate stood at 5 percent. By 1990, 28 percent of all children
were born out of wedlock, and illegitimacy among middle-class
women had become socially acceptable. Before the War on
Poverty and the expansion of welfare payments, the black illegitimacy rate stood at 25 percent. By 1990 the black illegitimacy
rate was 60 percent. A good many academic studies have concluded that fatherless children are more likely to live in poverty,
commit crime, and bear their own children out of wedlock.

Crime, especially violent crime, rose to new highs. Between
1960 and 1990 violent crime rose 560 percent. In cities such as
New Haven, robbery has increased 10,000 percent since 1960.
Crime hit Berkeley particularly hard. In 1960 Berkeley had 4
murders, 10 rapes, and 36 drug arrests. By 1970, with the flow-
ering of sexual liberation and the counterculture, Berkeley had
12 murders, 116 rapes, and 1,393 drug arrests. Only recently has
the national violent-crime rate begun to fall.

Despite the efforts of the War on Poverty, the pathologies of
urban America continued to worsen. Both middle-class whites
and blacks fled the cities. In 1945 Washington, D.C., had
900,000 residents. By 1998 Washington's population had fallen
to 528,000. Although many leftist activists and professors
blamed the declining urban population on racism, 140,000
blacks fled Washington between 1970 and 1998.

The New Left's identification with underclass criminality
and its propensity to regard militants such as Huey Newton as
"noble savages" and authentic representatives of black America
have not diminished with time. In the 1990s former SDS president Clark Kissinger created a Los Angeles–based organization
called "Refuse and Resist." Kissinger's group hailed the Crips

and other violent gangs as idealistic revolutionaries. People who criticized inner-city gangs were, Kissinger charged, "racist." Not surprisingly, given its take on white student protest in the 1960s, PBS offered a documentary series in the 1980s called "Eyes on the Prize, II" which glorified the Black Panthers.

American electoral politics has also been shaped by the style of the 1960s Boomer activists. Contemporary liberals blame Ronald Reagan, in his 1980 campaign, for introducing intolerance and shrillness into the electoral discourse. But the real culprits are the radicals and conservatives who came of age in the 1960s. Their rise to positions of power in the 1980s has, as *Washington Post* columnist David Broder has observed, created a slash-and-burn style of politics that makes intellectual discussion impossible and turns off an increasingly cynical and alienated electorate.

Lee Atwater of South Carolina is a case in point. In the 1960s Atwater played in a rock-and-roll band and charged his fraternity brothers admission to the pornographic movies he acquired. By 1988 Atwater, as George Bush's campaign strategist, gained fame for accusing Democratic presidential candidate and Massachusetts governor Michael Dukakis of allowing a black prisoner—Willie Horton—out on a weekend furlough to rape a white woman. Atwater cynically played to the fears and prejudices of the GOP's post-1960s base of white Protestant Southerners.

(Atwater's charge originated with Senator Albert Gore, Jr., who, during the Democratic primaries, had indicted Dukakis for Willie Horton's killing and rape spree. Gore also inspired Atwater to call Dukakis's patriotism into question, even though the GOP strategist had himself taken a student deferment to avoid the Vietnam War.)

On the Democratic side, civil rights activists Andrew Young and Roger Wilkins set new lows in political discourse. During the 1980 election, Young appeared at an Ohio State rally and warned that if Reagan became president, "it's going to be all right to kill niggers." Four years later Wilkins, a college professor and contributor to *The Nation*, claimed that Reagan practiced "smiling racism" in his efforts to "keep the niggers in their place." Other Boomer liberals joined this chorus in the 1980s and 1990s, accusing conservatives of being racists, anti-Semites, and extremists who incited violence against gays and women. With unintended irony, they frequently called their Republican foes "mean spirited."

Some veterans of the New Left deny that their tactics and philosophy succeeded in discrediting New Deal–Great Society reforms while enhancing the electoral prospects of Nixon and Reagan. Berkeley's Frank Bardacke, for instance, has complained, "Current wisdom is that all we produced was reaction, a law-and-order president. That's the way the bourgeoisie has tried to rewrite history."

The Bardackes of the 1960s revolt like to point out that they were able to elect Ronald Dellums, a black leftist, to the U.S. House of Representatives. The problem with that line of reasoning, though, is that while Dellums represented Berkeley in Congress, Ronald Reagan carried California in both the 1980 and 1984 elections. Perhaps what Bardacke meant to say was not that Dellums counterbalanced Reagan, but that the worst enemy of the New Left had been vanquished. That enemy was not the New Right but the center as epitomized by the New Deal–cold war Democrats.

Following the Democrats' embarrassing 1968 Chicago convention, South Dakota senator George McGovern led an effort to reform the party's method of selecting presidential candidates. McGovern and his allies persuaded their party to increase the number of primaries, reduce the power of the unions and party bosses, and impose gender and racial quotas on the selection of delegates. While primaries appeared to place the nomination machinery in the hands of ordinary people, the opposite proved true. Most working-class Democrats paid little attention to primaries. They had labor leaders and machine bosses to take care of the mundane business of choosing candidates. The typical voter did not follow campaigns until the general election. Those most likely to vote in a primary were middle class, college educated, and motivated by a cherished cause, whether it was ending the Vietnam War or legalizing abortion. Once the cold war Democrats were dispensed with, as former activist Peter Collier has vividly written, "like political body snatchers the left then inhabited the party's corpse through McGovernism."

The McGovern delegates to the 1972 Democratic National Convention generally came from the ranks of the highly educated professional class. (In contrast, just 29 percent of the electorate had ever set foot inside a college classroom, let alone obtained a degree.) McGovern's people were also far to the left of the party's rank and file and profoundly liberal in their attitudes toward social issues. Two of three McGovern delegates favored busing black children to white schools to promote integration, compared to 15 percent of blue-collar and middle-class Democrats. Three of four believed that the constitutional rights of criminals should take precedence over cries for law and order. After all, poverty and racial discrimination, not immoral behavior, bred crime. Only 36 percent of the party's traditional constituencies saw things this way. Fifty-seven percent of McGovern's delegates also dismissed any criticism of federal welfare programs, arguing that America had to abolish poverty by any means at hand. With nearly a quarter of McGovern's California delegation collecting welfare, their emphasis upon expanded anti-poverty programs was understandable.

To heap insult upon injury, the McGovern staff denied Chicago mayor Richard Daley and AFL-CIO president George Meany a role in the convention. Black activist Jesse Jackson took Daley's place at the Miami gathering while Gloria Steinem, a leader of the National Organization for Women and an abortion rights crusader, replaced Meany as power broker. The McGovern people thought that the humiliated Daley and Meany would have little choice but to support their candidate and platform. It was a miscalculation of epic proportions. Although the percentage of social liberals had swollen in the 1960s with the expansion of the professions, there were too few public-sector lawyers, humanities professors, and media people to win a general election. (Nineteen percent of the electorate was made up of professionals in 1972, compared to 16 percent in 1964.) McGovern believed his ability to win the Democratic primaries would translate into a general election triumph.

Underscoring its contempt for working-class Democrats, the McGovern campaign refused to give union officials passes to the convention floor and gallery. At the same time, long-haired writers from the countercultural press moved about freely. Benefiting from rigid quotas for the selection of delegates, feminists and blacks were strongly represented. Organized labor and big-city ethnics did not fare as well. At the outset of his campaign, McGovern had turned his back on the New Deal coalition, vowing to build an insurgent political movement "around the poor and the minorities and the young people and the anti-war movement."

When the campaign concluded and the votes were counted, Nixon had won 61 percent of the popular vote. Among evangelicals, Nixon captured 80 percent of their vote, beating McGovern 13 million votes to 3 million. McGovern lost the Catholic and working-class vote, with Nixon capturing 60 percent of the ethnic and blue-collar electorate. The Democratic presidential nominee also lost the white South.

There was some good news for liberals. First, McGovern managed to retain 40 percent of Catholic voters who remained suspicious of the anti-union, pro-business GOP. Subsequent Democratic presidential candidates would continue to get roughly half of America's Catholic voters to support them. While Republicans cut into the Catholic base of the Democratic party by denouncing lawless hippies and the black underclass, they came nowhere near the 80 percent—or even higher—tally Franklin Roosevelt had scored among Croatian, Polish, and Slovakian Catholics.

Second, McGovern was the first Democrat in living memory

to win the majority of upper-middle-class, college-educated voters—the core of what conservative antagonists called the "New Class." Harvard law students supported McGovern 698 to 131, while just 4 of their 38 professors voted for Nixon. Reporters for the national networks and prestige press were no more fond of Nixon. Eighty percent of the media elite voted for McGovern.

Despite their small numbers, the cultural liberals had the money, media influence, and social position to carry on a successful rearguard struggle against conservatism. At the same time, some free-market libertarians had the means to wage war on the New Deal economic order. Intellectuals on the right tended to overlook the fact that the Boomer generation contained many radical libertarians who were just as hostile to moral crusades as was the left.

Samuel Brittain, an assistant editor of the (London) *Financial Times*, for instance, explicitly championed a social-economic order unfettered by moral constraints. In 1973 Brittain, who would later be knighted, wrote:

> The values of competitive capitalism have a great deal in common with contemporary attitudes, and in particular with contemporary radical attitudes. Above all they share a similar stress on allowing people to do, to the maximum feasible extent, what they feel inclined to do rather than conform to the wishes of authority, custom or convention. Under a competitive system, the businessman will make money by catering for whatever it is that people wish to do— by providing pop records, or nude shows, or candy floss. He will not make anything by providing what the establishment thinks is good for them.

Under Reagan in the 1980s, the libertarians gained more than their social conservative colleagues. Although libertarians failed to dismantle the New Deal, they at least got major tax cuts. By contrast, moral traditionalists received a few comforting words from Reagan on why abortion was a great evil that could only be overcome through a constitutional amendment that he had no intention of championing.

Reagan's fudging, however, made political sense. It did not help the cause of social conservatism that it was (and continues to be) so closely identified in the public's mind with an often strident, intolerant Christian New Right. Even voters who might reject same-sex marriage and abortion-on-demand do not like to pronounce sweeping moral judgments on others. To that extent, the 1960s ethos of "live and let live" has permeated American culture. Correctly gauging the temperament of the electorate, Reagan never chastised gays or single mothers in the same way he condemned the "Evil Empire" of the Soviet Union. He thus avoided the stigma that many attached to the Moral Majority of the 1980s and the Christian Coalition of the 1990s. And the many sex scandals of Republican clergy and politicians in the 1980s and 1990s also undermined the cause of social conservatism and exposed cultural traditionalists to charges of being "moral hypocrites."

At the turn of the century, the problem facing the national Democratic party was that its most reliable voters were members of the passing World War II generation. (George Bush in 1992 and Bob Dole in 1996—both of whom were World War II combat veterans—lost their generational cohort to anti–Vietnam War protester Bill Clinton.) Boomers, in contrast, were a much more ideologically riven generation, dividing nearly evenly between Democrats and Republicans. Those born after 1960, however, tended to be hostile to *both* the Democratic party and Christian conservatives. In 1990, for the first time in sixty years, the majority of voters under thirty were Republican or independent, not Democratic. Many of the post-1960s generation of voters tended to fuse the cultural attitudes of the left with the economic values of the right. They supported abortion and gay rights, detested affirmative action, wrote off the urban underclass, demanded welfare "reform," and had doubts about the long-term solvency of Social Security.

By the end of the 1990s, the Democratic party, which had

since the 1930s been identified with workers and socially conservative white Southerners, found its fastest-growing constituency among voters earning more than $200,000 a year.
Republicans, meanwhile, long the party of the wealthy, were
losing their most affluent supporters while making substantial
gains among working-class and white Southern voters antago-
nized by the national Democratic party's stance on cultural issues.

Historian Christopher Lasch, before his death, concluded
that America's elites, as one result of the class divisions of the
1960s and the restructuring of the economy in the 1980s, no
longer had any sense of social responsibility and national iden-
tity. Regardless of whether the nation's elites were libertarian
stock analysts or liberal Hollywood directors, upwardly mobile
Boomers, Lasch contended, had seceded from the United
States:

> To an alarming extent, the privileged classes—by an expan-
> sive definition, the top twenty percent—have made them-
> selves independent not only of crumbling industrial cities
> but of public services in general. They send their children to
> private schools, insure themselves against medical emergen-
> cies by enrolling in company-supported plans, and hire pri-
> vate security guards to protect themselves against the
> mounting violence. It is not just that they see no point in pay-
> ing for public services they no longer use; many of them have
> ceased to think of themselves as Americans in any important
> sense, implicated in America's destiny for better or worse.
> Their ties to an international culture of work and leisure—
> of business, entertainment, information, and "information
> retrieval"—make many members of the elite deeply indif-
> ferent to the prospect of national decline.

Whether or not Lasch overstated his thesis on "the Revolt of
the Elites," it remains clear that the class and cultural divisions
of the 1960s have not disappeared—they have merely mutated.
Americans' continued fascination with the 1960s is due in no

small part to the fact that we still live with the consequences of campus protest, political unrest, and the tearing apart of America's social fabric. We will continue to feel the effects of the 1960s shock waves until the last Boomers are retired from campus, the newsroom, and political office.

A Note on Sources

AMONG MANY general histories of cold war–1960s America, those most sympathetic to the left are Joan Morrison and Robert K. Morrison, *From Camelot to Kent State: The Sixties Experience in the Words of Those Who Lived It* (New York, 1987); Paul Berman, *A Tale of Two Utopias: The Political Journey of the Generation of 1968* (New York, 1996); David Burner, *Making Peace with the '60s* (Princeton, 1996); Marcy Darnovksy, Barbara Epstein, and Richard Flacks, eds., *Cultural Politics and Social Movements* (Philadelphia, 1995); Godfrey Hodgson, *America in Our Time: From World War II to Nixon, What Happened and Why* (New York, 1976); Milton Viorst, *Fire in the Streets: America in the 1960's* (New York, 1979); Thomas G. Patterson, ed., *Cold War Critics: Alternatives to American Foreign Policy in the Truman Years* (Chicago, 1971); Maurice Isserman and Michael Kazin, *America Divided: The Civil War of the 1960s* (New York, 2000); Jerome Skolnick, *The Politics of Protest* (New York, 1969); and Todd Gitlin, *The Twilight of Common Dreams: Why America Is Wracked by Culture Wars* (New York, 1995). More critical of the left are William L. O'Neill, *Coming Apart: An Informal History of America in the 1960s* (Chicago, 1971); Richard Gid Powers, *Not Without Honor: The History of American Anti-Communism* (New York, 1995); Christopher Lasch, *The Revolt of the Elites and the Betrayal of Democracy* (New York, 1995); Ronald Radosh, *Divided They Fell: The Demise of the Democratic Party, 1964–1996* (New York, 1996); Louis Filler, *Vanguards and Followers: Youth in the American Tradition* (Chicago, 1978); Alonzo L. Hamby, *Liberalism and Its Challengers: From FDR to Bush* (New York, 1992); Nat Hentoff, *Free Speech for Me— But Not for Thee: How the American Left and Right Relentlessly Censor Each Other* (New York, 1993); and Alan Charles Kors and Harvey A. Silvergate, *The Shadow University: The Betrayal of Lib-*

erty on America's Campuses (New York, 1998). Other edited works and books on the cold war and the 1960s worth consulting are Larry Colton, *Goat Brothers* (New York, 1993); John Kenneth White, *Still Seeing Red: How the Cold War Shapes the New American Politics* (Boulder, Colo., 1997); David Steigerwald, *The Sixties and the End of Modern America* (New York, 1995); Stephen Macedo, ed., *Reassessing the Sixties: Debating the Political and Cultural Legacy* (New York, 1997); Fritz Fischer, *Making Them Like Us: Peace Corps Volunteers in the 1960s* (Washington, D.C., 1998); and "Academic Freedom Symposium," *William Mitchell Law Review* 22 (1996).

In a large body of literature on the Old Left, some works are of recent vintage and others were published closer in time to the 1960s: Loren Baritz, ed., *The American Left: Radical Political Thought in the Twentieth Century* (New York, 1971); Milton Cantor, *The Divided Left: American Radicalism, 1900–1975* (New York, 1978); Maurice Isserman, *If I Had a Hammer: The Death of the Old Left and the Birth of the New Left* (New York, 1987); Harvey Klehr and John Earl Haynes, *The American Communist Movement: Storming Heaven Itself* (New York, 1992); and Guenter Lewy, *The Cause That Failed: Communism in American Political Life* (New York, 1990).

Writing on the New Left has become a cottage industry. Participant-memoirs of the student left include Todd Gitlin, *The Sixties: Years of Hope, Days of Rage* (New York, 1989); Paul Buhle, ed., *History and the New Left: Madison, Wisconsin, 1950–1970* (Philadelphia, 1990); Jane Alpert, *Growing Up Underground* (New York, 1981); James Miller, *"Democracy Is in the Streets": From Port Huron to the Siege of Chicago* (New York, 1987); Tom Hayden, *Reunion: A Memoir* (New York, 1988); Peter Collier and David Horowitz, *Destructive Generation: Second Thoughts About the '60s* (New York, 1996); David Horowitz, *Radical Son: A Generational Odyssey* (New York: Touchstone, 1998); David Lance Goines, *The Free Speech Movement: Coming of Age in the 1960s* (Berkeley, 1993); Robert and Michael Meeropol, *We Are Your Sons: The Legacy of Ethel and Julius Rosenberg* (Boston, 1975); Ronald Fraser, ed., *1968: A Student Generation in Revolt* (New York, 1988); Judy Kaplan and Linn

Shapiro, *Red Diapers: Growing Up in the Communist Left* (Urbana, Ill., 1998); Dick Cluster, ed., *They Should Have Served That Cup of Coffee* (Boston, 1979); and Alexander Bloom and Wini Breines, eds., *"Takin' It to the Streets": A Sixties Reader* (New York, 1995).

Among the many histories of the New Left that tend to be kind to radical students are Terry H. Anderson, *The Movement and the Sixties: Protest in America from Greensboro to Wounded Knee* (New York, 1996); Robert V. Daniels, *Year of the Heroic Guerrilla: World Revolution and Counterrevolution in 1968* (New York, 1989); W. J. Rorabaugh, *Berkeley at War: The 1960's* (New York, 1989); Doug Rossinow, *The Politics of Authenticity: Liberalism, Christianity, and the New Left in America* (New York, 1998); and Kirkpatrick Sale, *SDS* (New York, 1974).

More critical studies of the New Left are Stanley Rothman and S. Robert Lichter, *Roots of Radicalism: Jews, Christians, and the New Left* (New York, 1982); Robert James Maddox, *The New Left and the Origins of the Cold War* (Princeton, 1973); Gerberding Smith, ed., *The Radical Left: The Abuse of Discontent* (Boston, 1970); Seymour Martin Lipset, *Rebellion in the University* (Boston, 1971); and Tom Bates, *Rads: The 1970 Bombing of the Army Math Research Center at the University of Wisconsin and Its Aftermath* (New York, 1992).

Interesting documentary collections on the New Left include Irwin Unger and Debi Unger, eds., *The Times Were a Changin': The Sixties Reader* (New York, 1998); James Weinstein and David W. Eakins, eds., *For a New America: Essays in History and Politics from "Studies on the Left," 1959–1967* (New York, 1970); and Massimo Teodori, ed., *The New Left: A Documentary History* (Indianapolis, 1969).

No study of the New Left would be complete without consulting the seminal book that shaped the radical analysis of American foreign policy, William Appleman Williams, *The Tragedy of American Diplomacy* (Cleveland, 1959).

Other works worth consulting include two books and two dissertations: Thomas Powers, *Diana: The Making of a Terrorist* (Boston, 1971), and Alan Adelson, *SDS: A Profile* (New York, 1972); and Caroline Hoefferle, "A Comparative History of Student Activism in Britain and the United States, 1960–1975," Ph.D. dissertation in history, Central Michigan University, 2000, and Joel Paul Rhodes, "The Voice of Violence: Performative Violence as Protest, 1968–1970," Ph.D. dissertation in history, University of Missouri at Kansas City, 2000.

Vietnam was America's longest war, and, not surprisingly, studies abound of both the Indochinese conflict and the American peace movement. Books critical of American foreign policy in Vietnam and that tend to champion the anti-war movement are Marcus G. Raskin and Bernard B. Fall, eds., *The Vietnam Reader: Articles and Documents on American Foreign Policy and the Vietnam Crisis* (New York, 1965); Charles DeBenedetti, with Charles Chatfield, *An American Ordeal: The Antiwar Movement of the Vietnam Era* (Syracuse, N.Y., 1990); Nancy Zaroulis and Gerald Sullivan, *Who Spoke Up? American Protest Against the War in Vietnam, 1963–1975* (Garden City, N.Y., 1984); Melvin Small and William D. Hoover, eds., *Give Peace a Chance: Exploring the Vietnam Antiwar Movement* (Syracuse, N.Y., 1992); David Caute, *The Year of the Barricades: A Journey Through 1968* (New York, 1988); Tom Wells, *The War Within: America's Battle Over Vietnam* (Berkeley, 1994); Marilyn B. Young, *The Vietnam Wars, 1945–1990* (New York, 1991); and Mitchell K. Hall, *Because of Their Faith: CALCAV and Religious Opposition to the Vietnam War* (New York, 1990).

Critics of the anti-war movement include Adam Garfinkle, *Telltale Hearts: The Origins and Impact of the Vietnam Antiwar Movement* (New York, 1997); Robert Timberg, *The Nightingale's Song* (New York, 1995); David Brock, *The Seduction of Hillary Rodham Clinton* (New York, 1996); Lawrence M. Baskir and William A. Strauss, *Chance and Circumstance: The Draft, the War, and the Vietnam Generation* (New York, 1978); and Walter A. McDougall, "Who Were We in Vietnam?" *New York Times*, April 26, 2000.

Several works are more mixed in their evaluation of the anti-war movement, among them Robert R. Tomes, *Apocalypse Then: American Intellectuals and the Vietnam War, 1954–1975* (New York, 1998); Kenneth J. Heineman, *Campus Wars: The Peace Movement*

at American State Universities in the Vietnam Era (New York, 1993);
and David W. Levy, *The Debate Over Vietnam* (Baltimore, 1991).

In recent years the literature on the New Right has grown, but
it still lags behind the sheer number of studies devoted to the New
Left. Participant-memoirs of the conservative 1960s have been
written by Irving Kristol, *Reflections of a Neoconservative: Looking
Back, Looking Ahead* (New York, 1983); John H. Bunzel, ed., *Polit-
ical Passages: Journeys of Change Through Two Decades, 1968–1988*
(New York, 1988); Alan Bloom, *The Closing of the American Mind:
How Higher Education Has Failed Democracy and Impoverished the
Souls of Today's Students* (New York, 1987); Irving Kristol, *Neocon-
servatism: The Autobiography of an Idea* (New York, 1995); and
Robert H. Bork, *Slouching Towards Gomorrah: Modern Liberalism
and American Decline* (New York, 1996).

For anyone interested in the conservative critique of 1960s libertarianism, Frank S. Meyer, "Libertarianism or Libertinism?"
National Review 21 (September 9, 1969); 910, is required reading.

The libertarian point of view is nicely presented in David Boaz,
ed., *The Libertarian Reader: Classic and Contemporary Writings from
Lao-Tzu to Milton Friedman* (New York, 1997).

Historical and sociological studies of the New Right include
Gary Dorrien, *The Neoconservative Mind: Politics, Culture, and the
War of Ideology* (Philadelphia, 1993); Kenneth J. Heineman, *God Is
a Conservative: Religion, Politics, and Morality in Contemporary
America* (New York, 1998); Gregory L. Schneider, *Cadres for Con-
servatism: Young Americans for Freedom and the Rise of the Contem-
porary Right* (New York, 1999); Rebecca E. Klatch, *A Generation
Divided: The New Left, the New Right, and the 1960s* (Berkeley,
1999); and Margaret M. Braungart and Richard G. Braungart,
"The Life-Course Development of Left- and Right-Wing Youth
Activist Leaders from the 1960s," *Political Psychology* 11 (1990):
243–282.

The civil rights movement has inspired a great many books.
Among the best are Robert Mann, *The Walls of Jericho: Lyndon
Johnson, Hubert Humphrey, and the Struggle for Civil Rights* (New
York, 1996); David J. Garrow, *Bearing the Cross: Martin Luther ·
King, Jr., and the Southern Christian Leadership Conference* (New

York, 1986); Doug McAdam, *Freedom Summer* (New York, 1988);
Paul Berman, ed., *Blacks and Jews: Alliances and Arguments* (New
York, 1994); Taylor Branch, *Parting the Waters: America in the King
Years, 1954–1963* (New York, 1988); Clayborne Carson, *In Struggle: SNCC and the Black Awakening of the 1960s* (Cambridge, Mass.,
1996); and Stephen B. Oates, *Let the Trumpet Sound: A Life of Martin Luther King, Jr.* (New York: HarperPerennial, 1994).

Works examining aspects of black power include Diane Rav-
itch, *The Troubled Crusade: American Education, 1945–1980* (New
York, 1983); Tom Wolfe, *Radical Chic and Mau-Mauing the Flak
Catchers* (New York, 1970); David Hilliard and Lewis Cole, *This
Side of Glory: The Autobiography of David Hilliard and the Story of
the Black Panther Party* (Boston, 1993); and Benjamin Ginsberg,
The Fatal Embrace: Jews and the State (Chicago, 1993).

For an excellent general history of the contemporary South, see
Dewey W. Grantham, *The South in Modern America: A Region at
Odds* (New York, 1994).

A book that means to praise the Great Society but ends up tear-
ing it apart is Irwin Unger, *The Best of Intentions: The Triumph and
Failure of the Great Society Under Kennedy, Johnson, and Nixon*
(New York, 1996).

Readers interested in rock and roll and the counterculture
should consult Charlie Gillett, *The Sound of the City: The Rise of
Rock and Roll* (New York, 1983); Robert Draper, *Rolling Stone
Magazine: The Uncensored History* (New York, 1990); Fred Goodman, *The Mansion on the Hill: Dylan, Young, Geffen, Springsteen,
and the Head-On Collision of Rock and Commerce* (New York,
1997); Charles Kaiser, *1968 in America: Music, Politics, Chaos,
Counterculture and the Shaping of a Generation* (New York, 1988);
and Raymond Obstfeld and Patricia Fitzgerald, *Jabber Rock: The
Ultimate Book of Rock 'n' Roll Quotations* (New York, 1997).

Works that examine particular lifestyle rebels and the ethos of
the counterculture include Morris Dickstein, *Gates of Eden: American Culture in the Sixties* (Cambridge, Mass., 1997); Abe Peck, *Un-
covering the Sixties: The Life and Times of the Underground Press*
(New York, 1985); Michael Wreszin, *A Rebel in the Defense of Tradition: The Life and Politics of Dwight Macdonald* (New York,

1994); Marty Jezer, *Abbie Hoffman, American Rebel* (New Brunswick, N.J., 1993); Jonah Raskin, *For the Hell of It: The Life and Times of Abbie Hoffman* (Berkeley, 1998); Christopher Lasch, *The Culture of Narcissism: American Life in an Age of Diminishing Expectations* (New York, 1978); Annie Gottlieb, *Do You Believe in Magic? Bringing the Sixties Back Home* (New York, 1987); and P. J. O'Rourke, *Age and Guile Beat Youth, Innocence, and a Bad Haircut* (New York, 1995).

The counterculture and 1960s television is discussed in Kenneth J. Bindas and Kenneth J. Heineman, "Image Is Everything? Television and the Counterculture Message in the 1960s," *Journal of Popular Film and Television* 22 (Spring 1994): 22–37.

Index

A NOTE ON THE AUTHOR

Kenneth J. Heineman was born in Lansing, Michigan, and studied at Michigan State University and the University of Pittsburgh, where he received a Ph.D. in history. He has also written *A Catholic New Deal, God Is a Conservative,* and *Campus Wars.* He is professor of history at Ohio University in Athens, Ohio.